For Better...
FOREVER

REVISED AND EXPANDED

For Better... FOREVER

A Catholic Guide to Lifelong Marriage

REVISED AND EXPANDED

Dr. Greg and Lisa Popcak

Our Sunday Visitor Publishing Division
Our Sunday Visitor, Inc.
Huntington, Indiana 46750

Nihil Obstat
Msgr. Michael Heintz, Ph.D.
Censor Librorum

Imprimatur
✠ Kevin C. Rhoades
Bishop of Fort Wayne-South Bend
June 1, 2015

The *Nihil Obstat* and *Imprimatur* are official declarations that a book is free from doctrinal or moral error. It is not implied that those who have granted the *Nihil Obstat* and *Imprimatur* agree with the contents, opinions, or statements expressed.

20 19 18 17 16 15 1 2 3 4 5 6 7 8 9

Our Sunday Visitor Publishing Division, Our Sunday Visitor, Inc., 200 Noll Plaza, Huntington, IN 46750; 1-800-348-2440

ISBN: 978-1-61278-906-4 (Inventory No. T1691)
eISBN: 978-1-61278-907-1
LCCN: 2015941968

Cover design: Amanda Falk
Cover art: Shutterstock
Interior design: Sherri L. Hoffman

PRINTED IN THE UNITED STATES OF AMERICA

First Edition

For Isaiah, whose short life helped us pursue a deeper path.
And for our children who remain with us. May God grant them
many blessed years, may they live in health and happiness,
and may they find the love he has for them.

Second Edition

To our children. May God bless them
with the love that comes from his very own heart.

Table of Contents

INTRODUCTION

"Happily Ever After": The Possible Dream

Every married couple wants to live "happily ever after." This book will show you what it takes.

This new, revised, and expanded edition of *For Better ... FOREVER* integrates even more cutting-edge-psychology with a clearer articulation of the Catholic vision of love and marriage in a way that we believe will surprise you, challenge you, and revitalize your relationship. More than a guide to an incredible Christian marriage, *For Better ... FOREVER* offers you a path to a complete and soulful marital spirituality. You will discover new and exciting ways to fill your home with the love that flows from God's own heart.

Is "Happily Ever After" Possible?

We opened this book by noting that every couple would like to make it to "happily ever after," but there are many people in this, the third generation of the culture of divorce, who wonder, "Are happily-ever-after marriages even possible?"

Much to everyone's surprise, they are, even today!

Recent research has identified a group of married couples we call the *Exceptional Seven Percent* (Popcak, 2002). These are exceptional couples in first-and-forever marriages who report significantly greater-than-average happiness, fulfillment, and longevity. These couples have very different ideas from their less-satisfied peers toward everything, from what they build their marriages around to how they handle conflict, from how they keep love alive to how they maintain the vitality of their marriages though the years.

Born That Way?

When you read about these *Exceptional* couples, you might very well be thinking, *Well, good for them and all, but they were probably born that way.*

Survey said (insert obnoxious buzzer noise here): "Wrong!" Studies suggest that only two factors set these remarkable couples apart: relationship skills and life experience. This finding is supported by the fact that another 7 to 8 percent of *second* marriages fall into the Exceptional category, bringing the Exceptional couples' tally to approximately 15 percent of all marriages. If these Exceptional couples were born to have uncommonly rewarding marriages, then half of them wouldn't have had to get divorced to learn how to do it! The good news is, even if you, as a couple, were not born to be what marriage experts refer to as "collaborative geniuses," or "marriage masters" (Lederer and Jackson, 1990; Gottman, 1995), you can learn how to become one. And, thanks to this book plus God's grace and your good efforts, you won't have to get divorced to do it! Better still, all of the attitudes and habits practiced by these couples are completely consistent with solid Christian teaching.

Marriage: The Adventure Begins!

This revised and expanded edition of *For Better ... FOREVER* is divided into three parts, each dedicated to empowering you to achieve a truly fulfilling, long-lasting, Christ-centered marriage.

In ***Part One*** of this book, ***Revealing the Vision*** will enable you to experience a marriage that will make the angels smile *and the neighbors sick with jealousy*! (We mean that in the best way possible, of course.)

Many people are surprised to discover that we Catholics have a very different, and very exciting, understanding of marriage that distinguishes us from other couples. In this first part, we'll look at the "Catholic difference" in marriage. What makes your Catholic marriage special, and why does it matter to you? What do Catholics believe is the *one reason* for marrying that *guarantees the lifelong success* of a marriage? How does your Catholic faith increase your chances of reaching the top of the marital food chain? Why does God care that you have a happy marriage, and what is his plan to help you achieve greatness as a couple? How can you and your mate experience the love that springs from God's own heart? Part One will answer these questions and more.

In **Part Two,** we'll look at ***Where Are We? How Did We Get Here? Where Are We Going?*** We'll reveal the hidden pathway to "happily ever after" and help you overcome any obstacles that stand in your way. You'll discover where your marriage falls on *The Relationship Pathway* and what you need to do to get from wherever you are to the *Exceptional Seven Percent* of marriages that exhibit uncommonly high degrees of happiness and stability. You'll also discover the *Seven Stages of Marriage Mountain* — that is, the seven stages every marriage encounters over the course of a lifetime. Plus, we'll show you how you can more easily overcome the challenges that accompany these stages, challenges that often prevent other couples from making it from one stage to the peak. All along the way, you'll uncover plenty of practical tips to help you make your love deeper and your relationship stronger. You'll develop the skills and confidence you need to keep your relationship going strong and growing stronger even in the face of all the challenges of life.

In ***Part Three***, we'll explore ***The Road to Intimacy.*** Do you know what it takes to create an uncommonly joyful, passionate, peaceful, and soul-satisfying relationship? God, the Author of love itself, wants your marriage to be an epic love story! Wherever you find yourself on *The Relationship Pathway* as you scale *Marriage Mountain*, there are certain habits — your special gear, if you will — that every couple needs to cultivate to get the most out of their relationship and make the journey simpler. We'll reveal those habits and show you, step-by-step, how to practice them. We'll expose the *true source of lifelong love*. You'll discover the *four qualities that create deep marital intimacy* and explore what it takes to stay in love every day of your lives together! Plus, we'll reveal the surprising skills that allow Exceptional couples to draw closer together *because* of their arguments rather than *in spite* of them. Finally, *For Better ... FOREVER* will expose the secrets to celebrating a *toe-curling, eye-popping, mind-blowing* (and, yes, *profoundly* spiritual) *sexuality*. Go figure!

A Possible Dream

When we underwent preparation for our marriage, the pastor guiding our experience said a remarkable thing: "I've never lost one of my couples [to divorce]. If you make it past me, I know you'll do just fine." More than 25 years later, through God's grace, we are pleased to say that we're making good on our pastor's promise to us moment by moment and day by day. We are more in love today than we were the day we said "I do," and every day reveals even more surprises, joys, and challenges and enables us to take our love to a new and deeper level.

We would like you to join us on this wonderful journey. It is our prayer that as you read these pages, your life, your faith, and your marriage will be transformed; made meaningful in ways you never thought possible. We know that sounds like a tall order, and it is. Ultimately, you will need to be the judge of how well we fulfill our mission to get you to "happily ever after"; but from the very beginning, we want you to know that God created you with all the qualities necessary to have a wonderful marriage. This is even truer if you are baptized, confirmed, married, and active in the life of the Church. Why? Because while the rest of the world has to figure love out for themselves, *Christians* are constantly being given the grace to discover what God infused into us at our baptism: traits that predispose us both to perfect love and enviable marriages. In fact, research bears this out. A major study by the National Marriage Project found that husbands and wives who regularly attend church together are both significantly happier in their marriages and significantly less likely to divorce than couples who either don't attend church or attend separately (Wilcox and Marquardt, 2011). We've heard it said that Jesus Christ is "the ultimate meaning of an interpersonal relationship." Well, of course he is. He created marriage! If we who follow His example can't have powerful, profoundly loving marriages, then no one can.

God Is Rooting for You!

The truth is, God is rooting for your marriage. He *wants* you to celebrate an uncommonly joyful, passionate, soul-satisfying life together. Why? *Because God wants to change the world through your marriage.* Through both the way you cherish each other every day and your faithful and steadfast love through trials, God wants to show the world that the kind of love that every human heart longs for — the kind of *free, total, faithful, and fruitful love* that comes from his own heart — is really possible to achieve. Your mission is to be a walking Jumbotron — a giant, bright, flashing, impossible-to-ignore sign to the world — that God's love is real, and that he wants to fill every heart to overflowing with a love that knows no bounds. He can only do that if he has couples like you to point to. Couples, like you, who aren't afraid to do the work and celebrate the blessings that an Exceptional Marriage entails.

So, are you ready to shake things up?

Do you want to wake up every morning thrilled to start a new day with your mate?

Do you want to know what God *really* intended when he created marriage?

Turn the page and discover the incredible journey God intends your marriage to be!

PART ONE

Revealing the Vision

What makes your Catholic marriage special, and why does it matter to you? What do Catholics believe is the one reason for marrying that guarantees the lifelong relevance and success of a marriage? How does your Catholic faith increase your chances of reaching the top of the marital food chain? Why does God care that you have a happy marriage, and what is his plan to help you achieve greatness as a couple? How can you and your mate experience the love that springs from God's own heart? Discover the answers to these questions and more.

CHAPTER 1

Marriage

Vive la *"Catholic Difference"*!

The word "marriage" means many different things to many different people. What does marriage mean to you? Have you ever wondered how your vision of marriage squares with the Church's vision? Then again, why should you even care?

Sharing the Vision: Why Does It Matter?

Catholics mean something specific when we use the word "marriage," and understanding that difference is critically important for you to be able to get the most out of your marriage. Why? Because how you think of marriage ultimately defines the way you build your life together. It sets up your expectations regarding the amount of effort you believe you should put into your relationship as well as the benefits you think you should anticipate from your marriage. For instance, a person who believes that marriage is just two people sharing their stuff and living under the same roof is going to be a very different kind of spouse than a person who believes marriage is supposed to be about working to achieve deep intimacy and helping each other become his or her best self. Imagine what would happen if the two people we just used as an example married each other. You'd end up with one spouse constantly chasing the other, begging for more love and intimacy, while the other felt perpetually nagged and pressured to make a fuss about something that wasn't really worth making a fuss about.

That's why it's important to have a shared vision about what marriage is supposed to be (Gottman, 2011). The Church can help you and your spouse get on the same page about your expectations for your marriage. Catholicism has some very well-developed and time-tested ideas about what a good marriage should look like, and it asks couples who get married in the Church to agree to live up to that vision so that God can use your marriage to change the world by being a sign of his love to everyone you meet.

Let's Go Shopping! or "Got Lost in the Marriage Market"

Imagine you went to the store to buy something. Cereal, software — it doesn't matter. Suppose that although you know what you want, you don't know which brand to buy. What do you do? Well, you could look at the checklist on the back of the box to see what this product is or does, compared to other similar products, so that you can get a sense of what you're buying.

Now, imagine you were going to The Marriage Store to "buy" a relationship. You see several different relationship-types on the shelf, all in their own brightly colored boxes. There's "Cohabitation," "Civil Marriage," "Romantic Marriage," "Faith-Based Marriage," and last but not least, "Catholic Marriage." As you compare the different "products," you might begin to notice that each of these relationship-types is largely defined by the kind of promises that it requires from the couples choosing it — or, more specifically, the vows the couple in that relationship make to each other. *The promises (vows) required by the relationship ultimately define the happiness and the stability the couple can expect from the relationship.*

Let's do a side-by-side "product comparison" to help you understand the important differences between Catholic Marriage and the other marriage-type relationships on the market and why it matters to you.

Cohabitation — The DIY Relationship

Of course, cohabitation isn't the same thing as marriage, but a lot of people don't know that. Many people go to our metaphorical Marriage Store and walk out with a box of Cohabitation, believing they got what they came for: a kind of self-styled, do-it-yourself relationship that means "we live together and whatever else *we decide* it should mean." It's an attractive relationship-type because it doesn't cost too much (in terms of the specific promises and commitment it requires) and seems to offer the greatest degree of freedom (in that "we can define it how we want").

The problem is the same as the benefit, however. Because it requires so little from the couple, it also takes very little to break it. Marriage researchers (Rhoades and Stanley, 2014) observe that the reason cohabiting couples tend to break up at a much higher rate than other couples is that they tend to "slide" into living together (and perhaps, eventual marriage), as opposed to "deciding" to live together (and/or marry). In other words, first the couple begins casually sleeping together. Then the one partner starts leaving more of their things at the other partner's apartment, and then more of their things, and more, until it "just makes sense" to stay where most of their things already are. After a while, maybe this couple has a child or two together, and now everyone (including, maybe, their kids) is asking when they're going to get married, so they do. In other words, at no point along the way does the cohabiting couple consciously choose anything, and the lack of clear expectation and relationship goals leads to a significant undercurrent of distress and instability. As one woman reported to University of Virginia sociologist Dr. Meg Jay:

> I felt like I was on this multiyear, never-ending audition to be his wife. We had all this furniture. We had our dogs and all the same friends. It just made it really, really difficult to break up. Then it was like we got married because we were living together once we got into our 30s. (Jay, 2013)

In the traditional path to marriage, couples have to *publicly and intentionally* choose to *increase* their commitment (to each other) and *decrease* their options (to date others) by doing things like "going steady" or getting engaged, and, ultimately, getting married, and submitting to all the rituals surrounding those public declarations. By contrast, the cohabiting couple doesn't really *choose* anything. The relationship just sort of happens to them — and they get locked in without expecting it. One day, one or both of the partners wakes up and says, "How did I get here?" This usually marks the beginning of the end of the relationship or, at least, leads to an extended period of time where one partner wants more from the other person but continually settles for less in the hopes that one day the other partner might decide to want those things too.

Although the Cohabitation package appears to be an attractive option in The Marriage Store for its freestyle, do-it-yourself nature, research shows that the lack of formal, public, conscious commitments ultimately undermines both the satisfaction and stability of the relationship, making cohabiting couples up to 200 percent more likely to separate than their married counterparts, even if they get married (Doughty, 2010).

Civil Marriage — Public Promises

Next, you pick up the box marked "Civil Marriage." It looks sturdy. It's been around a while (in fact, it's been recognized as a legal institution since about 1800 B.C., starting with Hammurabi, two-thirds of whose famous "code" involved marriage law). On the comparison chart on the back, you notice that Civil Marriage requires you to make a certain set of basic, but important, public promises. Essentially, if you purchase this marriage product, you must promise to share your stuff with each other and claim any children you produce together. Your things aren't just occupying your partner's space. You now must agree to give your partner a legal claim over those things. Likewise, any children you have are definitely your shared responsibility under the law. You don't just get to wander off quietly and hope someone else will take on the responsibility of parenthood — not without some difficulty, anyway.

With those responsibilities come certain rights. You have the right to expect your partner to help provide for your needs. You have a right to expect your partner to provide financially and emotionally for your children. These are significant and important promises, and you must agree to them if you want to "buy" this "product" from The Marriage Store. Making these specific promises in a public forum doesn't guarantee lifelong marriage, but studies consistently show it does significantly increase the likelihood that a couple will remain happily together over the long haul, because people are much more likely to stick to more specific promises, especially when they are made out loud and in the open.

Romantic Marriage — Making it Personal

Then, you look at the box marked "Romantic Marriage." Romantic marriage offers all the benefits and promises of civil marriage (which serves as its foundation) *plus* whatever else the couple decides to promise to each other. Those "extras" could be anything. We actually saw a wedding reality show where the wife vowed to bake the husband red velvet cake once a month, and the husband promised the wife to take the trash out ... *if it was raining.*

The point is, in Romantic Marriage the spouses put their stamp on the relationship and express, through their particular vows, what they think a happy marriage should be. These extra promises imply that there should be some kind of personal investment, some kind of intimacy, but these promises don't often clearly define what that investment should look like.

Despite this couple's best intentions, sometimes the extra promises are "too small" and don't allow for growth. For example, what if the husband in our example above decided he would prefer his wife to make German chocolate cake one month? Is that a breach of their agreement? Other times, these vows are so vague and general they sound good but mean little. For instance, what does it *really* mean to "always see you as my other self?" Those are pretty words, but what does it commit you to, *exactly*? What do you have a right to expect from each other for having made such a vow?

The problem with Romantic Marriage is that it tries to glue things on to basic Civil Marriage that the couple may or may not want 20 years from now or may not really understand even from day one. Although it sounds admirable enough to want make your marriage your own, writing vows that will remain relevant, compelling, and meaningful over the course of a lifetime requires a depth of wisdom and breadth of perspective that few, if any, couples really have, not to mention a degree of foresight that is impossible to have. That can lead to a lot of confused expectations and anger later on when the promises the couple make to each other can't stand up to the hard realities of a long life together.

Faith-Based Marriage — A Promise to Bear Witness

Next, you look at the box labeled "Faith-Based Marriage." In truth, there are as many different types of Faith-Based Marriages as there are faith traditions, but they all have two things in common.

First, they all agree to at least do what Civil Marriage does. Second, they require that the couple give up their right to define marriage as *they* want to. Instead, the couple must agree to build their lives around that particular faith's vision of what marriage should look like. *In a Faith-Based Marriage, the couple gives their religious community the right to tell them what their love for each other should look like.*

What would motivate a couple to do this? Presumably, because the couple believes what that faith-community believes about life and love, and because they would be proud to be examples of that vision in their own lives. The couple that actually chooses a Faith-Based Marriage (as opposed to couples who simply want a pretty church to serve as a backdrop to their self-styled Romantic Marriage) recognizes that, as much as they love each other, they still have a lot to learn about love, life, and marriage. They want to learn what their faith community — which has been praying about and discussing these topics for generations, if not for millennia — has to teach them.

There are several benefits to this approach. By agreeing to turn to their faith-community to help them learn what marriage should look like, the couple establishes a clear, shared vision of the kind of husband and wife they need to be to each other. Further, they receive an objective way to manage disputes more effectively, because their faith-community helps them manage each other's expectations. By surrendering their right to make their marriage up as they go, the couple in a Faith-Based Marriage has a clear vision, clear expectations, and a community of support and experts (pastors, resources) to facilitate their ability to live out the vision they have agreed to apprentice.

Catholic Marriage — Bearing Witness to Free, Total, Faithful, Fruitful Love

The last product on the shelf we'll look at is "Catholic Marriage." Catholic Marriage is a specific type of Faith-Based Marriage. The Catholic Church does not allow couples to write their own vows because Catholics believe that marriage is supposed to present a visible sign of God's own love for the world (*Catechism of the Catholic Church* [CCC] 1639), and so they must make promises to learn to live that love. That's a tall order — one that vows including sincere but incomplete human promises (like baking a monthly red velvet cake) can't begin to compete with. If a couple is going to be a faithful sign of God's own love for the world, then they need to learn what God's love looks like. Who better to teach them than the Church that has been carefully tending Jesus' legacy of love for 2,000 years?

First, in general, Catholics understand marital love, not primarily as a feeling but *as a commitment to help each other become everything God created you and your spouse to be in this life and to help each other get to heaven in the next.* God loves us even when we don't deserve it, or haven't earned it, or even don't act in particularly likable or lovable ways. No matter what we do, he is always working to help us become everything we were created to be in this life and to enable us to get to heaven in the next.

Learning to love one another as God loves us means that husbands and wives must be willing to learn to do the same for one another. We must be willing to do this whether we feel like it or not, and whether our spouse deserves it or not. And we must be willing to do it for life, just as God loves us as long as he lives — that is, forever. Of course, even for Catholics, love includes all those things that help us feel good about each other — romance, along with cherishing, respect, and caretaking — but it goes far beyond this as well.

As part of this loving mission for husbands and wives to become everything God created them to be in this life, and to help each other get to heaven in the next, we must understand four qualities that distinguish God's love for us, and we must agree (at least implicitly) to live those qualities as fully as possible in our relationships. In short, couples marrying in the Church must promise to love each other *freely, totally, faithfully, and fruitfully.*

Freely

God chooses to love us freely. No one makes him do it. He makes the commitment to love us of his own free will, and he willingly sticks to that commitment even when we behave in sinful, unlovable ways. He loves us without expecting us to do anything in return to "pay him back."

In the same way, when you marry in the Church, you are promising to learn from the Church's wisdom how to love each other freely, even when your spouse doesn't deserve it and you don't feel like it. You are promising to love your spouse even through those times when you get little or nothing back and even when your spouse really makes big mistakes. That's not to say that if you are struggling to get your needs met in your marriage you don't have a right to seek help. In fact, the Catholic idea that love means working for each other's good means that if you are unhappy in your marriage you have the *right to expect your partner to work through that with you*, just like God works with us through the hard times in our relationship with him. Loving each other freely and without limits isn't easy, and sometime we need to get help to figure out how to do it. Regardless, when promising to love each other freely, both of you are promising to be "all in" and willing to give yourselves to each other, even when doing so stretches you in surprising ways.

Totally

God loves us totally. He doesn't hold anything back. He wants to give every single part of himself to us, and he wants us to give every part of ourselves back to him. He longs for us to be totally one with him (Jn 17:21). Indeed, the entire point of the Christian walk is ultimate union with God. (For more on this, see Greg's book, *Broken Gods: Hope, Healing, and the Seven Longings of the Human Heart*).

Similarly, husbands and wives are called to love each other totally, with no reservations. It is tempting for husbands and wives to put limits on their love: "I won't share this part of my life, my thoughts, my feelings, my dreams, my body, or myself with you." Catholics understand this temptation as the result of the same sin that ruptured the union between God, man, and woman in the Garden of Eden at the dawn of creation. It may be natural to want to place these kinds of limits on our love for each other, but Catholic couples must view these limits as obstacles to be overcome, not as the expected state of affairs. God respects our limitations, but he expects us to transcend those limitations if they represent obstacles to his love. In the same way, couples can be respectful of each other's brokenness and limitations, but they have every right to expect that they both will do everything they can to heal from that brokenness and overcome those limitations if they present any kind of obstacle to their marital love. It is this total gift of self that makes God's love for us truly intimate and makes a marriage modeled after God's love an "intimate partnership" (*Gaudium et Spes*, n. 48).

Faithfully

God loves us always and no matter what (Ps 100:5). God, who has the busiest schedule in the universe, never lets anything come between himself and his commitment to love you totally (Rom 8:31-39). He won't ever abandon you so that he can go love someone else who is more lovable. He won't let all the things he has to do stop him from giving you as much of him as you want or need. God's love is indissoluble and never ending.

In the same way, a marriage founded on God's love must be unbreakable (Mk 10:9). Even more than simply being able to count on our spouse never abandoning us, the faithfulness that characterizes marital love tells us that we have a right to expect that our spouse will not let other people, commitments, or obligations get in the way of loving us fully — and vice versa. Our spouse comes first and has a right to the best of us, not just the rest of us. Our marriage must be given priority, because it is our best chance to learn how to love as God loves, to become everything we were created to be, and receive the support we need to get to heaven.

It is true that, in a fallen world, other responsibilities and other relationships may sometimes compete with, or outright threaten, the primacy of the marriage, but Catholic couples understand this as an obstacle to be overcome, not something to accept. Catholic husbands and wives have a right to expect that their marriage will reflect the faithful character of God's love, meaning that they will always work to place each other first and above *all* others.

Fruitfully

Because God is love, and love is the commitment to work for the good of another, God is always doing more, creating more, loving more (Gen 1-2). God's doesn't have to create — he doesn't have to do anything — but he loves to create, and he loves to love that creation. At the same time he is creating, he is doing things to help his creation flourish (Lk 12:27). God doesn't hoard all of his love to himself or to some small, select group. Love demands to be shared, so God looks for more and more ways to share his love with his creation. In all these ways, God's love is fruitful.

Similarly, Catholic couples recognize that as wonderful as their love for each other is, it demands to be shared. They know that the more they share their love, the more it grows. So they do two things.

First, they welcome children as a gift from the Lord. They know that one of the most beautiful ways to celebrate their love for each other is to allow God to create another person out of that love, born to be a witness and visible sign of the power of the couple's closeness and commitment to each other. The couple that is open to life is open to receiving everything each other has to give.

The second way the Catholic husband and wife exercise the fruitfulness of their love is by working to nurture not only their children but also each other and all of the people in their life so that everyone they come in contact with might come a little closer to being their best selves because of their influence. Catholic couples are committed to doing everything they can to help all with whom they are in a relationship to fulfill their potential as people of God. In this way, Catholic couples exercise their call to spiritual fatherhood and motherhood, as well as physical fatherhood and motherhood.

Your Mission

Imagine what a marriage that is committed to living out, in an authentic way, this ideal of *free, total, faithful, and fruitful* loving would look like. THAT is the kind of love that truly has the power to fill your hearts, change the world, and call others to Christ!

That said, the mission of living out the Catholic vision of marriage isn't easy; and because of both sin and our fallen human nature, it doesn't come naturally. In particular, there are two major enemies that will come against you as you strive to live this vision of a free, total, faithful, and fruitful love in your marriage every day — namely, *addiction to comfort*, and a game we call "Marital Chicken."

Addiction to Comfort

In our experience, more than communication breakdowns, infidelity, abuse, or any other issue, *the biggest problem facing marriage is that husbands and wives tend to love their comfort zones more than they love each other.* Human beings are absolutely addicted to their comfort. This is the root of almost every other marital problem that exists (and frankly, the primary enemy of living a holy life, which is why overcoming this tendency in marriage is so important spiritually as well as relationally).

All of us struggle to love our spouse the way he or she needs to be loved. Instead, we would rather do what *we* want to do for our spouse and then call that "being loving," regardless of what our mate actually needs from us. We *could* be more present, more romantic, more sexual, a better listener, or a more attentive mate; but, to be perfectly honest, we're tired and just a little too comfy in our own corner of the house. It happens to all of us — men *and* women. We are called to be Christ to our mate, but too often "Christ" is sacked out on the sofa, hiding out in a hobby or job, or out saving the rest of the world instead of actively searching for the hundred or so ways he or she could *literally* be a savior right at home.

Loving our comfort zone more than our spouse threatens our promise to love *freely, totally, faithfully, and fruitfully* by sending the message, "When push comes to shove, you can count on me to do what I want, not what you or our marriage needs."

Marital Chicken

The second insidious obstacle to love is the game of Marital Chicken. When a couple plays, grown-ups sit around whining, "If only *you* were more romantic [or sexual, helpful, complimentary, emotional, rational, etc.], maybe *I* would be more romantic [or sexual, helpful, complimentary, emotional, rational, etc.]. But I know *you*. You'll never change!"

Playing this game allows us to avoid confronting our own fears of intimacy while getting to feel self-righteous at the same time. As you can imagine, the game is fairly addicting. What couples playing Marital Chicken forget is that they are not really responsible to their partners for living out those loving qualities. Rather, such couples must become more affectionate (or sexual, helpful, complimentary, emotional, rational, etc.) because that is the person *they* want to be — because that is the person *God is calling the couples to be.* When we die and God asks us if we lived out our vocation to love, we really don't think the Almighty is going to accept an excuse such as "Well, Lord, I *would* have, if only *my spouse* had been more [fill in the blank]."

Part of being Christ to each other involves being loving, not because our mates deserve such generosity (we so seldom deserve to be loved) but because our Christian dignity requires this of us. As C. S. Lewis writes in *The Four Loves*, "All who have good parents, wives, husbands, or children may be sure that at some times … [they] are loved not because they are lovable but because Love Himself is in those who love them."

Loving our mates the way Christ would love them — whether they "deserve" it or not — is absolutely essential to our own growth as Christians. To reject this responsibility is to reject God's call in our lives and injure our relationship with him. "As you did it to one of the least of these ... you did it to me" (Mt 25:40).

By refusing to respond to our call to love, too many of us offend our own dignity, destroy our own self-esteem, and foster alienation in our marriages. We are constantly being tempted to play manipulative games with our mates, valuing our own convenience and comfort above all else. When we do this, husbands and wives slowly turn each other into "bitches," "avoiders," or — at best — shriveled-up, bitter, emotional scorekeepers. What we need to be doing is turning each other into saints. Thank God, by learning how to use the graces of marriage, we can. Nothing can come between those couples who believe the fulfillment of their identities in Christ is inextricably tied to the success of their marital partnership. Nothing can embitter those couples that understand their role in preparing each other to share the joy of God's heavenly kingdom. When a husband and wife respond to their innate call to love and work to fulfill each other's Christian destinies, they open the door to a truly vital, loving, spiritual, *sacramental* marriage. They guarantee that they will remain both faithful and joyful together through good times and bad, wealth and poverty, sickness and health, loving and cherishing each other until they deliver their mate to the heavenly Father, who will smile upon them and say, "Well done, [my] good and faithful servant" (Mt 25:21).

Living the Dream: Because You're Worth It!

Living this vision of marriage and overcoming the common challenges to this vision takes spending more time, commitment, and energy on your marriage than many people do. But isn't it worth it? If you do this work, you can have the kind of marriage that will make the angels smile *and* the neighbors sick with jealousy! If you commit to this work, you will have the kind of marriage that fills your days with true joy, real passion, incredible depth of meaning, and surprising strength in times of trial. In short, you will have the love your heart longs for — the love that comes from God's own heart. You will experience a love that will mold and shape both of you as a couple into everything you were created to be in this life and enable you to celebrate heaven as the Eternal Wedding Feast (Rev 19:6-9)!

CHAPTER 2

The Celebration of a Lifetime

The Two Become One

Weddings are a cause for celebration. Jesus himself showed what an occasion for joy weddings are when he performed his first miracle at the wedding feast at Cana, transforming jars of water into the choicest wine (Jn 2:1-12). We want to help you discover how you can celebrate your marriage and experience the incredible joy that comes from living the fullness of the Catholic vision of married love!

In the last chapter, we examined what made the Catholic vision of marriage special and unique among all the many different visions of love. Specifically, you discovered that Catholic couples promise to spend their lives learning how to love each other *freely, totally, faithfully,* and *fruitfully.* When a couple strives to live out this unique vision of love in their relationship, God blesses them in two special and important ways. First, he empowers them to celebrate an incredible Christian union — a miraculous degree of togetherness that melts two selves into one. Second, he empowers them to celebrate a life-giving love. Both of these blessings are cause for the couple to celebrate the gift of their marriage over the course of a lifetime!

Historically, these two blessings have been known as the "ends," or goals, of marriage (i.e., the unitive and procreative ends), but they are more than duties married couples serve or jobs married couples do. Rather, they are gifts that married couples receive from God for learning to love each other freely, totally, faithfully, and fruitfully.

In this chapter, we'll explore the ways God wants to give you the graces you need to celebrate an *incredible Christian union*. We'll look at celebrating the second blessing, life-giving love, in Chapter 3.

Celebrating an Incredible Christian Union

We know that, in marriage, two become one (Mk 10:8). While that sounds pretty and poetic, this idea has practical significance for your marriage. There are two major ways to celebrate an incredible Christian union.

The *first* is by striving to rebuild the *original unity* of man and woman.

The *second* is to actively and intentionally *work together to fulfill your identities in Christ*. Let's look at each of these.

Rebuilding the Original Unity of Man and Woman

It can sometimes feel like men and women are from two different planets — Mars and Venus, if you like. Some people even think that husbands and wives are so different that they should never expect to truly understand each other, much less be best friends. In this view, supposedly, women are communicative, sensitive, emotive, relational, nurturing, loving, and supportive. Men, on the other hand, like football.

And never the twain shall meet.

If this is true of our experience today — and sadly, for many, it is — then we need to remember that this is not the way God intended, or intends, it to be. In his Theology of the Body, St. John Paul the Great reminded us that before original sin entered the world, there was a perfect union and a deep, intimate connection between man and woman that was rooted in their mutual love for God and their desire to do his will. St. John Paul II referred to this state of intimate connection as the *original unity of man and woman* (St. John Paul II, 2006).

Illustrating this union, Genesis tells us that when God created woman, Adam said, "This at last is bone of my bones and flesh of my flesh" (Gen 2:23). Please note that Adam did not say — to quote *My Fair Lady*'s Professor Henry Higgins — "Why can't a woman be more like a man?"

The estrangement and confusion present-day men and women experience around one another is a direct result of original sin. Clearly, it is not the way things ought to be. The "regrettable apple incident" was to men and women what the Tower of Babel was to the world.

Winning the "Battle" of the Sexes

The good news is that God, through marriage, gives us the grace we need to begin to restore the authentic partnership Adam and Eve experienced with each other, and to overcome the *false differences* that keep men and women at odds (as opposed to the authentic differences that facilitate partnership between men and women). These false differences constitute the tension between men and women that people refer to as the "Battle of the Sexes." True, we post-fallen people can't achieve the complete union that Adam and Eve experienced with each other and God (at least not this side of heaven). But through God's grace and our good efforts, there is much we can do in this life to bridge the gap that exists between genders.

Theologically speaking, this is the grace underlying what is known as the "unitive end" of marriage. When a man and woman freely and completely give themselves to each other, they commit to spending their lives becoming fluent in each other's "languages." By doing this, men and women can learn to celebrate the deep level of friendship and understanding that is born of helping one another become fully human persons. By learning to love and serve one another more perfectly, day-by-day, they help each other develop the missing parts of themselves. "And the two shall become one" (Mt 19:5).

Of course, saying that God gives us the grace to overcome false, or invalid, differences between men and women is not to deny that there are real differences between the sexes. But the true differences between men and women are much more subtle and profound than the polarized, overly simplistic definitions to which many in our society cling (e.g., "Men are rational, and women are emotional"; "Men don't do housework and don't take care of small children, and women shouldn't work out of the home," etc.). As moral theologian William May explains in his book *Marriage: The Rock on Which the Family Is Built,* gender differences are supposed to be differences in "*emphasis.*"

Celebrating the True Differences Between Man and Woman

What does this mean? In the beginning, at the dawn of creation, God shared the *same* aspects of himself (i.e., the same sets of characteristics and virtues) with both male and female *human beings*. Remember, Genesis says, "male and female he created *them*" (Gen 1:27, emphasis ours).

In other words, although men and women express their shared humanity in different and complementary ways, men and women have all qualities that make them both fully human *and*, therefore, completely understandable to each other — unlike those lions, tigers, and bears (*oh, my!*) that Adam was trying to chat up before Eve came along.

As St. John Paul II argued, the fact that Adam said of Eve, "This at last is bone of my bones and flesh of my flesh" (Gen 2:23), dramatically shows that Eve — body, mind, and soul — was a being to whom Adam could relate completely. In Eve, Adam found a true helpmate, a partner who "got him" and whom he could "get" as well. At last! Someone made of the same essential biological, psychological, emotional, and spiritual *stuff* as himself! (Hip hip hooray!)

So, *in the beginning*, both men *and* women were given the ability to reason, emote, love, communicate, produce, set goals, nurture, and so on — all the qualities that made them a matched set of fully functioning and complete human persons. Likewise, both men *and* women were called to live out *all* of these qualities to the fullest. However, based on how God created their bodies, Adam and Eve had different *styles* of applying these qualities to everyday life. These complementary ways men and women live out all the qualities that make them human through the unique bodies God gave them are what we respectively call "masculinity" and "femininity."

Complementarity: The "Genius" of Men and Women

Although God makes both men and women fully capable of doing many, if not all, of the same things as each other — and all the things that make them fully functioning, emotional, spiritual, psychological, and relational human beings — when men and women work *together* to bring their masculine and feminine gifts (what St. John Paul II referred to as men and women's respective "genius") to bear on a particular task, they do a better job of revealing the fullness of the particular quality and representing that virtue as it exists in God's own heart.

For instance, God is fully nurturing to us, his children (cf. Lk 11:13), and he enables both men and women to be fully nurturing in their own ways through the unique body he gave each of us. God ordained a woman's body to be able to nurse her young, to nourish them with her body like he nourishes us with his Body in the Eucharist. And he made mom's body round and soft and cuddly to give baby a safe, comforting place to rest.

But even though men cannot lactate (much as their wives might wish otherwise at 3 a.m.), God still requires them to be abundantly present and active in the lives of their children, just as God, our Father, is present and active in our lives. And dads have their own nurturing "genius." For instance, because of their superior upper-body strength, dads can lift their children up over their heads and toss them gently in the air (and even catch them!), much to their little ones' delight! Because men have scratchy faces/beards, they can put their cheeks under babies' chins and on their tummies and — *Bzzzzzzzzrrrrrbbbbrrt* — tickle them in ways moms can't, making their children giggle with affectionate joy ("Do it again, Daddy!").

God gave both men and women the ability — their respective "genius" — to be *fully* nurturing and loving (and every other quality), each in their own way; but he ordained the sexes to express this nurturance in equally valuable yet different and complementary ways, so that, taken together, their children could experience a more complete example of the nurturance that God exhibits in his own heart for all of us. As St. John Paul II taught us, men and women must prayerfully contemplate and emphasize their *bodies' unique capabilities* to first understand true masculinity and femininity. Then, we must use our masculinity and femininity as the prism through which we express our *full humanity*. By doing this together, men and women reflect God's image and likeness more perfectly. They create a deeper union with each other and with God — a union that shines out as a powerful witness to the world of God's own glory.

False Differences: Mars vs. Venus

As you read above, the pre-fallen Adam and Eve fully exhibited all the qualities God gave them, although they tended to emphasize these qualities differently. But after the fall of humankind, masculine and feminine "emphases" stopped being that and became whole other languages that — because as Augustine put it, "Sin makes you stupid" (well, he said, "Sin darkens the intellect," but same difference) — men and women couldn't speak and didn't understand.

After the Fall, men and women staked out separate domains defined by the borders of their comfort zones and forbade each other from ever crossing the line — as if either ever would want to. This tragic estrangement continued throughout history, worsening and worsening until men and women began to feel as if they were born on two completely different planets and spoke two completely different languages (Martian and Venusian, if you like).

But God never intended for masculinity and femininity to be different languages, much less different planets. Rather, he intended that they should be complementary expressions of a shared *humanity*. The true, godly differences between men and women are the ones that enable them to work better together because of those differences, not stare at each other in frustrated confusion. Through marriage, God gives husbands and wives the grace necessary to begin to restore the original unity experienced by our first parents. God does not give us an insufficient grace, allowing us to merely hook up at the Interplanetary High School Prom ("This Year's Theme: *Counting Stars!*"). Instead, God gives husbands and wives all the grace they need to transcend false differences, to discover that they were really earthlings all along, and to speak one language again: a language of joyful, mutual love and generous service, a language spoken into being by the Father, exemplified by the Son, and inspired by the Holy Spirit.

Celebrating Complementarity: Overcoming the False Differences

God gives us men and women the unifying grace we need to overcome the Battle of the Sexes, but we must be willing to do the work that grace empowers us to do. Unfortunately, too many Christian husbands and wives do not have *complementary* roles; instead, they have *compensatory* roles that inhibit their growth, both as human persons and as Christians. For example, certain wives never learn to do or become *A*, *B*, or *C*, because, as they put it, "That's what my husband is for." Similarly, certain husbands never learn to do or become *X*, *Y*, or *Z* because "That's what my wife is for." What such individuals forget is that they are passing up the chance God gives them to become the people he created them to be: competent, fully formed human beings, eager to challenge the limitations original sin placed upon their bodies, minds, spirits, and relationships. Sanctification is not just about overcoming spiritual obstacles; it is about overcoming physical, emotional, and psychological ones as well. Are you taking advantage of the marital grace God gives you to become fully human? Or are you hiding behind the sad and alienating excuse, "That's just not what women [or men] are supposed to be"?

Such a statement is a cop-out unworthy of our Christian dignity. Men must be men like Jesus Christ is a man. And women must be women like the Virgin Mary or the Proverbs 31 wife is a woman. Only then will Christian husbands and wives be able to experience the truth of complementarity and the fullness of marital grace.

If you are a Christian married person, God is giving you the grace to do the work. In order to understand the *specific* work you must do, consider the following.

EXERCISE: Winning the Battle of the Sexes

The true, godly differences between men and women should be a catalyst, not an obstacle, for healthy intimacy and partnership. The following questions can help you have a better sense of how God wants your and your mate's masculinity and femininity to be a blessing to each other.

STEP ONE: *Embrace Your Masculinity or Femininity*

Prayerfully contemplate your body. What can you do with your body that your spouse simply cannot do, or do as well, with his or hers? This is God's definition of masculinity and femininity. Emphasize these things in your life.

STEP TWO: *Embrace Your Humanity*

- What domestic jobs (e.g., cooking and housekeeping, taking care of the finances, nurturing and playing with the children, etc.) are you *physically capable* of doing but don't do (or do extremely rarely) simply because you lack practice or don't like doing them?
- What tasks do you require your mate to do for you, simply because you lack practice or don't like doing them?
- What qualities (e.g., emotionality, rationality, communicativeness, affection, etc.) do you lack in your life, or excuse yourself for not having because "That's not how women [or men] are supposed to be"?

STEP THREE: *Embrace the Unity of Man and Woman*

The tasks, domestic responsibilities, and personal qualities you listed above are exactly the areas you must develop in your life in order to become the human being God created you to be, in order to have a marriage based on complementarity and sanctification, instead of simple compensation or spiritual enabling. To develop these aspects of yourself is to participate fully in the grace God gives you through the unitive end of marriage. Do you have the guts to become the new Adam and new Eve on your block? As a Christian married couple, you are being called by God to nothing less. Will you accept his call?

An Incredible Christian Union, Part Two: A Shared Mission

So far, we've been looking at ways you can celebrate an uncommon Christian union in your marriage by working to restore the original unity between the sexes. But there is a second way every married couple can create an even deeper union. Recall that earlier in this chapter we said that the source of Adam and Eve's unity before the Fall was their mutual love for God and their shared desire to do his will. In addition to winning the Battle of the Sexes, you can achieve greater intimacy and unity with your spouse by cultivating a shared mission that reflects your desire for God's will to shine out in your lives together.

The Secret of a Divorce-Proof Marriage

Marriage researchers have discovered that couples who create a shared vision for their lives enjoy much happier and stable marriages (Gottman, 2011). For the Christian, this means that there is really only *one reason for marrying* that guarantees the lifelong happiness and relevance of a marriage, only one reason that even comes close to addressing the true meaning of a Christian marriage. More than love and companionship, the real function of a Christian marriage is *for a husband and wife to help each other become the people God created them to be in this life and help get each other to heaven in the next.*

God didn't go to all the trouble of instituting the Sacrament of Matrimony just so that you could have a guaranteed date for bowling night. The real dignity of your Christian marriage comes from promising to spend every single day of your lives discovering and fulfilling your identities in Christ. In other words, marriage is a partnership in actualizing your Christian destiny.

Scripture tells us that "whether we live or whether we die, we are the Lord's" (Rom 14:8). Through marriage, God gives each one of us a sacred trust: to prepare our mate to spend eternity in heaven with *him* or *her*. This is what that nice-sounding phrase exhorting husbands and wives to "be Christ to one another" means. In essence, God says to every person who marries in the Church, "I am choosing *you* to play a central role in your partner's sanctification. Your spouse may not make it without you. Be sure that he or she makes it *with* you." All people who are married in the Church have the right to expect that their mate will be their best hope — second only to the saving grace of Jesus Christ and their own free will — of helping them become everything they were created to be in this life and get to heaven in the next.

This responsibility should not come as a huge surprise to you; after all, sanctification is the chief work of any sacrament. When you marry in the Church, you are not simply saying, "We love each other," or "We're best friends," or even "We're really hot for each other." Of course, all of these things should be true. But even more importantly, when you marry in the Church, you are acknowledging that from now until the day you die, *God has made you responsible* (second only to the saving work of Jesus Christ and your partner's free will) to see that your husband or wife becomes the person God created him or her to be. And you are acknowledging that you sincerely believe you have a better chance, with each other than without, of becoming all God intends *you both* to be. As one Protestant minister's wife said to us, "Jesus saved me, but my husband has everything to do with what shape I'm in when I get there." Amen, sister.

In His Image

So, what did God create you to be? How do you know what your identity in Christ is? The answer lies in the Scripture passage that tells us we are created in God's image and likeness. We might not be able to identify God in a lineup. We don't know the color of his skin and hair, or his weight, or the size of his nose — but we do know what he looks like. We "see" God every day in his compassion, mercy, justice, truth, love, creativity, wisdom, and so on. Being created in God's image means that each of us is called to reflect those aspects of him, those virtues (love, truth, wisdom, justice, compassion, etc.), which he encoded in our DNA at conception (metaphorically speaking). As C. S. Lewis writes in *Mere Christianity*, "[God] lends us a little of his reasoning powers and that is how we think: He puts a little of His love into us and that is how we love one another."

Wade in the Water: Our Baptismal Identity

Baptism is the foundation of our Christian identity. When we were baptized, God gave us some incredible gifts. In addition to washing our souls clean of original sin, he infused us with sanctifying grace; gave us the three theological virtues of faith, hope, and love; bestowed upon us the seven gifts of the Holy Spirit (wisdom, understanding, counsel, fortitude, knowledge, piety, and fear of the Lord); granted us moral virtues (e.g., prudence, justice, temperance, fortitude); and empowered us to bear the twelve fruits of the Holy Spirit (charity, joy, peace, patience, kindness, goodness, generosity, gentleness, faithfulness, modesty, self-control, and chastity). To have an identity in Christ is to live out these freely given virtues and qualities in the unique way the circumstances of our lives demand. You know you have the *seeds of an identity* if you can say that, between now and the day you die, you'd like to be known for *these particular* virtues, qualities, ideals, and beliefs. You know the *strength of your identity* by how much your daily life reflects the active pursuit of those virtues, qualities, ideals, and beliefs. If someone made a reality show of your life (*Real Housewives — and Husbands — of Vatican City!*), would viewers be able to tell what you stood for just by watching the choices you make, the priorities you set, and the way you live?

The more our daily choices and behaviors reflect these God-given values, virtues, dreams, and goals, the more solid our Christian identity. While each one of us is individually responsible to God for living out this identity, it is the job of a sacramental marriage to support, nurture, and encourage us in this pursuit.

"Pretty words," you may comment. "But why should I care?"

"You ... Complete Me"

Practically speaking, being partners in fulfilling your Christian identities means that when your spouse asks for more from you, you are obliged to give it, so that you can respond to God's invitation — written on your spouse's heart — to grow in ways you never would on your own. You respond to this invitation not necessarily because your spouse always deserves such generosity (we so seldom deserve to be loved), but because you have a responsibility to God to demonstrate that generosity. You may not *feel* like doing more romantic things for your mate, but through these gestures you participate in God's plan for letting your partner know how special she is to God. You may fear the vulnerability you feel in lovemaking, but that vulnerability is the very thing you and your partner must learn to enjoy if you want to become open to God's eternal love. Whenever you hold back in your married life, you prevent God from loving your mate the way he wants to love him — the way your mate needs to be loved. Remember, God requires you to be Christ to your spouse. When was the last time Christ refused you a sign of his affection? When did he ever refuse to share the comfort of his precious body with you? You may not have deserved it, and God may or may not have felt like doing it, but, oddly, these issues never came up.

And this is just the beginning. Do you encourage the creativity of your mate — as God does — or do you say, "Why would you want to do something silly like that?" Do you affirm the beauty of your husband or wife — as God does — or do you criticize your spouse and/or treat her or him with benign neglect? Do you seek to fulfill your partner's dreams, goals, and needs — as God does — or do you cling to your own comfort, asking your spouse to be limited to what you deem acceptable or "reasonable"?

For the Christian, being a master of marital skills has little to do with being a good earthbound companion and everything to do with being a collaborator in God's plan of salvation for you and your mate. If your spouse isn't even worth a couple of flowers, a card, some good conversation, or some physical affection from you, how will your mate ever learn to accept the immense bounty of love that God has prepared for her in his heavenly kingdom?

Helping your mate get to heaven involves a great deal more than getting to church on Sunday and praying your Rosary. It involves all that — *plus* being the loving, attentive, generous spouse Christ would be if he were married to your partner. Have you ever really appreciated the importance of your role as a husband or wife in God's plan? Grasping this importance is the essential first step of answering the call of the Church, "Families, become what you are" (*Familiaris Consortio*, n. 17).

EXERCISE: Creating Shared Meaning — Partners in Christ

At the beginning of this section, we mentioned research showing that couples who create shared meaning for their lives and marriage have much happier and more stable relationships than other couples who are less intentional about sharing a mission (VanderDrift and Lewandowsky, 2010; Gottman, 2011). The following exercise is intended to serve two needs. First, it will help you to clarify both your identity in Christ and what you must do to live out that identity more consistently in your life and marriage. Next, it will help you identify how to make your marriage a partnership in fulfilling that Christian destiny. In essence, by the end of this exercise, you will have developed a basic "mission statement" (or "marital imperative") around which to build your life and marriage. Don't expect to fulfill every part of that mission statement today. Rather, view it as a plan of action, an itinerary for what you will be working toward over the course of your lives together.

PART ONE: *Your Christian Identity*

Directions: Just like there are different religious orders (e.g., Jesuits, Dominicans, Franciscans, etc.), with each emphasizing a different mission or *charism* (teaching, preaching, hospitality, simplicity, etc.) that witnesses to another facet of God's face to the world, God calls each family to be its own religious community (i.e., "domestic church," cf. *Lumen Gentium*) that witnesses to his goodness through the qualities they live out in their household (generosity, faithfulness, hospitality, joy, etc.). Take some time to prayerfully meditate on the questions below. Do not share your answers with your mate at this time. This first part is about *your* identity in Christ, the identity that you would be responsible for living out, whether or not you were ever married.

1. Most of the virtues listed below were given to you freely and automatically at your baptism. Of them all, which virtues do you believe God has made dearest to your heart? Identify a few virtues that are *most important* to you. Use the list below, or write your own in the space provided. (If you have a hard time answering, try thinking of the qualities you wish to be *most* known for at the end of your life.)

   __Love __Faith __Hope
   __Wisdom __Understanding __Fortitude
   __Integrity __Counsel __Holiness
   __Fear of the Lord __Prudence __Knowledge
   __Justice __Moderation __Charity
   __Joy __Peace __Patience
   __Kindness __Goodness __Generosity
   __Gentleness __Faithfulness __Modesty
   __Self-control __Chastity __Service
   __Hospitality __Compassion __Creativity

   Others: ____

   ____

2. Write the virtues you indicated in the form of a personal motto. (For example: "With God's help, I will spend my life pursuing the following virtues: love, wisdom, and service.") Now it's your turn.

   "With God's help, I will spend my life pursuing the following virtues: ______

   ____."

3a. Recall the things that irritate you most about your spouse. Annoying habits, traits, infuriating opinions or behaviors, etc. Write one or two of the most trying examples here: ______________________________

____

____

____

3b. When your spouse does these annoying things, how, specifically, will you change your behavior to more adequately reflect your chosen motto? (For example: "How can I respond more lovingly when my wife is late?")

4. We all hold back from our mates. What do you hold back? How will God's grace and the virtues you identified help you overcome this selfishness? How will you motivate yourself to give more generously to your mate?

5. What steps must you take so that your work life, parenting life, and personal life can more adequately reflect your personal motto? (For example: take a parenting class, go on a couples' retreat, do more spiritual reading, go to daily Mass, get additional job training, etc.) What role would you like your spouse to play in helping you achieve these goals?

6. What goals or accomplishments do you believe God is asking you to pursue at this time in your life? (Think of those most heartfelt desires that you have dismissed as silly but somehow won't go away.) What role would you like your spouse to play in helping you achieve these goals?

PART TWO: *Your Partnership*

Directions: You and your mate should now share and discuss your answers to Part One. During this discussion, keep in mind that your mate has arrived at her answers to Part One through prayerful discernment. Her answers reflect her genuine beliefs about the identity God is making her responsible for fulfilling. This identity may involve things you don't appreciate, think are silly, or don't like; but God didn't ask your opinion when he gave your mate this mission. He only demands that you be faithful to the promises you made in your marriage and help your partner fulfill her identity. Remember, your mate may not make it without you, but you are responsible to God to make certain she makes it with you.

Discuss: In order to become the partner God asks you to be to your mate, what specific actions must you take, what skills must you develop, or what choices must you make in your daily life? What must you do to increase your mate's chances of fulfilling his identity in Christ?

PART THREE: ***A Promise***

Take turns pledging the following:

[*Say your partner's name*] I genuinely respect the person you are, and the person God wants you to be. To that end, I promise that I will work to see the good in the things you value, especially when I don't understand. I will never say that the dreams, goals, or values God has placed in your heart are silly or unworthy of my time and attention. I promise to be the most important influence in your life, second only to our Savior, Jesus Christ, because I love and honor who you are and who God is calling you to become. I promise that I will love you and support you with all of my life, all the days of my life. And I promise that with the Lord's help, I will be your best hope for arriving, properly attired, at the heavenly banquet.

______________________________ / ______________________________

Husband's Signature Wife's Signature

Conclusion

In this chapter, you discovered that the phrase "the two shall become one" is more than mere poetry. It is a promise. God wants to use your marriage to restore the unity that existed at the beginning of time between Adam and Eve, and to show the world that men and women are not meant to be enemies or mysteries to one another, *but true, intimate helpmates for each other.* Further, he wants to unite you in a mission that will bring his face to the world in ways only you and your spouse can, and to empower your marriage to be a blessing to everyone who encounters you. And by committing your lives to all of this, God plans to give you the grace each of you needs to help each other become everything you were created to be in this life and to enable each other to get to heaven in the next! Clearly, God is giving you a great deal to celebrate!

But wait! There's more!

In the next chapter, we'll explore the second blessing God wants to give you, a blessing that will be a cause for celebration for generations — literally — to come; the blessing that accompany *a life-giving love.*

CHAPTER 3

The Celebration Continues

A Life-Giving Love

In the last chapter, you discovered that as married couples commit to living out the free, total, faithful, and fruitful love that comes from God's own heart, he gives them two special blessings to celebrate throughout their lives; an *incredible Christian union* and *a life-giving love*. So far, we've looked at the ways marital grace empowers you to experience an uncommon degree of unity between you and your mate by winning the Battle of the Sexes and creating shared meaning by growing together in your Christian identities.

Don't Stop the Party

But, as evidenced by our abundance of feast days, Catholics love a party. So naturally, there is still a second celebration to which all Catholic couples are invited: the celebration of a *life-giving love*. These two goals of marriage — unity and procreativity — are really inseparable from each other and feed into one another. *A true, unifying love must also be a life-giving love* (and vice versa), not just metaphorically, but literally, in the procreative sense. Children represent the miraculous unity between a husband and wife like nothing else.

In his *Letter to Families*, St. John Paul the Great told us:

> Rather than closing [spouses] up in themselves, [a couple's unity] opens them towards new life, towards a new person. As parents, they will be capable of giving life to a being like themselves, not only bone of their bones and flesh of their flesh ... but an image and likeness of God — a person. (n. 8)

Of course, Jesus himself said that anyone who welcomes a little child welcomes him (Mt 18:5). Spouses who truly love each other and love our Lord will welcome the children he wants to give them.

This is a timely message. Challenging the low birth rates that are causing social problems throughout Europe, Pope Francis asserted, "In a world often marked by egoism, a large family is a school of solidarity and of mission that's of benefit to the entire society" (comments to the National Association of Large Families, 2014).

Over the years, certain people have taken a lot of swings at what they think is "the Church's position" on sex and procreation. Unfortunately, these people are often too blinded by their own ignorance to see that what they are swinging at isn't the Church's teaching at all, but rather a Monty Pythonized (cf. *The Meaning of Life*), pop-culture bastardization of Church teaching. Later on, we'll look at how you can experience a truly joyful, intimate, soulful sexual life with your spouse. For now, we want to simply explore a few brief points about how welcoming children as a gift from the Lord can help you celebrate the fullness of your marriage.

Celebrating the Joy of Creative Love

"Because God is a lover, he is also a creator" (*Our Sunday Visitor's Encyclopedia of Catholic Doctrine*). God is love, so part of his very nature is to create new things to be loved. This is why God seems to be endlessly fascinated with creating new things. It gives him more to love.

God especially loves to create people. As the Church tells us in the Vatican Council II document *Gaudium et Spes*, the human being is "the only creature on earth which God willed for itself." Why? Because we are the only creatures he gets to spend an eternity loving. We are the only earthly beings built to last — so to speak. One can only guess that for God it is a joy beyond words to create creatures whom he can love *eternally*. This same God, who generously longs to share all of his joy with us, gives husbands and wives a taste of the particular joy that encompasses creating and loving the creation by inviting us to bring his children into the world.

Pope Francis noted that "each child is a great miracle ... that changes life" (2014)! When a couple conceives a child, they are making a statement. They are saying, "This child is a living witness to the intimacy and love we share." There is no more real way for two to become one than in the act of creating a child together.

This isn't just a theological point. In her book *The Good Marriage*, secular relationship researcher Judith Wallerstein argued that when married couples close their hearts to children, their relationships take on the form of a "romantic anti-marriage" that becomes cold and isolating with time.

Rather than being antithetical to joy and intimacy, being open to life makes lovemaking a powerful, spiritual, earth-shattering, even redemptive, event. All of the books in the popular press about "spiritual sex" and "tantric lovemaking" have nothing on the sheer joy, vulnerability, spirituality, and total self-gift that accompany knowing that "tonight we are making a baby." Likewise, there are many books that proclaim the virtues of "simultaneous orgasm" — and, to be honest, they speak a truth. But nothing, absolutely nothing, compares to the profound joy that occurs when *a husband, a wife, and God climax together* — and a life is created. How sad it is that our sexuality has been so perverted by the pagans and misrepresented by the media that such a statement might actually be shocking to many of you reading this book. But the fact remains: sex is a good that God gave to the godly. The pagans stole it from us when we weren't looking, and it's time we take it back (see more in Chapter 11). Through the procreative work of marriage, God gives us the grace to do just that. To paraphrase theologian Scott Hahn, God empowers us to experience a love so profound that in nine months it has to be given its own name.

Celebrating Partnership Through Creative Love

But what about those times when a couple isn't ready to have another child?

Even when a couple has valid reasons for delaying or postponing pregnancy, appreciating the value of "openness to life" can help the couple celebrate a more intimate sexual partnership. In fact, a great help to couples wishing to celebrate this unique sexual partnership is the practice of Natural Family Planning, or NFP.

NFP and artificial contraception (the pill, condoms, etc.) exemplify two radically different mind-sets about sexuality. Contraception is isolating. It prevents a husband and wife from giving themselves totally to each other, and it is almost always one spouse's responsibility (usually the woman's). Contraception promotes a fear-based approach to sexuality by treating pregnancy as a disease that should be prevented — an optional by-product of pleasure. Various forms of artificial contraception (the pill, for instance) often have harmful side effects (NIH, 2015); increase women's risk of breast, cervical, and ovarian cancer as well as a 200 percent increased risk of brain tumors (NCI, 2012; Andersen, Fiis, and Hallas, 2014); they poison the environment (Parry, 2012); they are prone to failure (up to 30 percent for condoms — CDC, 2013); they make sex habitual rather than special; and they can present physical barriers to intimacy.

By contrast, NFP promotes the union of the couple by making family planning a shared responsibility of a husband and wife. As the Church's *Letter to Families* puts it, NFP makes it so that "Both [spouses] are responsible for their potential and later actual fatherhood and motherhood. The husband cannot fail to acknowledge and accept the result of a decision that has also been his own. He cannot hide behind such expressions as: 'I don't know,' 'I didn't want it,' or 'You're the one who wanted it.' "

NFP facilitates ongoing, prayerful communication between husbands and wives about their fertility. Studies show that NFP is as effective as hormonal contraception — over 99 percent (Hermann, Heil, and Gnoth, 2007) — and it is becoming both more practical and effective than ever because of simple-to-use electronic fertility monitors and NFP-related apps powered by sophisticated and highly accurate computer algorithms.

Interestingly enough, while many Catholics believe the Church is behind the times, the secular world is beginning to wake up to how cutting edge the Church's views really are. More and more, secular physicians are promoting Fertility Awareness Methods of family planning — which is really just NFP without the spiritual dimension (Kunang, 2015). Secular feminists are promoting the method. As one woman put it in in an article on FAM on the popular wellness site Well+Good, "How can we consider ourselves to be the feminists we are if we don't know the cycles of our body?" (Gallagher, 2015). Additionally, many women are beginning to wonder why they are putting so much energy into exercising, eating organic foods, avoiding pesticides, preservatives, and genetically-modified foods, while simultaneously pumping their bodies full of cancer-causing artificial hormones (Grigg-Spall, 2013).

But despite its health benefits and its effectiveness as a method of helping couples to both *avoid* and *achieve* pregnancy, NFP's true benefits come from its constant encouragement for husbands and wives to continually talk and pray about their priorities and becoming or being parents. NFP couples must simply be more intentional — more *mindful* — about their sexual relationship, which facilitates greater closeness and intimacy. Couples who practice NFP constantly seek after God's will for their lives in a way that is very difficult, if not impossible, for contracepting couples. They experience a sharing of one another and a level of communication that no contracepting couple ever could. So, even when a couple has a legitimate reason to hold off on becoming pregnant, having a more procreative view of sexuality facilitates the closer union of the husband and wife. In light of this deeper level of sharing facilitated by NFP, it is little wonder that a significant number of NFP couples report that NFP helps them experience a much more satisfying and stable marriage (VandeVusse, Hanson, and Fehring, 2004).

Celebrating Responsible Parenthood

Of course, the true joy of Catholic procreation (and this is the part you'll *never* hear about in the media) is that it doesn't stop at conception. When we Catholics say "yes" to the gift of a child, the Church reminds us that we must also be in a position to say "yes" to the forming of that child's body, mind, and soul. Doing this requires the couple to work hard on the health and strength of their relationship with each other and with any children they may already have. The communication and partnership required by this effort is another way that a love that is open to life calls couples and families to experience deeper union with each other.

The Church refers to the process of forming persons as *integral procreation*. In other words, Catholics view procreation as *a continuous process of ongoing formation that extends from the moment of conception to the time our children are returned to God.* Procreation is the process of cooperating with God to form minds and souls, not just bodies. As St. John Paul II put it, "Fatherhood and motherhood represent a *responsibility which is not simply physical but spiritual in nature*" (*Letter to Families*; emphasis in original).

Indeed, Sirach 16:1-3 provides important support for the idea of responsible parenthood, reminding us that the blessing of children is intimately tied to our ability to raise them to love the Lord.

> Do not yearn for worthless children,
> or rejoice in wicked offspring.
> Even if they be many, do not rejoice in them
> if they do not have fear of the LORD.
> Do not count on long life for them,
> or have any hope for their future.
> For one can be better than a thousand;
> rather die childless than have impious children! (NABRE)

Because the formation of whole persons is so important, the Church teaches "responsible parenthood" (cf. *Humanae Vitae*, *Familiaris Consortio*, *Letter to Families*). That is, in discerning God's will for the size of our families, we are obliged to consider the resources (or lack thereof) he has given us to provide for the physical, emotional, and spiritual needs of a child. The Church reminds us that in considering whether it is time to have a child, a husband and wife will

> thoughtfully take into account both their own welfare and that of their children, those already born and those which the future may bring. For this accounting they need to reckon with both the material and the spiritual conditions of the times as well as of their state in life. Finally, they should consult the interests of the family group, of temporal society, and of the Church herself. The parents themselves and no one else should ultimately make this judgment in the sight of God. (*Gaudium et Spes*, n. 50)

Again, all of this requires a degree of constant prayer and communication that can't help but strengthen the closeness a couple has with each other.

Celebrating the Selflessness of Creative Love

Even if couples decide that they aren't able to have another child in the short or longer term, by respecting the procreative dimension of marital love they will continue to grow closer to each other because of their willingness to put each other first over even their own desires. How can they do this? Again, by practicing Natural Family Planning.

There are about a million ways we can use our sexuality to abuse ourselves and others, and married couples are not immune to this. Most commonly, we treat our sexuality as if it were a street drug we take to make us happy. Or we use it to inflate a pathetic self-image ("Hey! I can't be all bad. I got some!"). This attitude hurts the unity we can have with our spouse because it turns our mate into a thing to be used (or a thing to be resented when he or she refuses to be used) instead of a person to be loved, cherished, and respected.

Any abuse of self or others decreases our ability to be happy either in marriage or with God in heaven. That's why husbands and wives are encouraged by the Church to make use of periodic abstinence (the time — usually about a week or so each month, during the fertile phase of a woman's cycle — when the couple will refrain from having sex, if they have determined that they have godly reasons to avoid pregnancy) as a *spiritual exercise* to help each other master, purify, and perfect their sexuality, so that they can love each other more honestly, more generously, and more respectfully. By the way, although the forms of this vary, periodic abstinence is not just a Catholic phenomenon. Hinduism, Buddhism, and several popular Eastern texts on spiritual sexuality all speak of the benefits of sexual abstinence in various forms. Virtually every major spiritual system on earth values some form of abstinence as a means of purifying both sexuality and the human person. Aristotle, who lived some four centuries before Christ, tells us: "The man who abstains from bodily pleasures and delights in this very fact is temperate, while the man who is annoyed at it is self-indulgent" (*Nicomachean Ethics*).

In over 20 years of marriage ministry and counseling, we have never met a couple who loves each other more *because* they drink too much, eat too much, play too much, sleep too much, or otherwise abuse themselves. Caving in to every whim of our bodies is one of the quickest ways to destroy both self-esteem and mutual respect. That's why people who eat, drink, play, and sleep in moderation are happier and healthier than people who don't do enough of those things, or do them too much. The same is true about sex. When couples are willing to make the sacrifices necessary to learn to put each other's good before their own immediate pleasure, they dedicate themselves to cultivating the sacrificial attitude that lies at the heart of the Christian vision of love. They learn to trust each other on a deeper level, a level that says, "You can count on me to always put you and what's good for our marriage first. I will never pressure you, guilt you, or manipulate you into doing something just because I feel like it."

It isn't always easy to live this kind of love. Sometimes it can be a real challenge. But from both personal experience and the witness of thousands of couples we've worked with over the years, we know it's a challenge worth accepting. The couple that is willing to take up this challenge for the good of each other and their marriage fosters an incredible Christian union. Clearly, in the hands of someone who knows what he or she is doing, marriage is an awe-inspiring thing. It is one of the best tools we have for perfecting each other in love.

Get the Party Started

The last two chapters have explored the two major blessings God wants to gift your marriage with; an uncommon union and life-giving love. Celebrating these blessings throughout your life together will help you become the people God is calling you to be and help each of you prepare the other to participate in the Eternal Wedding Feast of Heaven. Additionally, celebrating these blessings will enable you to call the world to Christ through the uniquely close, intimate, grace-filled intimacy you and your spouse share.

We know, both from our personal and professional experience, that living out the call to Catholic marriage isn't always easy, but it is amazing. In good times and bad, sickness and health, for richer or poorer, God will use the lives you are building together to open your hearts to a love you couldn't even begin to imagine: a love that has the power to make every day of your life a celebration of God's providence and passion. God wants to teach you how to have an uncommonly amazing marriage, both by sharing his vision for married love with you and then giving you the grace you need to fulfill it. Will you let him? Let your lives be your "yes" to his invitation to love.

CHAPTER 4

At the Feet of the Master

Lessons in Love

"The family that prays together stays together."
SERVANT OF GOD PATRICK PEYTON, C.S.C.

Living the unique vision of marriage we've described in the last few chapters doesn't come naturally. Many of us didn't witness this in our parents' marriage, and we certainly don't see it on television, in the movies, or on the Internet! The fact is, no matter how much you and your spouse love each other, there is a point in every marriage where every couple hits the wall — a point where it feels like all the human love you can summon on your own just isn't enough to make it. In those times, couples need to plug into a power source that is bigger than both of them put together. They need to create a direct line that taps into the love that comes from God's own heart.

In order to have any hope of succeeding at living out the radically different, deeply soulful, and ultimately transformative, *free*, *total*, *faithful*, and *fruitful* marital love to which we're called, we are going to have to sit, together, as a couple, at the feet of the Master, and learn from him one day at a time. *We're going to have to learn to pray together as a couple*, every day, about every aspect of our marriage and the life we are building together as a couple.

But Isn't Prayer "Too Private"?

Many Catholics mistakenly believe that prayer is a private affair that is simply too personal and too intimate to be shared with one's spouse, but nothing could be further from the truth. As Catholics, we believe that while prayer is certainly an intimate affair, and deeply personal, it is never private.

Even when you think you are praying alone, in reality, the entire communion of saints is praying with you! Prayer is always a *communal* activity. As the *Catechism* tells us, "Prayer is *Christian* insofar as it is communion with Christ and extends throughout the Church, which is his Body" (2565, emphasis in original). By definition, then, prayer is an activity that draws us into deeper intimacy with God *and* others. While there is certainly a place and a time for praying on your own, there is really no such thing as a prayer that you keep to yourself. It would not be a stretch to say that you are never less alone than when you pray.

If a couple truly wishes to live a full and joyful Catholic marriage, praying *together* is anything but optional. This is more than just a pious sentiment. There's actually a solid body of evidence that backs up the practical benefits of couple-prayer.

Science Says — Benefits of Couple-Prayer

If there was a completely affordable pill that was completely without side effects and proven to make you up to 20 percent happier, would you take it? Well, God has something even better for you.

A joint study by the University of Virginia and the University of Texas at San Antonio found that up to 83 percent of couples who pray together are happy with their marriage compared to only 69 percent of couples that do not pray together. On average, couples who pray together tend to be about 15 to 20 percent happier with their relationships than couples who don't (Rushnell and DuArt, 2011). Likewise, research by the Florida State University Family Institute shows that couples who pray together display higher levels of marital commitment and are significantly less likely to fall prey to infidelity (Fincham, Lambert, Beach, 2010). These are just two examples of literally hundreds of studies that show that when couples pray together, they are dramatically more secure and happy with each other than couples that don't. In fact, according to sociologist Andrew Greeley, of all the factors known to contribute to marital happiness and stability, couple-prayer has been found to be "the most powerful correlate of marital happiness that we have yet discovered" (1992).

Couple Prayer: How Do You Begin? What Do You Say?

First of all, relax. Just like there is no one right way to talk to a friend, there isn't one right way to pray. God, who indeed calls us "friends" (Jn 15:15), is happy to receive our prayers as long as they come from our heart.

Try to choose a regular time (e.g., 9:00 p.m.) or at least a regular time of the day (e.g., "right after dinner" or "right before bed") and a consistent place. This way you can create a prayer ritual, and it will be easier to remember. Don't worry if one of you tends to remember to initiate prayer more than the other. Although, ultimately, it is both of your jobs to make prayer happen, the most important thing is that it happens.

Once you've managed to find a good time and place, then what? What do you say? The short answer is, "Whatever you want."

Because there isn't a right way to pray, you have a lot of freedom about what your prayer time might look like. That said, here are some things you might like to keep in mind so that you and your beloved can get the most out of couple-prayer.

1. Remember the Point

No matter what you do, always remember that the point of couple-prayer is not about checking off certain boxes or jumping through certain spiritual hoops. At its best, couple-prayer is a shared, intimate conversation with God that brings you closer to him and to *each other*. Keep thinking about what kinds of prayer might have the greatest chance of helping you accomplish those ends.

Do you have a favorite prayer from childhood? A particular devotion (like the Rosary or Divine Mercy Chaplet) that you'd like to try? Is there a Scripture study guide or prayer book you're familiar with or that someone has recommended to you? Maybe you're just more comfortable talking out loud to God in your own words. Feel free to experiment. It's normal to feel awkward the first few times you try to pray together as a couple. But if, after a while, you aren't feeling inspired by your present efforts, try a different approach. The beautiful thing about our faith is that there are so many ways Catholics can pray, you'll never run out of options.

2. Formal or Informal Prayer?

There are two basic forms of simple (aka "vocal") prayer: formal and informal. Formal prayer involves prayers that have been provided by the Church — such as the Hail Mary, the Our Father, or the Rosary — or perhaps other devotions or a Scripture study. Formal prayer isn't formal in the sense that it's fancy and requires you to wear a tuxedo or ball gown, but in the sense that it follows a particular form. We like to think of formal prayer as a love poem or a love song. Even though someone else wrote it, singing "your song" to each other or quoting lines from a meaningful passage of a favorite poem can be a beautiful way to share your heart with someone you love. In the same way, using different types of formal prayers can be both a great way to get started with couple-prayer (because it eliminates the guesswork) and a great way to go deeper (because you are praying with the mind of the Church). Some of the greatest couple-pray-ers began with something as simple as a nightly commitment to say one Hail Mary or Our Father together for "the intention of our marriage."

That said, it would be a little odd if, when you want to tell each other how much you love each other or say something important, you *only* sing love songs or quote poetry. You need to talk to each other in your own words too. In fact, it's all the personal conversations you've shared and all the meaningful moments you've created together that give those songs and poetry their power. That's why informal prayer (that is, prayer in your own words without a predetermined form) can also be an important part of couple-prayer. Informal prayers can become most meaningful when they help you recall all the times you've shared your heart with God in your own words. If you're not used to praying in your own words, you might begin with some simple statements like "God, thank you for *X*" or "God, please help me/us with *Y*" or "Please bless my friend, so-and-so." You don't have to be flowery or even wordy. Just put your heart into it like you would any really good conversation with a really good, mutual friend, and let things develop from there.

3. Take Turns

For some people, the most intimidating thing about couple-prayer is figuring out who says what and when. Be casual about this. You can even work it out while you pray by looking at each other and asking, "Do you have anything you want to say/add?" The normal way couples approach figuring out who-says-what-and-when is by simply taking turns. For instance, one of you might say the first half of the Hail Mary (up to "... the fruit of thy womb Jesus"), and the other might say the second half (from "Holy Mary ... hour of our death, Amen"). Or you might spend a minute or two thanking God for the blessings of the day in your own words and then, before moving on to whatever the next part of your prayer might be, you could stop and give your spouse an opportunity to thank God for something in his or her own words. Once both of you have said your piece, you can move on to the next part of your prayer time. Like learning a new dance, with practice you'll be able to be more flexible about who-says-what-and-when. But for starters, taking turns responding to each part of the prayer can be a great way to kick things off.

4. Think About Your Goal

Each time you pray, it can be helpful to think a little bit about what you hope to take away from your prayer time. For instance, sometimes we pray to thank God either for a particular blessing or just for being God and loving us. Sometimes we ask God for help, for us or a friend who is suffering. Other times, we need to ask God for his forgiveness and his help to not let us commit the same sin again. It can be good to think a little bit about what is the most important thing to communicate to God today. If you're stuck, that's okay too. Just tell God that you're not sure what to say and ask him to put the words he'd like you to say into your heart. Sometimes the best prayer times come when words fail us and we just let the Holy Spirit do all the work in us. Regardless, when a couple prays together, it can be good to start your prayer time with a brief discussion about what you'd like to take from the experience. You don't have to have a spiritual plan ready for filing in triplicate with the Home Office, but knowing what you'd like the focus of your prayer time to be can help couple-prayer be a more meaningful experience.

5. Be Flexible

Some nights you'll have more energy and time than others. It's okay to vary how you pray from day to day. Perhaps there's a day you can only manage to say a Glory Be. The next day might be the same. The following day you might pray in your own words together. Maybe the time after that, you'll both want to pray a Rosary, and the next day you might be back to the Glory Be. Making the commitment to a regular couple-prayer ritual is more important in the long term than how you pray on any given day. Just try to build on what you usually do as time progresses. Learning the process of prayer — especially couple-prayer — is more of a journey than a destination. No matter how simply you start out, you will find that in time, with a regular commitment, God will take you deeper into his own time, as you are ready. Trust him. In fact, that's one of the most important parts of the process.

The PRAISE Format

In our own efforts to cultivate couple-prayer, we use all the ideas we've recommended above, but something else that has been very helpful for us is having a semi-structured prayer time. Many couples that pray together find that they get the most out of it if they spend a little time with different dimensions of prayer. Because of that, we like to use the acronym PRAISE to serve as a guide to our couple-prayer time:

P = PRAISE and thank God for his blessings.
R = REPENT of the small ways you've let God or each other down.
A = ASK for God's help with special concerns that are on your heart.
I = INTERCEDE for others.
S = SEEK his will about bigger decisions/questions that are on your heart.
E = EXPRESS your desire to serve him until you meet again in prayer.

Depending upon our energy on a given day, this format could take as little as five minutes or as much as an hour or more. It can include elements of both formal and informal prayer, as you see fit. Over the next few pages, we'll take a look at each step and give you a brief example of what it might look like in practice.

P = Praise and Thank God

Praise refers to honoring who God is, while *thanksgiving* refers to honoring God for what he has done. Take a moment to praise God for who he is to you and to thank God for the little blessings you've experienced throughout the day. Again, don't feel that you have to say anything fancy.

Just take turns between you and your spouse, thanking God for the ways he has shown that he is taking care of you. For instance:

Husband: "Thank you, Lord, for letting work go so well today. I'm really grateful for your help."

Wife: "Yes, Lord. And thank you for helping me get everything together for the class I'm teaching in the parish school of religion."

Husband: "And, God, I just want to thank you for letting my wife and me get some time for a date this weekend. Thanks for giving us the time we need to take care of each other."

As we said, this doesn't have to be fancy. You can thank God for everything from the great parking spot you got that was close to the mall entrance to the miraculous recovery your mom made from that illness. Big or small, it doesn't matter. Being thankful is a simple way of giving God the praise he deserves. God doesn't need our praise. But when we praise him, it reminds us of all the little ways he is present in our lives, and it enables us to trust him more — and as a bonus, taking a moment to recall the things you are grateful for is good for your mental health. One study has shown that the simple exercise of listing things to be grateful for increases the average daily level of happiness a person experiences by 25 percent (Eammons, 2007).

Happier spouses make for happier marriages!

R = Repentance

We're not talking about confessing your sins here. You can save that for confession. But this would be a good time to reflect together on the little ways you might not have done as good a job taking care of each other, and asking God to help you do better the next time similar circumstances arise:

Husband: "Lord, I'm sorry for being short-tempered with my wife when I got home from work today. She really didn't deserve it. Thank you for not letting it turn into a 'thing.' Help me to do a better job taking care of her when I feel frustrated about my work."

Wife: "And Lord, I'm sorry for not trying to be more understanding. I know that he wasn't really upset with me, but it's hard not to react. I'm grateful too that you gave us the grace to not turn it into an argument, but help me to be more understanding and sensitive next time."

Keep in mind that this PRAISE format is just a guideline. You don't have to use all the steps all the time (or at all). Some days, you might not feel that you have anything to repent of, but most days there will probably be something you'd like to get God's help with. Admitting your simple flaws in front of your spouse and God requires humility — but so does having a great marriage. Letting God, and your spouse, know of your commitment to do better the next time is a great way to keep resentments from building up — God will give you the grace to overcome those weaknesses so that, in time, they won't be weaknesses anymore.

A = Ask

This step comes fairly easy to most people. We're good at asking God for things. Take a moment to ask God for help with any practical concerns you might have. They don't have to be particularly noble or spiritual concerns. Just invite God into your everyday life and acknowledge that you can't do anything — even the smallest things — without him:

Husband: "Lord, please help me to get everything done. I feel really overwhelmed by all the things going on right now, and I really need your help clearing my head so I can get on top of it all."

Wife: "Yes, Lord. Please help my husband have a peace about all he has to do and help me be a good support to him. Also, Lord, please help me get over this cold quickly. I'm really feeling run down, and it's really hard to be the person I want to be when I feel like this."

Husband: "And help me to be sensitive to the fact that she's feeling poorly and to find ways to take care of her and let her know how much I love her."

When possible, don't just ask God for help with the specific concerns; ask him to help you do a better job of *being there for each other* and supporting each other as you address those concerns. God wants you to be each other's helpmate. Let him teach you how to do it.

I = Intercede for Others

Don't forget to pray for the people in your life who have special needs or concerns. Take a moment to not only ask him for his grace and blessing on them, but to give you the grace and wisdom you need to find ways to be a blessing to those people whenever possible:

Husband: "Please bless Andy. His son is giving him and his wife such a hard time. Give them your wisdom and grace to know what to do. Lord, sometimes it's hard to know what to say to him. Help me support him in ways that enable him to draw closer to you through it all."

Wife: "And Lord, please bless Ann at church. She is having so many struggles with her health. Strengthen her, and help me find ways to be there for her and make things a little easier on her."

S = Seek His Will

This is similar to asking for God's help, but it has to do with bigger concerns, which might take a little longer to figure out what God wants you to do about them. Learning the steps of hearing God's voice (i.e., discernment) is beyond the scope of this book (for more information on this, check out our book, *The Life God Wants You to Have*), but suffice it to say that when you consistently ask God for his advice and counsel, he will find ways to get through to you. When you're Christian, everything doesn't have to be up to you anymore. God wants to help. And when you seek God's will together, God will speak to both of you so that you can check each other's math, so to speak.

Husband: "Lord, we aren't really sure if we should start looking for a new house. We're starting to outgrow this one, but everything is so expensive. Help us to know your will, whether that is to stay here or to go somewhere else. Find us the home you would want us to raise your children in. And even though I'm nervous about looking at homes, please give me the wisdom to know what's really best for us and the courage to do your will, whatever it is."

Wife: "Yes, Lord, help us to really know what you want. And even though I really want to move, help me to be sensitive and considerate to my husband's concerns. Help me to be open to all the ways you want to provide for us. And let us work well together as we try to understand what you want us to do."

In addition to asking God to let you know his will, make sure to bring your desires to him in a way that says, "This is what I would like, but your will, not mine." The good news is that even when God's will is different from yours, it will still make you happy. He made you, after all. He knows better than anyone else what it is going to take to make you authentically happy. Don't be afraid to pray for his will.

While you're at it, as we showed in the example, when you and your spouse are of different minds about a bigger decision, ask for God's grace to be sensitive to each other's concerns and to find ways to be a support to each other as you find your way forward. This will go a long way to preventing those arguments where you each stake out an opposite position and then just verbally hammer away at each other until one of you — resentfully and angrily — surrenders.

Couple-prayer is especially important when you're seeking God's will about any decision that affects your marriage and family life (which is pretty much everything, when you think about it). We regularly talk to couples who pray individually about such big decisions but come to different places in their prayer time. For instance, a wife says that, in prayer, God is telling her it's time to have a child (or another one) while the husband says that God is telling him to wait. What's going on here? Is someone lying? Is God sending mixed messages?

Assuming that both the husband and wife are sincerely seeking God's will, even if they are coming to different places in their prayer, it may not be that one is mistaken, and it is certainly not that God is sending mixed messages. What we usually find is that God is showing the husband and wife difference pieces of the same puzzle, but that the husband and wife are mistaking their piece for the whole picture. For instance, in the example above, it may be that God is showing the wife that it is time to have another child, but he is showing the husband that it will be important to overcome a particular challenge in the marriage (e.g., already not getting any time together, frequent arguments, etc.), or difficulties with a child they already have, as a way of clearing the road for that next child.

It isn't that God is saying "yes" to two different and mutually exclusive ends. Rather, God is giving the husband and wife different pieces of the same puzzle and then asking them to exercise their communication and couple-prayer muscles so that they can learn to be better helpmates to each other, as he teaches them how these two different pieces of the puzzle fit together.

E = Express Your Desire to Serve Him Until You Meet Again in Prayer

This is basically where you wrap up. Couple-prayer shouldn't just be limited to the specific time that you're sitting together praying. Because your marriage is a sacrament, *your whole marriage is a prayer.* God wants to use everything that happens in your marriage as a way of opening your hearts to him and to each other. Because of that, it's a good idea to not just end your prayer and put it away like it was a piece of exercise equipment. Instead, end your prayer with the understanding that God wants to keep reaching out to you both throughout your day. Ask him to help you be attentive to what he is trying to tell you so that the next time you meet in prayer, you will have more to share, more to be thankful for, and more questions to put before him. This way, your whole married life can be the prayer that it is because your whole married life can be an ongoing conversation with God.

Husband and/or Wife: "Lord, thank you for this time together. Help us to know what you're saying to us through the things that happen in our lives and all the movements of our heart. Help us to always put your will first. Amen."

Concluding your prayer in this manner helps prepare your hearts to receive whatever God might wish to share with you and makes you mindful that God wants to spend every moment of every day with you — not just at prayer time. When you wrap up your couple-prayer time with a request to stay open to the movement of the Holy Spirit, you begin to make a personal connection to the idea that married life is, itself, a prayer. It helps you see the truth in what Archbishop Fulton Sheen once said, that "every moment is pregnant with divine purpose."

Although the PRAISE template is largely a template to guide informal prayer, some couples get a great deal out of adding formal prayers to the template. For instance, you might open your PRAISE time with an Our Father to get things started and close with a Hail Mary or Glory Be. Some like to follow their time in PRAISE with a Rosary, or Chaplet of Divine Mercy, brief Scripture reflection, or other meaningful devotion. The point it, this is your prayer time. You should feel free to do whatever makes this time more meaningful to you and your spouse. Just remember to be generous to each other. If something is meaningful to your spouse but maybe not so much to you, open your heart to the possibility that God might want to reach out to you in some new ways. Rather than turning up your nose at a prayer or type of prayer that is meaningful to your spouse, be generous and learn from each other. You'll be glad that you did, as you give God even more avenues to bring his grace into your own heart and your life together.

Livin' on a Prayer ...

If you thoughtfully consider the suggestions we've made in this chapter, you might begin to see why couples that pray together really are happier in their marriages than couples that don't. If you pray together daily, especially using the PRAISE format we outlined, you can see that your prayer doesn't just draw you closer to God. It also puts you in a different mind-set about your marriage. It makes you more generous. It makes you more considerate. It helps you be more aware of each other's concerns. It helps you reflect more deeply and meaningfully on how you might be able to support each other through those cares and concerns. It gives you a simple way to deal with and heal from those little ways you might have disappointed each other. It can help soften your heart so that when you disagree, you can still leave a little part of yourself open to the possibility that you might be wrong, or that God wants to show you an even better option. And, of course, it can help remind you both of the little ways God is taking care of you every day and enable you to truly stop and celebrate — even if only for a moment — the little blessings of each day that make life, and married life in particular, worth living. All that (and more) in as little as about ten minutes a day!

John 12:36 says, "Put your trust in the light ... so that you may become children of the light." Remember, God wants to change the world through your marriage. He wants to teach you how to live his unique vision of marriage, rooted in the *free*, *total*, *faithful*, and *fruitful* love that burns in his heart for you. Making a commitment to couple-prayer will enable you to let the light of Christ shine brightly in your home. Your love for each other will be warmed in its glow, and you — often without even knowing it — will be a light to the world: a world that is aching for the love God is teaching you — day by day — how to live.

PART TWO

Where Are We? How Did We Get Here? Where Are We Going?

Now you have discovered the unique vision God has for your Catholic marriage and learned how to sit at the feet of the Master while he tutors you in the art of loving each other with his love. Part Two will help you identify the unique strengths and challenges of your marriage and what you will have to do to fulfill God's plan for marriage in your unique life together.

Every couple wants to make it to "happily ever after," and in Part Two we'll help you identify where you and your spouse are on that journey. You'll discover where your marriage falls on *The Relationship Pathway* and what you need to do to get from wherever you are to the *Exceptional Seven Percent* of marriages that exhibit uncommonly high degrees of happiness and stability. You'll also discover the Seven Stages of Marriage Mountain — that is, the seven stages every marriage grows through — and how you can more easily overcome the challenges that accompany these stages, challenges that often prevent other couples from making it from one stage to the peak. All along, you'll receive plenty of practical tips to help you make your love deeper and your relationship stronger so that you will have the confidence you need to stand strong in the face of all the challenges of life.

CHAPTER 5

The Relationship Pathway

Now that you have discovered God's vision for marriage, this chapter will help you identify both the strengths and areas for growth in your relationship so that you can create an individualized action plan for actually living out this vision in your lives together.

Vive la Différence?

Most people intuit that not all marriages are the same, and many books describe different marital types. The problem is that until the first edition of *For Better ... FOREVER* and its companion, *The Exceptional Seven Percent: Nine Secrets of the World's Happiest Couples*, were published, no one had identified any meaningful connection between them. So, for example, Dr. Sigmund Q. Psychologist might be able to tell you that you have a "Green Marriage" (whatever that means) and that it is distinctly different from, and perhaps inferior to, a "Blue Marriage" (whatever that means). But the good doctor would probably not be able to tell you what predisposes you to your "Green Marriage" or how to move yourself into a "Blue Marriage" (except, maybe, by suggesting that you "take more time together" or "marry someone else").

To organize the different marital types in a meaningful way and show couples how to move from one stage to the next, we developed *The Relationship Pathway*. *The Relationship Pathway* orders the different categories of marriage along a continuum of identity strength.

If you've ever read a pop psychology book — or for that matter, watched daytime talk shows — you know that it is important to have an "identity" before you enter into a marriage. Psychologists tell us that

1. You know you have at least the *seeds* of an identity if you can identify, without having to think too hard about it, the dreams, goals, virtues, and values that are important to you.
2. You know the *strength* of your identity by the degree to which your daily life, choices, and relationships *reflect* those dreams, goals, virtues, and values.

For the Christian, an identity in Christ (as we discussed in Chapter 2) and psychological identity are supposed to be the same thing. In fact, a strong, personal commitment to our God-given baptismal virtues almost always guarantees a solid psychological identity.

But as the work of many developmental psychologists (especially Abraham "Hierarchy of Needs" Maslow) shows us, not everyone builds his or her identity around the same things. Some people build their identities around escape, their sole concern being to numb themselves with enough drugs, alcohol, sex, or chaos to get through the day. Other people center themselves around the basic needs of life — pursuing a "guarantee" of financial or emotional security and/or the acceptance of others. Still others build their lives around pursuing "success," as defined by the society and/or institutions to which they belong. And finally, people in the highest-functioning group build their identities around a clear, coherent, and practically lived set of values, ideals, and life principles — a personal "mission statement," if you will.

What you build *your* life around is directly related to the type of marriage you have, as well as the happiness and longevity you can expect from that marriage. For you, as a Christian, what you build your identity around is also directly related to the degree of sacramental grace to which you are currently opening yourself in your marriage. If it is true that the purpose of marriage is to "*help each other become all God created you to be in this life and help get each other to heaven in the next*" (and it is), then every married couple — especially the Christian married couple — is capable of and responsible for spending married life moving up *The Relationship Pathway*.

The Relationship Pathway: Step-by-Step

There are five major types of marriages (each of these comes in different varieties, but we'll deal with that later), each of which is pegged to a stage in Maslow's Hierarchy of Needs (see below).

The Relationship Pathway

Stage (Level)	**Maslow's Hierarchy of Needs** *Pre-Occupying Need*	**Popcak Relationship Pathway** *Relationship/Life Theme*	
5	**Actualization** — Primarily concerned with pursuing a deeply and personally held set of beliefs and values.	**Romantic Peer Marriage** — Theme: Mutual growth and fulfillment of shared mission.	**EXCEPTIONAL** (Satisfaction/Stability)
4	**Respect/Esteem** — Primarily concerned with becoming a model/exemplary member of the groups to which you belong.	**Partnership Marriage** — Theme: Cultivating deeper intimacy by learning to love partner more than comfort zone. *Two types:* (a) Traditional Type (b) Contemporary Type	
3	**Love/Belonging** — Primarily concerned with finding a community to belong to/to care and be cared for.	**Apprenticeship Marriage** — Theme: Supporting each other's place in the world (work and roles). *Two types:* (a) Contemporary Type (b) Traditional Type	**CONVENTIONAL** (Satisfaction/Stability)
2	**Safety/Security** — Primarily concerned with maintaining sense of stability, well-being, and security.	**Lifeboat Marriage** — Theme: Maintaining stability through either financial gain or avoidance of stress. *Two types:* (a) Materialistic Type (b) Avoidant Type	**IMPOVERISHED** (Satisfaction/Stability)
1	**Basic Needs** — Primarily concerned with achieving basic food, shelter, basic health, and finding comfort from the hardships of life.	**Crisis Marriage** — Theme: Survival and escape. *Two types:* (a) Chaotic Type (b) Codependent Type	

Maslow's Hierarchy of Needs identifies the particular needs a person is *pre-occupied* with securing and achieving in his or her life. The particular need you are focused most on achieving or maintaining — that is, the *need you most value* — becomes the major theme around which you focus your daily life. It also becomes the best predictor of the level of happiness, intimacy, and/or stability you can expect from your marriage. Relating Maslow's Hierarchy to relationship satisfaction was a novel idea when the first edition of *For Better ... FOREVER* was published, but subsequent research has proposed a direct connection between the two, even asserting that securing a stable and satisfying marital relationship was essential for achieving actualization (Kenrick, Griskevicius, Neuberg, 2010).

The stage people occupy on both Maslow's Hierarchy and *The Relationship Pathway* depends less on what they actually have acquired in life and more on what they are *pre-occupied with maintaining*. As Scripture says, "For where your treasure is, there your heart will be also" (Mt 6:21). Your place on both Maslow's Hierarchy and *The Relationship Pathway* depends upon what you value the most and what you spend the greatest amount of time, effort, and emotional energy maintaining. For instance, you may have plenty of money and look, for all the world, like you have "achieved" Maslow's level of Safety/Security (Stage 2) and, therefore, ought to have moved on to Maslow's Love/Belonging Stage (Stage 3), but this might not be true. If your *most important pre-occupation* — the thing you spend most of your time and emotional energy on pursuing — *continues to be accumulating wealth* despite having achieved basic security, you will never move beyond the Safety/Security Stage (Stage 2) in Maslow's Hierarchy and the Lifeboat Stage on *The Relationship Pathway*. Even if you have also achieved the needs associated with later stages — e.g., a certain level of belonging and respect, a certain degree of religious faith — you will not achieve the full benefit of satisfying these higher-level needs because, in your mind, these all remain secondary to maintaining a sense of safety and security in your life.

By contrast, a person may be concerned with how he is going to meet his expenses from month-to-month and look to everyone who sees him as though he is struggling to achieve the level of basic Security (Stage 2). But if, in spite of his financial struggles, he has found a way to find peace with his month-to-month existence and is *primarily pre-occupied* with becoming a living, breathing example of a deeply held, personally significant value system, then this person may find himself seeking to meet his Actualization need (Stage 5) despite his precarious financial impecunious circumstances

In sum, just having acquired the resources to meet a certain need does not predict your place on Maslow's Hierarchy or *The Relationship Pathway* as much as your perception of which needs are the most emotionally important to you and the pursuit of which needs receive the lion's share of your time, energy, and attention.

Moving Up *The Relationship Pathway*

Every couple starts out at a different point on *The Relationship Pathway*, and generally speaking, we all move along *The Pathway* one stage at a time. Each stage represents the mastery of different skills and presents new challenges. That said, it is possible that a powerful, life-changing experience (for example, a deeply emotional and personally meaningful conversion experience) could radically change the need a person focuses the lion's share of his energy and effort on fulfilling and, therefore, radically change his place on *The Relationship Pathway* as well. Such a rapid shift would, by necessity, be life altering and involve both great blessings as well as significant challenges because, of course, each stage does not merely reflect a change in attitude about relationships, but also a change in attitude about your whole view of life.

As you read over the following pages with an eye toward picking out what stage your marriage might be at, keep these following tips in mind:

1. *Resist the urge to overestimate or underestimate your marital strengths.* Try to be as honest as possible. Nobody's keeping score. Pay close attention to the recommendations given at the end of each marital type. If they apply to you, start working on them, even if all the descriptions in a particular category don't seem to apply to you.
2. *Don't demonize your mate and canonize yourself.* It is tempting for people to try to place themselves at the top of *The Relationship Pathway* and their mate at the bottom. This is not the way it works. We all marry people whose identities are built around similar things to our own. Your entire circle of friends probably does not include people more than one full stage up or down from you. Without professional support, most couples feel as if they're

"growing apart" if one spouse is a half-a-stage higher or lower than the other spouse and risk total irrelevancy if there is a gap of a full stage or more between them.

3. *You may be in between two stages.* Because it takes so much energy to move from one stage to the next, and because these stages are organized along a continuum, don't be surprised if you find yourself between two stages. Simply choose the stage you think you lean more toward and start working on the recommendations listed in that section first.

In order to help you understand the progression from one stage to the next, we'll start at the bottom and work our way up. As you go through the sections, try to think of couples you know who can serve as an example of each type to make the categories more relatable.

IMPOVERISHED MARRIAGES (Stages 1 and 2)

Couples in *Impoverished Marriages* build their lives around one of two themes. Impoverished Couples in *Crisis Marriages* (Stage 1) build their lives around the theme of securing basic needs and seeking relief from the hardships of life (often through drugs, alcohol, or other addictions), while couples in *Lifeboat Marriages* (Stage 2) focus on maintaining basic security by accumulating wealth or seeking to lead quieter, more stress-free lives. Both Crisis Marriages and Lifeboat Marriages tend to experience lower levels of satisfaction and stability (which is what makes them "impoverished"), because the couple often sees pursuing deeper intimacy or emotional connection as either unnecessary or, at best, a distant second to achieving and maintaining the necessities for a secure life.

Crisis Marriages (Stage 1)

Couples in Crisis Marriages (formerly, "Deadly Marriages") build their lives around basic survival and their relationships around escaping reality, either through using each other, abusing drugs or alcohol, or by surrounding themselves with people who have so many problems that they never have to deal with their own. Most marriages at this stage exhibit both extremely low longevity and extremely low satisfaction.

The Relationship Pathway

Stage (Level)	Maslow's Hierarchy of Needs *Pre-Occupying Need*	Popcak Relationship Pathway *Relationship/Life Theme*	
5	**Actualization** — Primarily concerned with pursuing a deeply and personally held set of beliefs and values.	**Romantic Peer Marriage** — Theme: Mutual growth and fulfillment of shared mission.	**EXCEPTIONAL** (Satisfaction/Stability)
4	**Respect/Esteem** — Primarily concerned with becoming a model/exemplary member of the groups to which you belong.	**Partnership Marriage** — Theme: Cultivating deeper intimacy by learning to love partner more than comfort zone. *Two types:* (a) Traditional Type (b) Contemporary Type	
3	**Love/Belonging** — Primarily concerned with finding a community to belong to/to care and be cared for.	**Apprenticeship Marriage** — Theme: Supporting each other's place in the world (work and roles). *Two types:* (a) Contemporary Type (b) Traditional Type	**CONVENTIONAL** (Satisfaction/Stability)
2	**Safety/Security** — Primarily concerned with maintaining sense of stability, well-being, and security.	**Lifeboat Marriage** — Theme: Maintaining stability through either financial gain or avoidance of stress. *Two types:* (a) Materialistic Type (b) Avoidant Type	**IMPOVERISHED** (Satisfaction/Stability)
1	**Basic Needs** — Primarily concerned with achieving basic food, shelter, basic health, and finding comfort from the hardships of life.	**Crisis Marriage** — Theme: Survival and escape. *Two types:* (a) Chaotic Type (b) Codependent Type	

Couples in Crisis Marriages are usually more impulsive and tend not to set longer-term goals. Seeking personally meaningful work is not usually a major consideration, and most individuals in this category are happy to have enough cash to get through the day. Drugs, alcohol, sex, and other serious addictions are often major players and serve to anesthetize the couple from the hardness of life. Crisis Marriages come in two varieties: *Chaotic* and *Codependent.*

Chaotic Marriages are characterized by mutual addictions and dysfunction on the part of both partners. By contrast, *Codependent Marriages* occur when one spouse — whose psychological life is, itself, often in chaos — builds his or her life around saving the other spouse from his or her chaotic, self-destructive tendencies. Codependents usually are not addicted to any chemicals themselves but are escapists just the same. They put off solving any of their own laundry list of dysfunctions by escaping into someone else's even more hopeless life. They become addicted to saving the addict.

Question to Consider: Can you think of a couple you know who might fit into either the Chaotic- or Codependent-type Crisis Marriage?

Recommendations for Crisis Marriages

If you are in either type of Crisis Marriage (i.e., Chaotic or Codependent), you will need tremendous support to heal. You may need to take advantage of a good addiction recovery program (including, but not limited to, a hospital-based rehabilitation program, Alcoholics Anonymous, or Narcotics Anonymous), and/or a codependent recovery group such as Al-Anon.

Additionally, you will need to seek individual therapy to address your deeper personal wounds. The pain in your life has caused you to focus on escape, preventing you from expecting even the basics from life. Things like food, income, shelter, and safety are not luxuries. In order to move to the next stage in your life, you must at least develop enough strength to acquire these for yourself so that your relationships can be about more than just getting by and providing a distraction from a difficult life.

Let's take a look at the next stage up, the second category of Impoverished Marriages: Lifeboat Marriages.

Lifeboat Marriages (Stage 2)

Lifeboat Marriages (formerly, "Shipwrecked") are significantly more stable than Crisis Marriages, and while these marriages can be happy if they receive proper support and encouragement over the years, couples in this category face significant challenges.

The husband and wife in a Lifeboat Marriage tend to find themselves at Maslow's Safety/Security Stage (Stage 2). The couple tends to see the world as hostile — a stormy sea — and marriage more as a place to retreat for safety — a lifeboat — than a place to grow and change. The husband and wife in a Lifeboat Marriage may come from deprived or traumatic backgrounds, where basic needs were not necessarily guaranteed. The relationship itself is built around getting, accumulating, and securing the basics in life (financial security and/or safety/peace and quiet), and this is fine to a point. The problem comes from the fact that this is almost all these marriages are about. After the initial honeymoon warmth wears off, the couple may deteriorate into a functional, brother/sister relationship that focuses on guaranteeing security at the cost of any real intimacy, passion, or growth. Very often, requests to grow in deeper intimacy, friendship, passion, or depth are rebuffed or even treated as a betrayal. For many couples, growth or change, especially personal growth and change, tends to be seen as a dangerous thing. It requires shaking things up, and Lifeboat couples have already been shaken enough in their lives.

Additionally, although this is not universal, it is not uncommon that the constant internal pressure Lifeboat spouses feel to keep the perceived wolves from the door (i.e., stress or want) can lead some of them into addictions. That said, they are usually more-functional addicts who know how to maintain the veneer of normalcy to the outside world.

There are two types of Lifeboat Marriages based on the kind of security/safety the couple finds to be more important. Lifeboat Marriages of the more *Materialistic Type* tend to cultivate security by accruing wealth. Almost everything besides working, saving, and accumulating wealth to protect against potential misfortune is a distant second for these couples. If Materialistic-Type Lifeboat spouses have the good fortune to hold higher-status jobs (doctor, lawyer, etc.), they tend to be more proud of the money and power that comes with the career than with the value of the work itself.

By contrast, Lifeboat Marriages of the *Avoidant Type* tend to concentrate on building security by leading as safe, quiet, and stress-free a life as possible. Contrary to their Materialistic counterparts, they tend to not worry about money beyond what they might need to pay their bills and meet basic goals. Instead, having often come from chaotic or traumatic backgrounds of one kind or another, they devote themselves to pursuing quiet above all else. They have raised the normal tendency to live within one's comfort zone to a high art form and tend to work hard to avoid conflict as much as humanly possible.

In addition to the focus on securing and maintaining the financial means or peace they need to achieve a safe and secure life, Lifeboat couples (of both varieties) tend to experience a *significant degree of estrangement between men and women*. This is the group most likely to see men and women as separate species who simply cannot really understand each other, much less become true, intimate friends and helpmates. Their protection of their respective comfort zones (the place they feel most safe and secure) prohibits them from venturing far enough into each other's worlds to become true partners. Instead, they rely on fairly rigidly defined roles. The more well defined these roles, the more peaceable these relationships tend to be — though it costs them true intimacy. Even so, successfully achieving this level of role-definition can be difficult for couples in this feminist culture, which tends to view role definition as oppressive but doesn't give people who need roles any healthy alternatives. This leaves many couples at this stage literally fighting it out for themselves.

Lifeboat couples (of both types) also tend to use *sex as a substitute for real intimacy*. Because they struggle to leave their comfort zones long enough to develop real mutual understanding and partnership, they lean heavily on their physical relationship to make up for the disconnect that exists in the many other areas of their lives together. They may not talk or share much, but if the sex is relatively good, then they usually consider the marriage to be good as well. Eventually, however, these relationships can devolve into sexless marriages because it is just too difficult to create a true, long-term sexual partnership when the day-to-day emotional partnership doesn't exist. Alternatively, some couples lean more heavily on kinkier sexual activities to maintain the sexual high in the absence of general marital intimacy.

Finally, regarding their relationship to their faith and moral values, Lifeboat couples *tend to struggle — outside of their prayer or worship lives (which may appear to be very devout) — to live their faith and values in meaningful and effective ways in their daily lives and relationships*. They may be faithful, devout, and knowledgeable about their faith, but their even stronger devotion to their comfort zones makes it extremely difficult to be truly self-giving in their daily lives. Usually, if asked to do anything that isn't inside their wheelhouse, they tend to draw strong boundaries or feign incompetence or preciousness, to the point of being unwilling to even try new things without significant pressure. More contented Lifeboat couples compensate for this tendency by having very rigidly-defined roles, staying in them, and excelling at them. While this can be a workable arrangement, it often masks a deeper emotional and spiritual disconnect that runs throughout the marriage and can present itself in surprising and frustrating ways. Similarly, if Lifeboat couples buy into the Church's moral teachings, they tend to see them as rigid rules that must be followed without really understanding the heart behind those rules. They do a better job of adhering to the letter of the moral law than the spirit.

Question to Consider: Can you think of a couple you know who might fit into either the Materialistic or Avoidant type of Lifeboat Marriage?

Prognosis and Recommendations for Lifeboat Marriages

Historically, Lifeboat Marriages lasted forever, whether or not they were happy. In contemporary times, these marriages don't last like they used to. The increased social outlets for women, combined with the decreased social pressure to keep marriages together, often provide a deadly one-two punch to the Lifeboat Marriage.

At the ten-year mark, many Lifeboat Marriages can hit a crisis as one spouse feels sated with the security they have achieved and wants to pursue deeper intimacy or more adventure while the other wants to keep doing what they've always done. This can be the start of a period of significant tension that often requires professional assistance to resolve successfully because of the deeper psychological issues involved. Generally speaking, the problems experienced by couples with Lifeboat Marriages cannot be addressed with simple skill-building strategies. Instead, these couples need to learn new ways to think about life and relationship, as well as learning to leave their comfort zones for the sake of a richer marriage, deeper intimacy, and a more rewarding life. They need to overcome the often tremendous amount of fear that keeps them fixated on keeping and maintaining basic security in one form or another.

That said, Lifeboat Marriages are *absolutely worth saving*, and the couples in them can learn, with proper support and skills, to have much deeper and more satisfying relationships. The following four tips, as well as the ideas throughout the rest of this book, will be helpful to you.

1. Expect More from Life

You have learned that it was either foolish or selfish to want more than "security" from life, but marriage is not supposed to suck the life out of you to sustain itself. Sacramental marriage is supposed to be a life-giving thing that empowers you to grow and change, to become what God created you to be. Lifeboat couples are often tempted to dismiss the vision of marriage we describe as "too idealistic." They have a hard time believing that it makes sense to make this much of a fuss about relationships, thinking that "a good marriage either works or it doesn't. You shouldn't have to work so hard." If this is your attitude toward relationships and your faith, you will need to challenge this in order to move to the next stage.

The first step in moving forward is to stop thinking of your dreams, goals, virtues, and values as some sort of "lovely fantasy" that maybe you'll take up one day after you win the lottery. You must prayerfully identify those things God has placed in your heart as important to your fulfillment *and* you must begin making plans to fulfill them. Finding ways to make a meaningful connection with the work and roles you occupy — as opposed to seeing them as the means by which you achieve basic security — is essential to entering the next stage of your marriage.

The transition to a more *Conventional Stage* on *The Relationship Pathway* can be a difficult one, but it is absolutely worth the effort and definitely possible for you to accomplish with the right support. Your pastor, supportive groups (such as Marriage Encounter and Retrouvaille), and a good, marriage-friendly counselor, can help. Don't let your pride stop you from making use of these resources.

2. Relate to Your Mate

Lifeboat spouses spend far too much time standing around, wondering what their mates want from them. Because they tend to be so addicted to their comfort zones, requests made by their spouse that are too far outside their comfort zone just don't compute. They may hear their spouse recite a list of specific needs and then stare blankly at their mate and say, "I just don't know what you want." It isn't that they didn't hear what was said. They just can't imagine ever wanting to do those things, so they reflexively ignore them and try to steer the conversation back to what they are comfortable doing.

If this describes your marriage, books like Christian counselor Willard Harley's *His Needs, Her Needs*, John Gray's *Mars and Venus* series, programs like PAIRS (an acronym for Practical Application of Intimate Relationship Skills), or Retrouvaille will be particularly helpful (see Appendix 2). Take advantage of them today. Also, seek individual and/or marriage counseling to help you be accountable for the changes you want to make.

3. Seek Deeper Conversion

You may have a personally meaningful faith, but you may struggle in having it impact your life and relationships in positive, healthy ways. Faith is more than devotion, and morality is more than rules. Both are a call to deeper conversion of heart. Pray that God would give you the courage to both apply your faith to your daily life in practical ways and/or empower you to move past a more rule-based faith to a faith that satisfies your spiritual obligations out of love rather than duty.

CONVENTIONAL MARRIAGES (Stage 3)

Apprenticeship Marriages (Stage 3)

At least in the early years, most basically happy, stable marriages begin in the *Conventional/Apprenticeship* category. Most *Conventional Marriages* are solid, happy marriages with a potential for greatness if the couple is willing to do the work. Individually, husbands and wives are at Maslow's *Love/Belonging* Stage (Stage 3), in which they are primarily concerned with finding a community to belong to and achieving acceptance from the people they associate with in their work and roles.

Even though couples in Conventional Marriages exhibit many of the skills necessary for a good or even great marriage, the couples in them have not mastered these skills to the level that couples higher up on *The*

The Relationship Pathway

Stage (Level)	Maslow's Hierarchy of Needs *Pre-Occupying Need*	Popcak Relationship Pathway *Relationship/Life Theme*	
5	**Actualization** — Primarily concerned with pursuing a deeply and personally held set of beliefs and values.	**Romantic Peer Marriage** — Theme: Mutual growth and fulfillment of shared mission.	**EXCEPTIONAL** (Satisfaction/Stability)
4	**Respect/Esteem** — Primarily concerned with becoming a model/exemplary member of the groups to which you belong.	**Partnership Marriage** — Theme: Cultivating deeper intimacy by learning to love partner more than comfort zone. *Two types:* (a) Traditional Type (b) Contemporary Type	
3	**Love/Belonging** — Primarily concerned with finding a community to belong to/to care and be cared for.	**Apprenticeship Marriage** — Theme: Supporting each other's place in the world (work and roles). *Two types:* (a) Contemporary Type (b) Traditional Type	**CONVENTIONAL** (Satisfaction/Stability)
2	**Safety/Security** — Primarily concerned with maintaining sense of stability, well-being, and security.	**Lifeboat Marriage** — Theme: Maintaining stability through either financial gain or avoidance of stress. *Two types:* (a) Materialistic Type (b) Avoidant Type	**IMPOVERISHED** (Satisfaction/Stability)
1	**Basic Needs** — Primarily concerned with achieving basic food, shelter, basic health, and finding comfort from the hardships of life.	**Crisis Marriage** — Theme: Survival and escape. *Two types:* (a) Chaotic Type (b) Codependent Type	

Relationship Pathway have, which is why we refer to them as *Apprenticeship Marriages*. The fact that they have not yet mastered their partnership skills makes them vulnerable to threats like competing priorities, communication breakdowns, as well as some degree of scorekeeping and what we call Marital Chicken (but more on that in a moment).

There are two types of Apprenticeship Marriages: *Traditional* and *Contemporary*. *Traditional* Apprenticeship Marriages tend to adopt the husband-as-sole-provider/stay-at-home-mom model, in which there is a fairly straightforward division of labor. *Contemporary* Apprenticeship Marriages, for their part, tend to ally themselves with a more quasi-feminist, two-career household model, in which there is a somewhat greater sharing of responsibilities — although research on these couples shows that the wife still often has greater household and childcare responsibilities, despite working outside the home (Hochschild, 2012). But beneath these different appearances, the dynamic of both types of couples is strikingly similar.

Even though only the Contemporary wife works outside the home (except, perhaps, for the traditional wife's occasional/part-time work) both types of Apprenticeship Marriages consist of two people who are basically confident in their ability to meet their own needs (financial and emotional). Individuals in this category know who they *are* primarily by what they do (e.g., their work, preferences, or roles they play in society).

Because the husband and wife both feel like competent people who can meet their own needs if necessary, this is the first relationship on the continuum that is primarily centered on love (defined as a willingness to work for each other's good, as opposed to mere companionship and hanging around each other), although the couple may tend to define love as "making each other happy." Apprenticeship Marriages enjoy an average-to-good degree of satisfaction/stability. As long as each spouse feels "taken care of" by the other, all will go well. However, fairness is a major concern for most apprenticeship couples. If one spouse is seen as dropping the relationship ball, things can go downhill rather quickly, as this upsets the implicit *quid pro quo* arrangement, and taps into the couple's fears of being taken advantage of (or taken for granted).

There are three "entrance requirements" to the Conventional/Apprenticeship category: (1) meaningful work and roles, (2) negotiating basic gender differences, and (3) beginnings of a *lived* system of faith and values that impacts the couple's life and marriage:

1. *Both men and women fulfill meaningful work and roles.* Pursuing work — or another social role (for example, parenthood) — that is viewed as meaningful for its own sake is the single most important

distinction of the Apprenticeship couple. Whereas Lifeboat couples work to establish and maintain their ongoing security, Apprenticeship couples work because they have found something they truly enjoy doing and find personally meaningful. This is the difference, for instance, between a (Lifeboat) physician who practices medicine for the money, power, and esteem and the (Apprenticeship or higher) physician who loves the art of medicine. For that matter, it is the difference between the (Lifeboat) mother who stays at home by default and the (Apprenticeship or higher) mother who stays at home because she genuinely values the work of mothering and invests her whole self in it. The tendency of Apprenticeship couples to identify with their work has the potential to be either the saving grace of the marriage (it gives them something interesting to talk about) or, if they aren't careful, its downfall (it takes too much time away from the relationship).

2. *They have negotiated the basic differences between men and women.* Unlike their Lifeboat counterparts, individuals in this category no longer relate to the opposite sex as creatures from another planet. They may occasionally feel that they do not completely understand where the opposite sex is coming from — and this may be the source of some relatively good-natured joking as well as mild exasperation — but this is more the exception than the rule. While not as accomplished at this as higher functioning couples on *The Relationship Pathway*, both men and women in this group are better at expressing their emotions, communicating, and advocating for their needs than are their Lifeboat counterparts. Apprenticeship men and women genuinely try to understand and be sensitive to the experiences of the opposite sex. They are beginning to be in touch with both their masculine and feminine sides.
3. *They have begun to develop a more integrated value system.* Remember, Lifeboat couples may give the appearance of having personally meaningful faith and values, but there is usually a wide disparity between their professed beliefs and their actual lives. For example, a Lifeboat wife may talk about equal dignity of men and women, but then she will let her husband habitually treat her poorly. Likewise, a Lifeboat husband might talk about marriage being

> "a partnership," but he would see nothing wrong with letting his wife do all the housework and pouting about being asked to help in the smallest way.

Alternatively, Apprenticeship couples' lives tend to reflect a more holistic, albeit incomplete, integration of the values and teaching of their church or other values group. They take their faith and values seriously, and they at least try to apply these values to their daily life in meaningful, positive ways. Sometimes their personal preferences, emotions, and competing comfort zones get in the way of their attempts to do this, but for the most part the spirit is genuinely willing to at least engage their stated values, even though the flesh is often weak.

Because they do try to apprentice to a more objective value system and have a clearer personal sense of justice, Apprenticeship couples are fairly good at setting respectful boundaries, both regarding offenses and the division of household labor (arguments about this are common, but at least the couple is arguing on the same page).

Likewise, Apprenticeship couples may tend to spend a great deal of time out in their parish or community furthering their social agenda. However, they often struggle with prioritizing marriage and family life with so many other important things to do.

Apprenticeship Couples: Through the Years

Couples in this category genuinely love each other, and their marriages are often envied by their less socially established friends. But as the name implies, Apprenticeship couples will need to develop their skills a bit before they can master the intimacy that people in the Exceptional Marriages have achieved.

There are three phases of life to each relationship on *The Relationship Pathway*. And while we will not address them for the other types of marriages because we simply don't have the space here, we will address them for the Apprenticeship Marriage because it is such a common first-marriage type.

Phase One: The Early Phase

This is often the phase of the "warm-fuzzy marriage." At this point, couples are still in the early stages of their career/social roles, and though their futures look promising, they are not yet actualized. To make up for the lack of challenge in the other parts of their lives, Apprenticeship couples pour themselves into their new roles of husband and wife. They tend to be somewhat rule-based with regard to defining their roles and ways of managing life, and they can sometimes confuse their preferences with their identity, to the degree that they may feel like they are "losing themselves" if they are asked to make too many changes in their schedules/preferences. This can be a source of some conflict in the early years, but unlike Lifeboat Couples, most Apprenticeship Couples are mature enough to get past most of these challenges to their comfort zones with effort.

Phase Two: The Middle Phase

Things are starting to take off now. Careers are cooking, kids are being cranked out, and the community-at-large is callin' your name. This is a very heady time of life for Apprenticeship couples; they are finally getting to harvest the fruit they have been cultivating for so long now. The problem is that instead of enjoying each other's glory, the spouses often spend so much time taking care of business — as it were — that they forget their primary obligation to each other. Often, one mate's attempts to ask the other to spend more time concentrating on the marriage are rebuffed by such comments as, "I would love to, but this is just a terrible time. [Of course there's never really a *good* time.] Can't you see how busy I am? You should *know* I love you. Why are you being so needy (*or controlling or demanding*) just when everything is starting to take off for me?"

Rather than allowing this to be the beginning of the end, Apprenticeship Couples need to understand this is a normal part of their marriage's evolution. Developing healthy marriage and family-friendly priorities is a major challenge and goal of this phase.

Phase Three: The Late Phase

Assuming the spouses in an Apprenticeship Marriage survive the middle-phase crisis of balancing personal success with intimacy, they enter a phase of questioning. They look at all their accomplishments, possessions, awards, and titles and say, "Is this all there is to life?"

This presents a real opportunity. Although many couples do give up on the relationship at this stage, other couples dig deeper. They may read philosophy, study the theology of their church, or seek to discover the spirituality of work and parenthood. It is this pursuit of a personal commitment to internalizing their value system that will motivate them to give more of themselves than they are initially comfortable giving to their mate. This self-gift will change the dynamic of the marriage and raise it to a new level of intimacy (the *Partnership Marriages*).

This effort to deepen their connection to their spiritual values is what leads to the deeper intimacy that Exceptional couples are known for. True intimacy requires a willingness to be loving even when doing so makes you uncomfortable — even when your partner doesn't deserve such generosity. This is difficult for many Apprenticeship couples because they are afraid of losing themselves in a marriage or being taken advantage of. What these couples must eventually come to learn is that a person with a solid identity, rooted in a real commitment to living out an internalized value system, cannot get lost in a relationship.

Question to Consider: Can you think of a couple you know who might fit into either the Contemporary or Traditional Apprenticeship Marriage?

Recommendations for Apprenticeship Marriages

Apprenticeship couples would benefit from a clearer understanding of the concept of marriage as a partnership in fulfilling Christian identities. Modern-day Apprentices tend to be very psychologically savvy and are very interested in "personal growth and fulfillment." Explaining marriage to them in these terms often makes things come together as they begin to appreciate how the theology of marriage really can impact their daily lives together. Saying that the two become one in Christ, or that husbands and wives are supposed to be Christ to one another, or even that the husband-and-wife relationship is supposed to mirror Christ's relationship with the Church is all true enough, but Apprenticeship couples need more specific assistance in understanding what this means on a practical level.

Beyond this, if you find yourself in either type of Apprenticeship Marriage, you may benefit from the following suggestions.

1. Make Time for Each Other.

Because couples at this stage are very eager to find their place in the world and establish themselves in their chosen work or roles, Apprenticeship Marriages can get very lonely if you aren't careful. So be careful. Create *rituals of connection* (see Chapter 6 for more information) that enable you to establish regular, scheduled time for work, play, talk, and prayer. Couples at this stage need to remember that the world will not stop revolving if you turn down a project, or stand up to certain members of your family (Mom or Dad, for instance). Make decisions with your marriage in mind. This applies to Apprenticeship stay-at-home moms as well, who may tend to ignore their marriages and get lost in their mothering and housekeeping roles. Schedule regular, consistent time to be with each other.

2. Develop Your Intimacy Skills

Are you afraid of losing yourself in your marriage? Are you afraid of loving your mate "too much" and being taken advantage of? Are you uncomfortable sharing your feelings, fears and failures, hopes and dreams, emotional/psychological and spiritual needs? Do you play Marital Chicken (the game where you *would* change if only your mate changed first but that will never happen)? Do you have a hard time saying "no" to everyone except your mate?

If you answered "yes" to one or more of the questions above, you may have some work to do on cultivating your intimacy skills. That is, you will need to learn to be less self-protective, more self-donative, and more comfortable making yourself vulnerable in healthy ways, especially as all of these relate to sharing the more intimate aspects of your life and relationship with your spouse.

Additionally, your relationship would benefit from developing your sense of partnership. Specifically, you need to learn how to help meet your partner's needs while remaining true to your own. Apprenticeship Couples often struggle to frame competing needs as a both/and instead of an either/or. For example, how can you balance your mate's need for you to spend more time with her and your need to complete certain projects? How can you balance your need to communicate more with your mate's need for more physical intimacy? How can you balance your desire for career advancement with your mate's own desire for career advancement, and still have a family life? Chapter 10 in this book, "The Secrets of Red-

Hot Loving (How to Be Loving When Conflict Heats Things Up)," will be a good resource for you. Likewise, Greg's book, *When Divorce Is Not an Option: How to Heal Your Marriage and Nurture Lasting Love* can be a great resource for advanced problem solving. Finally, a good counselor can help you if you get stuck, or just want to know more.

3. You Must Learn to be Loving Even When Doing so Makes You Uncomfortable

Apprenticeship spouses often work very hard at loving their partners the way they themselves want to be loved, but they tend to ignore the things their partners really want them to do. For example, a Conventional wife may kill herself redecorating the house for her husband only to be greeted with minimal thanks because it just isn't that meaningful to him. Now, *he* would just fall in love with her all over again if she would cook chicken wings and watch *Monday Night Football* with him, but she would never do that because "You know I hate football." She won't resent his liking it, but she will do what she can to keep her distance. (Early-stage Apprenticeship men stereotypically do the same thing around church.) What happens over time is the husband becomes resentful because "She never does anything to show me she loves me," and the wife becomes resentful because "He never appreciates the things I do to show him I love him." Apprenticeship husbands act in similar ways toward their wives. There are a million examples of this in every Apprenticeship Marriage. The problem is — to put it in management terms — the couple is working hard but not working smart. If you want a successful marriage, you need to love your mate in a way that is meaningful *to her*, not simply in a way that you think *should* be meaningful (see Chapter 7, "What You Can Do To Maintain the Woo!"). You are going to need to do this even when it makes you uncomfortable, not because your spouse necessarily *deserves* such generosity (it is so rare that people deserve to be loved), but because that is the kind of loving, generous, self-giving person *you* want to be at the end of your life. People always say to us, "But what if I do all these loving things for her and she doesn't do anything for me? That would make me look pathetic."

Look, do you *really* think your mate is such a putz that she would not lovingly respond to your loving efforts? More likely, you are simply using this statement as an excuse to avoid dealing with your *own* fears of intimacy, of upsetting the balance of power in your marriage and becoming a victim. Now's the time to leave those fears behind. Admittedly, this can be a big step. Ask God for help; certainly he knows what it's like to give more love than he gets. If you can't do it on your own, a good counselor can help you.

4. Deepen Your Sense of Identity

Because you get so much of your identity from what you do, you have a tendency to confuse preferences with identity. For example, you might say things like, "My husband [wife] and I are completely different people. He [she] is a person who likes football [shopping, classical music, country music, yellow, red, etc.]. That's just not *me*."

Those may be things you like or enjoy, but remember that they don't define who you *are*. Who *are* you, really? You *are* a person who values love, wisdom, generosity, etc., who might be willing to challenge your *dislike* of football, shopping, classical music, country music, yellow, red, etc., if it meant giving you an opportunity to *become* more loving, wise, generous, and so on.

Two-year-olds know who they *are* because of their preferences and the things they do. A two-year-old may, for example, identify himself as "the boy who only eats sandwiches with the peanut butter on *top* of the jelly and the crust cut off." If you mess with this order, he will act as if you have destroyed his whole world. Lifeboat couples live in this space, but Conventional husbands and wives are often at least moderately tempted to give in to this attitude. "I would *never* be caught dead eating *X*, watching *Y*, shopping at *A*, doing *Z*. That's just not me!" This attitude limits a person's growth, and plants the seeds of estrangement in a marriage. To get more out of your life and marriage, you will need to work a little harder to identify with your values, not your preferences.

5. Bring Your Values Home

This is the *single, most important challenge* that confronts you. It will enable you to overcome all of the challenges we have described thus far. To move to the next stage, you are going to have to learn more about applying your faith (and/or beliefs) to your everyday life and start practicing it even when it stretches you, even if that means you can no longer be a "smorgasbord Christian," picking and choosing among the various beliefs held by your church (or other "values group"). Here's why.

Your current value system may not be strong enough to motivate you to be loving and faithful to your mate even when you are angry with her — even when she doesn't "deserve" this generosity. Right now, you tend to be loving to her when she is loving to you. You can be giving to her as long as she is equally giving to you. But to get to the next level, one of you is going to have to start giving more of yourself than would seem reasonable at first. The only way to do this and maintain your integrity is if you see this self-gift as an exercise in spiritual growth, an opportunity to become a better example of the values you claim to hold, more of the person you believe God created you to be. If you do not make yourself truly accountable to the values held by your church, you will find it difficult to give more of yourself than your mate has earned without feeling like you are being taken advantage of.

Conclusion to Apprenticeship Marriages

Exceptional Marriages — the next stop on *The Relationship Pathway* — will show how all the principles we described above work in real life. But before we go there, read the following passage from *The Velveteen Rabbit*. It is the story of a toy rabbit that very desperately wants to become real. We refer to it when we're tempted to choose our own comfort over intimacy. In this excerpt, the Velveteen Rabbit seeks advice from the oldest toy in the nursery: a shabby leather-covered rocking horse:

> "Real isn't how you are made," said the Skin Horse. "It's a thing that happens to you. When a child loves you for a long, long time, not just to play with, but *really* loves you, then you become Real."
>
> Does it hurt?" asked the Rabbit.
>
> "Sometimes," said the Skin Horse, for he was always truthful. "When you are Real you don't mind being hurt."
>
> "Does it happen all at once … or bit by bit?"
>
> "It doesn't happen all at once," said the Skin Horse. "You become. It takes a long time. *That's why it doesn't happen often to people who break easily, or have sharp edges, or who have to be carefully kept"* [italics in the original].

A good marriage happens about the time we stop carefully keeping ourselves. Let's take a look at some of those marriages that have been, as the Skin Horse in *The Velveteen Rabbit* would say, "loved into Real."

EXCEPTIONAL MARRIAGES (Stages 4 and 5)

Exceptional couples in both *Partnership* and *Romantic Peer* categories are the marriages Apprenticeship couples are trying to emulate. The relationships in this category are primarily concerned with pursuing intimacy and living out a deeply held, well-integrated system of faith and values. Once you can meet your basic needs and have a solid sense of your own place in the world, you are ready to begin building something larger than yourself: an *Exceptional Marriage* (also referred to in the literature as a *Peer Marriage*). Besides the high value they place on intimacy, couples in Exceptional Marriages have another quality that sets them apart. In an Exceptional Marriage, husbands and wives are *equally skilled* at communicating and respectfully expressing their emotions.

While *Partner* and *Romantic Peer Marriages* are different from each other in important ways, they do share some common ground. Couples in both marriages make decisions on their time, energy, and work by considering their marriage and family first. They are comfortable turning down projects, invitations to social functions, or even certain friendships and career moves that would take too much time away from their marriage. To varying degrees, what allows these couples to make such bold decisions is their own *deeply personal commitment to a value system*. They rely on this set of beliefs for guidance in making all major decisions — not in a rigid, rule-based way as Lifeboat couples do or in the somewhat halting, am-I-getting-this-right way Apprenticeship couples do (because they are still learning to find their feet), but the more confident, holistic, and flexible way that shows a masterful and heartfelt understanding of their beliefs. In a word, both categories of Exceptional couples have achieved a degree of *wisdom*, which is perhaps best understood as the practical side of moral goodness — a sense of how to pursue and apply one's ideals in a more natural, compassionate, and human way.

An Exceptional Marriage might be based on qualities esteemed by the women's movement, or a more theologically oriented system. Either way, the values will include egalitarianism and mutual respect — and if the spouses belong to an organization supporting their beliefs, the couple's commitment will be more of a personal nature as opposed

The Relationship Pathway

Stage (Level)	**Maslow's Hierarchy of Needs** *Pre-Occupying Need*	**Popcak Relationship Pathway** *Relationship/Life Theme*	
5	**Actualization** — Primarily concerned with pursuing a deeply and personally held set of beliefs and values.	**Romantic Peer Marriage** — Theme: Mutual growth and fulfillment of shared mission.	**EXCEPTIONAL** (Satisfaction/Stability)
4	**Respect/Esteem** — Primarily concerned with becoming a model/exemplary member of the groups to which you belong.	**Partnership Marriage** — Theme: Cultivating deeper intimacy by learning to love partner more than comfort zone. *Two types:* (a) Traditional Type (b) Contemporary Type	
3	**Love/Belonging** — Primarily concerned with finding a community to belong to/to care and be cared for.	**Apprenticeship Marriage** — Theme: Supporting each other's place in the world (work and roles). *Two types:* (a) Contemporary Type (b) Traditional Type	**CONVENTIONAL** (Satisfaction/Stability)
2	**Safety/Security** — Primarily concerned with maintaining sense of stability, well-being, and security.	**Lifeboat Marriage** — Theme: Maintaining stability through either financial gain or avoidance of stress. *Two types:* (a) Materialistic Type (b) Avoidant Type	**IMPOVERISHED** (Satisfaction/Stability)
1	**Basic Needs** — Primarily concerned with achieving basic food, shelter, basic health, and finding comfort from the hardships of life.	**Crisis Marriage** — Theme: Survival and escape. *Two types:* (a) Chaotic Type (b) Codependent Type	

to Apprenticeship couples that view their memberships as important roles they play. In addition to making decisions with their marriage in mind, the spouses' adherence to a value system allows them to do the following:

1. They are comfortable loving even when it requires them to grow or it seems "unfair."

Couples in Exceptional Marriages are secure enough to know they will not allow themselves to be walked over. They would be financially and emotionally capable of leaving a marriage today if they decided it was necessary. Because they are secure in themselves, they do not keep a running tally of offenses like couples in lesser marriages do. Likewise, they are willing to challenge their own preferences, weaknesses, and ways of doing things. This commitment to a value system frees up people in Exceptional Marriages to act in loving ways, not because their spouses always deserve it, but because they see themselves as individuals who value intimacy, compassion, love, and commitment. Not to live up to those values is to disappoint themselves.

2. They value each other as essential partners in helping them live up to all of their values and goals in life.

Exceptional Marriages are unique for their uncommon longevity and happiness. What makes them so special? As we suggested earlier in the chapter, it is the goals these couples have built their marriages around.

Most marriages enter a crisis when couples run out of goals. That's why so many relationships end after the couple builds a home, graduates school, has children, has children leave the nest, or even when one or both spouses retire. All of these milestones are goals on which people base their less-good marriages. Research shows that in order to be sustainable, couples must always have the sense that they are learning, growing, and discovering things together (VanderDrift, Lewandowski, Agnew, 2010). When a couple's major, pre-occupying goal is completed, they often experience a major shake-up as they scramble to figure out "Now what?"

In both categories of Exceptional Marriages, the primary goal in life — more than having a nice home, raising kids, or traveling after retirement — is *becoming a loving, genuinely self-donative, godly person* (among other qualities). This goal lasts a lifetime. Marriages built around such a goal will always be relevant.

How do you know if you are building your marriage around such a value system? A more Conventional couple will read the above statement about being a loving person and think, "Oh, yeah, well, I want that too." But a person in an Exceptional Marriage will think, "Yes. That's what I want more than anything else. And I would be willing to get off the fast track in my career, reduce the number of friends I have, and decrease my involvement in other activities to get it."

Just as important as having a value system is viewing your mate as an essential partner in helping you live up to those values. Couples in Exceptional Marriages believe that their partners are instrumental in helping them achieve their goal of being a more loving and/or secure, confident, creative, fun, open, intimate person.

There are a few other items that make Exceptional Marriages unique, but you will read about those as we explore the two major categories of Exceptional Marriages. Because the central theme of an Exceptional Marriage is living out and mastering a particular value system, whether the spouses are still learning to apply the ins and outs of a value system or have internalized it (own it) will determine whether they have a Partnership Marriage or a Romantic Peer Marriage.

Partnership Marriages

Partnership Marriages exhibit high longevity and high satisfaction. Partnership couples' marriages model the idea that a good marriage isn't a fifty-fifty effort as much as it is a hundred-hundred effort, in which both the husband and the wife work hard to contribute everything they have to give regardless of the situation. There are two major differences that set Partnership couples apart from Apprentice couples.

First, Apprentices believed they were faithful members of "Values Group X" because they attended meetings faithfully, raised money for X's causes, and chaired various committees. Partners tend to be established leaders in their groups, plus they bring their values home. They aren't afraid to ask hard questions about how their lives and roles as husbands and wives actually measure up to the values espoused by their group, and they are working to make deep changes in their lives and marriages accordingly.

Second, while Apprentices try to be good partners to each other, they often get caught up in arguments about how much is "fair" to give because they are still afraid of losing themselves to the relationship. Alternatively, Partners have moved beyond this fear. They have learned how to be wholly themselves while simultaneously working hard to meet their spouse's needs.

Partnership couples (of both *Traditional* and *Contemporary* types) are at Maslow's Respect/Esteem Stage (Stage 4). They do not pursue respect and esteem for the sake of status, but because of their efforts to truly own their respective value system and their demonstrated capacity for wisdom, they have earned the respect of those in their values groups (e.g., church, professional groups). Without seeking it, these couples are often held up as examples by fellow members of these groups, who recommend them to leadership positions in their respective groups. Because of their desire to prove themselves, Apprenticeship couples would be drawn to these leadership opportunities like an addict to cocaine, but Partnership couples are much better at weighing these opportunities against their need to be present to each other, their children, and whatever other most important priorities they have. They are just as content to serve as they are to take a back seat, if there are more pressing needs at home.

Question to Consider: Can you think of a couple you know who might fit into either the Contemporary or Traditional Partnership Marriage?

Recommendations for Modern and Traditional Partnership Marriages

Partnership Marriages of both types are generally very stable and satisfying. Furthermore, in both types of Partnerships, the husband and wife are quite capable of taking care of themselves and like it that way. They see their marriage neither as a way of protecting themselves against a hostile world as Lifeboat couples do nor as a means of establishing their place in the world like Apprenticeship couples, but rather as a genuine *partnership in mutual growth* in which they are working toward goals of intimacy, equality, and mutual service and respect.

Both types of Partnership Marriages are busy. But unlike their counterparts in Apprenticeship Marriages, the spouses are not only willing to take time for each other, but are religious about actively maintaining their daily and weekly rituals of connection around work, play, talk, and prayer. Sometimes this means turning down work or other obligations that conflict with their *rendezvous*. "Unforeseen circumstances" that prevent couples from having their scheduled time are extremely rare.

Partners are very well skilled when it comes to negotiating conflict (see Chapter 10, "The Secrets of Red-Hot Loving"). There are very few problems, big or small, that this couple cannot resolve to the satisfaction of both. Despite this fact, two issues may eventually bring some partners to counseling.

The first is that, ironically, their deep friendship can have a dampening effect on their sex life. For many people, even so-called "evolved" people, sex still has overtones of being something "bad," "naughty, " or "rebellious." At the very least, sex is often used as a way to prove one's desirability to a mate. Since so little in Partnership Marriages is lacking, and the couple's mutual respect leaves little left to prove, Partners often experience what Dr. Pepper Schwartz calls "an incest taboo." As one Partnership wife put it, "I love sex and I really don't have any hang-ups about it; it's just that I have a hard time 'getting nasty' with someone I respect so much."

What helps Partnership spouses through this phase is redeeming their idea of what it is to be sexual. Partnership couples with happy sex lives view lovemaking as a spiritual act, a celebration, and a logical outcome of all that is good in their marriage. Chapter 11 of this book will help you understand this transition better, but it will do for now to know that one of the major tasks for Partnership couples is to change their understanding of sex as "getting nasty" to sex as a "free and open celebration of our love."

Assuming that Partnership couples continue to ask hard questions about what it means to apply their values system to their life and relationship and seek to go deeper in their understanding of how to apply their values to the challenges of everyday life, they will most likely evolve into the Romantic Peer Stage, at which point they develop real wisdom and a true depth of intimacy.

Romantic Peer Marriages

As far as current research goes, this is the top of the marital food chain. *Romantic Peers* focus on intimacy in the context of self-actualization and sanctification — of becoming everything that God is calling them to be. To this couple, nothing is more important than helping each other live out a deeply held set of values. Other couples have values; but what makes Romantic Peers different from Partners is that while Partners still need — at least to some degree — to look to a church or other social group to clarify their value system, Romantic Peers have almost completely internalized — or "own" — their values. Christian Peers will remain active in their churches because Christianity values fellowship and community so much. But for the most part, Christian Peers have incorporated the tenets of the group into their lives and no longer have to check with anyone else to see if they are "doing it right." They do what they do, not because they are *supposed* to, or to fit in, but because they have a deep, personal understanding of what living by a certain set of values means *in their unique set of circumstances.*

Even so, these individuals are sensitive to the possibility of falling victim to pride ("Look at how wonderfully I'm living out all my Christian values!"). As such, many Christian Peers seek regular, individual spiritual direction. Typically, this stage of marriage coincides with the stages of spiritual growth that Father Benedict Groeschel called the "Illuminative Way," or even the "Unitive Way," in his book *Spiritual Passages.*

Three qualities are the hallmarks of these marriages: simplification, competence, and egalitarianism.

First, let's look at *simplification.* Both husband and wife are definitely off the fast track. They *could* work more, but they have come to the conclusion that the time and money isn't worth the cost to their pursuit of intimacy and other values. Romantic Peers aren't deadbeats — they just have more important things to do, such as loving each other and their children. Romantic Peers are not martyrs. They don't give up anything they really need; but they know how to give up everything that is not valuable, like approval, or more money than their needs — and, most important, their wants — require.

Second, both husband and wife are *competent* at all aspects of family life. Romantic Peers are co-partners in the extreme. They have raised their ability to attend to the tasks and chores of daily domestic life to an art form, a dance that is inspiring to witness. And they are adept at seeing the opportunities for spiritual growth behind the mundane tasks of everyday life. Their lives are inspiring examples of the "little way" of holiness that can be found in the domestic church.

Third, they value *egalitarianism over equality*. What does this mean? Basically, people who value equality know they are equal because they *do* the same things or the same amount of things as someone else. People who value egalitarianism know they *are* equal, and they don't feel the need to prove it by dividing jobs up into nice even piles or by declaring certain tasks to be beneath them. Here is a practical, albeit somewhat silly example of how a couple going up *The Relationship Pathway* grows in egalitarianism. The Lifeboat wife might rather die a slow, torturous death than change a light bulb if she considered it her husband's job; but she would exhaust 300 times as much energy nagging him to do it. The Apprenticeship wife would change the bulb if her husband didn't get to it when she asked, but she would secretly resent his dereliction of duty. The Partnership wife changes the bulb without a second thought. The Romantic Peer wife would not only change the bulb without thinking about it but also might see to having the whole house rewired — to code — by the time her husband came home. Likewise, the Lifeboat husband would consider watching his children akin to "babysitting," something beneath his dignity. He is loath to do it and looks for the earliest opportunity to sack out on the sofa. The Apprenticeship husband knows that he *should* want to watch his kids, but it would only be a matter of time before he got bored and sent them to play in the basement so he could get some work done. The Partnership husband would eagerly play with the children and would be happy to give his wife a break whenever she needed it. And the Romantic Peer husband would be begging his wife to go out so that he could get some time alone with his kids (and the house would be immaculate when she got back).

These examples are meant as somewhat tongue-in-cheek illustrations, not diagnostic criteria, but they provide examples of the attitude each stage of marriage on the Pathway has toward the idea of partnership.

Egalitarianism means that spouses do not quibble over who does what and how much. They both do whatever needs to be done when it needs to be done and respect each other's ability to do it. To them, masculinity or femininity is not a matter of the jobs a person does; it is a matter of emphasis of certain qualities (see "Celebrating an Incredible Christian Union" in Chapter 2).

Some Christians have a difficult time understanding how this is an acceptable way for husbands and wives to behave. How can husbands and wives be so independently competent and still be faithful to both their "male and female roles" and the exhortation found in the Letter to the Ephesians? "Be subject to one another out of reverence for Christ. Wives, be subject to your husbands, as to the Lord. For the husband is the head of the wife …" (5:21-23).

Catholics understand this passage in terms of the mutual deference described in verse 21, to submit to one another out of reverence for Christ. How does this work in real life?

Essentially, in any human structure there is a naturally occurring authority, somebody who is, ultimately, the person looked to for a final decision in emergencies or when there is a deadlock. Even contemporary research on marriage finds that this order naturally expresses itself in marriage even when the couples don't cultivate it (Gottman, 2011). This kind of authority is a simple sociological fact and is *distinctly different from power or domination*, both of which are unacceptable qualities for any Christian to exhibit. Considering this, all decisions that affect the family should be made with the full cooperation of both husband and wife (and possibly the children). Further, decisions must *not* be made on the basis of who has more power, or whose turn it is to "win"; rather, they should be made on the basis of whose idea more clearly benefits the general good of the family.

Therefore, in most instances, the husband and wife will be just as willing to defer to each other, just as Christ demands (Eph 5:21). However, there will be times when either emergencies occur or when consultation among the family members yields no clear winning answer. In these times, assuming the man is deferring to Christ (Eph 5:21) and has the good of the family foremost in his heart and mind, the man would cast the deciding ballot. This designation is a result of the qualities God ordained Adam to emphasize, qualities that, assuming he is acting in deference to Christ and truly has the good of the family as his foremost thought, make him more likely to be able to discern God's will for his family.

Equality can be at odds with this notion of headship because it values distribution of power over everything else. When equality is the highest value, *the good of the family* often falls victim to the "whoever got his or her way last time must lose this time" mentality. Egalitarianism is not at odds with this model of headship, however, because decisions are never made on the basis of power. The reason for a decision should never come down to "Because I can." When egalitarianism is valued over either simple "equality" or oversimplified "gender roles," every decision is made with the genuine welfare and happiness of all concerned as the first and only consideration.

The level of competence couples in this category have attained has other benefits. Romantic Peers are so good at taking care of themselves and each other that to outsiders their marriages just seem to happen magically. They are what Drs. Lederer and Jackson of the Palo Alto Mental Research Center described as "collaborative geniuses." Of course, a great deal of very hard work goes into making these marriages, but it is most definitely a labor of love. Romantic Peers are each other's best friends, have virtually no secrets from each other, and have achieved a level of spiritual sexuality that is truly enviable. Unlike couples in less-good marriages that go through periods of boredom with each other, Romantic Peers' relationships actually become more vital, exciting, fun, and fulfilling as the years go by.

If they struggle with anything, it is their relative social isolation. Romantic Peers are too busy loving each other and living their own lives to have the energy for the *Sturm und Drang* that comes with having too many acquaintances. This is in contrast to Lifeboat couples, who avoid others because they fear them, and Apprenticeship couples, who gorge themselves on a frenzy of acquaintances.

Abraham Maslow's description of self-actualizing people applies to Romantic Peers as well. They are at peace in times of uncertainty, are good at accepting themselves and others, can be both spontaneous and creative, have a good sense of humor, value their privacy, can take care of themselves, are capable of deeply intimate relationships, and have an open, positive attitude about life.

Whether or not you think you will ever arrive at such a place in your life, you could learn a lot from such people. The rest of this book concerns itself with teaching you how both Partners and Romantic Peers solve problems, keep love alive, and maintain the relevance of their marriage throughout the years.

Question to Consider: Can you think of a couple you know who might fit into the category of Romantic Peer Marriage?

The Relationship Pathway: Some Final Considerations.

We hope that by covering the main points of each marriage type on *The Relationship Pathway*, you have a better idea where you come from, where you are at this point in your marriage, and where you will be going from here. The point of this chapter is not to diagnose you or stress you out, but to give you a sense of the next steps on your marital journey and the specific work you might need to accomplish to get where God is calling you to go. Marriage is about perfecting one another in Christ. *The Relationship Pathway* is one attempt to convey the process by which that transformation in grace takes place.

If, after reflecting on your place on *The Relationship Pathway* you feel you would like some assistance in addressing the obstacles that stand between you and becoming an Exceptional Couple, we are available for "technical support." If you would like to discuss your situation more thoroughly with a faithful counselor, please call the Pastoral Solutions Institute at 740-266-6461 for a telephone consultation, or look us up online at www.ExceptionalMarriages.com.

Having identified both the ideal for your marriage and where your marriage actually is on *The Relationship Pathway*, next we'll examine the challenges that all marriages encounter over the course of a couple's life together, and ways you can prepare yourself to weather those challenges with courage, grace, and most of all, God's abundant love.

CHAPTER 6

On the Road to "Happily Ever After"

Marriage Mountain and the Stages of Married Life

Christian psychologist Paul Tournier once quipped, "I've been married six times — all to the same woman!" Tournier and his wife didn't divorce and remarry six times. Rather, he meant that even though he was only married one time, to one woman, the character of his marriage changed dramatically over the course of their years together.

Regardless of your place on *The Relationship Pathway* (i.e., Crisis, Lifeboat, Apprentice, Partnership, or Romantic Peer), *every* marriage will travel though particular stages, evolving in dramatic ways over time. You will need to be ready for those changes in order for you to experience the potential blessings that accompany each stage of married life.

Climbing Marriage Mountain

Over the course of our years together, we've observed that being married is like climbing a mountain. There are times when the climb is exhilarating and the views are breathtaking. Other times you're scared out of your wits and it's all you can do to hang on and keep from falling to your death. In order to make it to the top, you can't look down. You've got to keep your eyes on the next peak and keep climbing. Sometimes you'll wonder why you ever decided to do this crazy thing, but once you've made it, you're never sorry.

When the marital climb gets difficult, it has been our experience that too many people panic and jump. They don't think beyond the immediate crisis; they just know they're scared and uncomfortable, and they don't want to be scared and uncomfortable anymore, and so it would be easier to fling themselves into the great unknown than to keep going. Of course, when you're 10,000 feet up, the first step is a doozy.

Your place on *The Relationship Pathway* gives you an idea of your readiness to ascend the various stages of Marriage Mountain. By analogy, climbing Mount Everest requires similar things from every climber. But some climbers are definitely better prepared for the climb than others. For instance, couples in Crisis Marriages are like climbers hoping to make it to the top of the mountain wearing nothing but a swimsuit and flip-flops, while Romantic Peer couples come outfitted with a matched set of climbing gear and a half-dozen Sherpas to guide them.

Regardless of the stage you find yourself on *The Relationship Pathway*, any couple that is going to do such a crazy thing as get married ought to at least have a map, some resource to let the partners know what common obstacles they will encounter while making the ascent up Marriage Mountain. Otherwise, it is too easy to take a normal part of the climbing experience — hair-raising as it might be — and make a crisis out of it, with one or the other spouse complaining, "This rock face is too sheer. This path is too narrow. We must be going the wrong way. *And it's all your fault!*"

Your Journey: An Itinerary

The illustration on page 102 shows the different stages that every marriage encounters. You *will* go through these stages, no matter what type of marriage you have. As we examine each stage, you will see how they affect each marriage on *The Relationship Pathway*, and you will discover how to gracefully negotiate the challenges you will face and increase the likelihood of arriving successfully at the top of the mountain.

Stage One: Beginning the Climb

Honeymoon Stage

- *Major Task for Self-Esteem:* Pursuing intimacy.
- *Time into Marriage:* Newlywed to six months (approximately).
- *Major Relationship Challenges at This Stage:* (1) Establishing the

strength, priority, and independence of your marriage. (2) Reconciling romantic notions with marital realities.

When you first begin your climb, you are excited, to say the least. It's a clear, sunny day, and you have all the energy in the world. It's a good thing too, because the work begins with the first step you take on Marriage Mountain.

The *Honeymoon Stage* of marriage encompasses two challenges. The first is to establish the strength, priority, and independence of your marriage. The second is reconciling the reality of marriage with your romantic ideal of it. Most of you reading this will already be through the Honeymoon Stage, so we will not belabor it except to say that a couple's commitment to marital fidelity receives its first challenges here (for a closer look at the first three stages of marriage, please check out our book *Just Married: The Catholic Guide to Surviving and Thriving in the First Five Years of Marriage*). We don't mean fidelity in the simple sense of not sleeping with other people; we mean fidelity in the sense of a willingness to forsake *all* others, including families of origin, friends, extracurricular activities, and even certain job placements — *if* they interfere with the primacy of the marriage. Devaluing the non-marital attachments held dear for much of one's life can be a terrifying experience; but for the sake of the marriage's future, it must be done.

Even though many newlyweds feel that they have nothing but time together, they must make a concerted effort to establish *rituals of connection* — regular, scheduled, daily and weekly appointments to work, play, talk, and pray together. By doing so, they learn to establish the structures that will protect the priority of their relationship and maintain it as their lives become busy with children, work, and other responsibilities. Couples who do not use this time to establish solid rituals of connection around work, play, talk, and prayer will find that it is difficult to retrofit these things into their lives once the family starts to grow and their commitments increase. Waiting until you feel like you're growing apart to start trying to squeeze in time to work, play, talk, and pray together is rarely a good idea, and can cause the couple to experience a real crisis of marital relevancy and intimacy.

At this stage, it is especially important for a couple to remember that they got married because they believe they are each other's best hope

(Continued on page 104)

SCALING MARRIAGE MOUNTAIN

The Stages of Married Life

Note: All time frames are approximate. Actual beginnings and endings of stages may vary greatly from couple to couple.

1 • HONEYMOON STAGE (0–6 months)

Major Goals: Establish strength and independence of your marriage.

Individual Goals**:** Foster intimacy and fidelity.

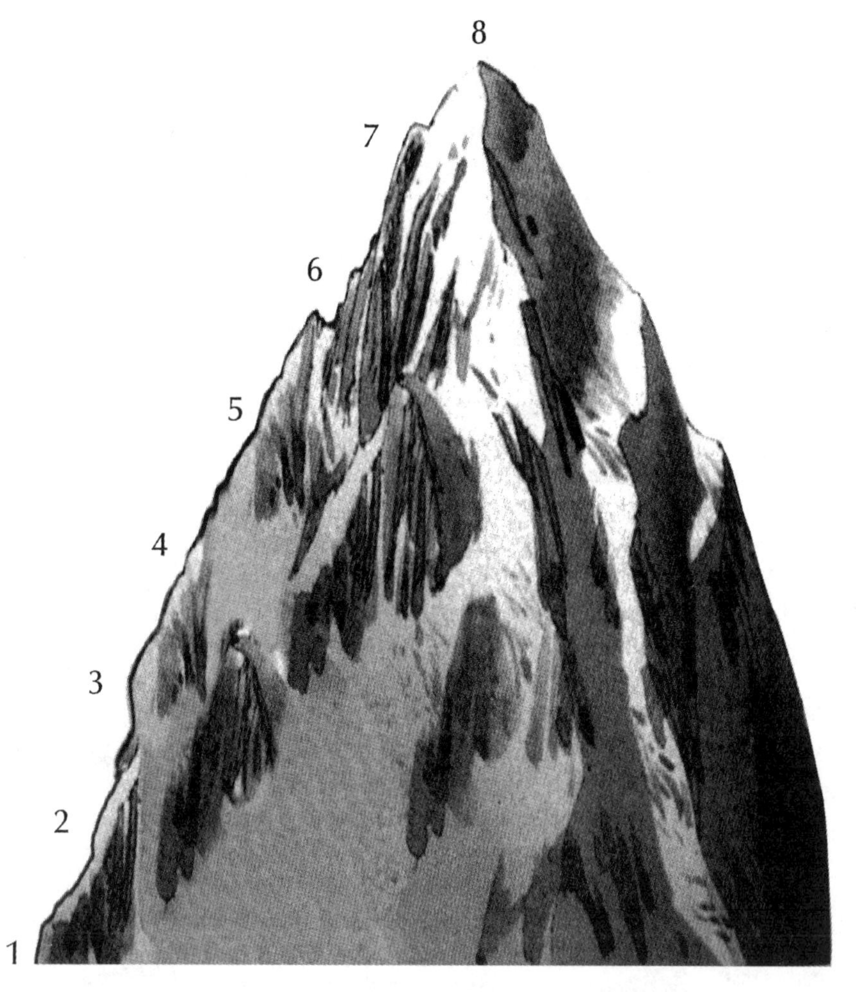

2 • CONFLICT AND NEGOTIATION STAGE (6 months–3 to 5 years)

Major Goals: Learn safe, effective problem-solving skills. Work out unique character of your relationship.

Individual Goals: Maintain intimacy in spite of conflict.

3 • NEW PATTERN STAGE (4–8 years)

Major Goals: Take time to let patterns negotiated in last stage take hold before starting too many other new ventures.

4 • CREATIVE STAGE (7–15+ years)

Major Goals: Maintain intimacy while pursuing goals that are important to personal fulfillment.

Individual Goals: Develop relationship with community at large. Increase potential for caring, nurturing, and creativity. (Warning: Extremely difficult phase for Shipwrecked/Rescue couples; moderately difficult for Conventional couples in later phases of stage.)

5 • HOMECOMING STAGE (14–25+ years)

Major Goals: Jettison unnecessary commitments for the sake of greater intimacy and time with family. Zero in on what's "really" important. Also, begin thinking about life after children leave home.

6 • LAUNCHING STAGE (20–30+ years)

Major Goals: Successfully launching children into the world. Answering question "Now what?" about life and marriage. Midlife crises common. Second major danger area for Shipwrecked and lower-functioning Conventional couples.

Individual Goals: Maintain intimacy while figuring out what to do with second half of life.

7 • SECOND HONEYMOON STAGE (30–45+ years)

Major Goals: Maintaining intimacy, creativity, and relevance in the world as late midlife/later life is approaching. Finding new ways to deepen intimacy and beginning new projects that you didn't feel comfortable starting while children were still around.

8 • "HAPPILY EVER AFTER" STAGE (45+ years)

Major Goals: Enjoying late years together. Confronting loss and death. Maintaining hope and meaning as end of life draws near.

Individual Goals: Reviewing life. Developing and passing on your wisdom.

(Continued from page 101)
for becoming the people God wants them to be by the end of their lives and helping each other enjoy heaven in the next. This is the only reason strong enough to motivate a couple to establish the necessary boundaries between them and their friends, employers, and families of origin.

Cutting loose from old attachments is hard work, and the pain involved often brings the first challenge to people's romantic ideals of marriage. But doing this work builds a solid foundation of security in the marriage. A couple can't embrace the vulnerability involved in pursuing mutual growth and intimacy unless they know that they are really each other's number one priority, after their love of God. Fortunately, the warm-fuzzy feelings that accompany this stage often make the difficult choice of forsaking all others more bearable than it might otherwise be. Making the mutual choice to gently but firmly stand up to Mom and Dad, less-supportive friends, and other obstacles to establishing the primacy of the marriage creates the security necessary for the couple to negotiate the next stage of married life as a team, instead of as self-protective individuals.

Stage Two: Climbing to the First Peak

Conflict and Negotiation Stage

- *Major Task for Self-Esteem:* Pursuing intimacy.
- *Time into Marriage:* Approximately six months to three to five years.
- *Major Relationship Challenges at This Stage:* (1) Learning that disagreements and/or differences do not equal death. (2) Establishing rules that keep arguments safe and productive.

One of the keys to successful mountain climbing is packing light. Unfortunately, on this part of your ascent up Marriage Mountain, you are beginning to discover that you have brought along a little more baggage than is absolutely necessary. Before going any further, you are going to have to decide what to keep and what to leave behind.

Following quickly on the heels of "honeymoondom" is the "I never knew *that* about you" stage. Suddenly, you begin discovering things about your mate of which you were previously unaware. Some of these discoveries are pleasant, some are surprising, and some are decidedly unwelcome. As you marvel at your spouse's hitherto unknown obsessiveness, eccentricities, and harebrained ideas, you begin to wonder who this wacko is that you married and if there is any hope for your future.

This is the stage where couples tend to lose a lot of blood fighting over such issues as the "correct" way to wind the vacuum cleaner cord, roll a tube of toothpaste, drive the car, manage your schedules, pay the bills, and assorted other life-or-death catastrophes. These arguments are never as simple as they seem because there is more going on than toothpaste. Arguments in this phase are often really about vulnerability and safety. In other words, couples engaging in such petty battles are often saying to one another, "I've never trusted so much of myself to anyone else before. I want to be certain I didn't make a bad choice. So I am going to make a big fuss about nonsense to see if you treat me with respect even when I am acting like a complete idiot."

We all play this game at one point in our marriages. Fortunately, most of us survive it. Better still, we become more mature and more confident in our marriages as a result.

The second factor that complicates arguments in the *Conflict and Negotiation Stage* is that we are often unclear about the differences between our identities and mere preferences. This stage involves so many challenges to how we used to organize our single lives that some people begin feeling as if they are "losing themselves." Learning to identify what is an essential part of our identities versus what are merely our preferences is a major goal of this stage. "How much can I let go of without losing myself?" is an important question to ponder. Obviously, how you define yourself will determine how successful you are at negotiating this stage. If, like Lifeboat couples, your life is built around maintaining your comfort, then this stage can be a living hell for your marriage. Every stylistic difference, from how you wash dishes to the "correct" way to conduct your morning routine, will be experienced as a real threat to your sense of self. If, like Apprentices, you build your life around meaningful work and roles, things will go relatively well, until you begin arguing over your inherited ideas of what husbands and wives are "supposed" to do for each other or how work schedules should be arranged. If, like Partners and Romantic Peers, you build your lives around fulfilling a particular value system, then you will limit yourself to arguments that infringe on your ability to live up to your values, ideals, and goals. You will be able to see that everything else is either unimportant or simply a matter of taste, and there is no sense arguing about that.

No matter what category of marriage you fall into, to keep a proper perspective about the many changes you undergo in Conflict and Negotiation, you have to ask yourself the following question: "Does negotiating this issue in any way decrease the possibility of fulfilling my dreams, goals, or values?" If the answer is "yes," then by all means argue about it. If the answer is "no," you would probably do better to get over yourself and exercise a bit of flexibility. Save your energy for the battles that really count.

Again, the Conflict and Negotiation Stage is only moderately uncomfortable for most Apprenticeship, Partner, and Romantic Peer Marriages. But it can be devastating to Crisis Marriages, and it often initiates the long slide into estrangement for Lifeboat couples, who view challenges to their personal comfort and style as life-or-death issues. This attitude often causes them to choose either quiet resentment or violent, recurring arguments over practical, equitable solutions.

This brings us to the second task of the Conflict and Negotiation Stage: establishing rules for effective problem solving. As you and your mate discuss your different preferences, styles, and attitudes toward household tasks and life, you will have to work out what "fair fighting" means to you. The implicit or explicit "rules of engagement" you develop in the Conflict and Negotiation Stage set the precedent for solving large and small problems in the future. The wise couple will take this opportunity to learn the difference between problem solving and arguing. Chapter 10 talks more about this subject, specifically how those in the *Exceptional Seven Percent* learn to feel closer *because* of conflict rather than in spite of it. Likewise, our book *When Divorce Is Not an Option: How to Heal Your Marriage and Nurture Lasting Love* offers additional supports for cultivating habits for effective conflict resolution and *Just Married: The Catholic Guide to Surviving and Thriving in the First Five Years of Marriage* discusses ways to resolve the challenges of this stage in detail.

Stage Three: The First Plateau

New Pattern Stage

- *Major Task for Self-Esteem:* Pursuing intimacy.
- *Time into Marriage:* Approximately four to eight years.
- *Major Relationship Challenges at This Stage:* (1) Solidifying the

unique identity of your relationship. (2) Seeking "second-nature" status of rituals and routines

The climb to this first plateau of Marriage Mountain was a little harder than you would have liked it to be. Still, you are grateful to have made it this far. Time for a little rest. As you finish pitching the tent and begin to warm yourself by the fire, you and your partner talk about the things you have learned so far and how these lessons will enable you to work together more efficiently when you start climbing again.

In the *New Pattern Stage*, your marriage begins to take on an organized identity that is unique to the two of you. Because — in the last stage — you were so conscientious about negotiating mutually satisfying "standard operating procedures" (i.e., acceptable ways of solving problems, resolving conflict, and conducting your everyday life as a couple), you now generally know what is expected *of* each other and what you can expect *from* the other. The main task of the New Pattern Stage is taking time to let these "standard operating procedures" — these rituals and routines that define the unique way you complete tasks together and hang on to your marriage throughout the challenges of life — become second nature.

As satisfying as this stage can be, it takes a great deal of work to get here. Couples don't usually find their feet until between three and five years into the marriage, after a whole lot more Conflict and Negotiation than they would have liked. This is the major reason that so many first-time marriages don't make it to the five-year mark — especially Crisis and Lifeboat Couples. Couples become frightened that the conflict stage will never end. But, of course, with patience, diligence, and sincere effort, it does, and the spouses find that through all their Conflict and Negotiation Stage they have created a truly unique relationship that is not based on old, inherited expectations, but on what works well for them.

The most important thing that spouses can do in the New Pattern Stage is to relax and take some time to become accustomed to their new ways of doing things. The next stage of marital development causes partners to begin distancing themselves from each other a bit. To prepare for this, it can be helpful to avoid taking on any new, major stressors for a while so that a couple's routine can solidify. This is not always possible, but when it is, it is most certainly desirable.

Stage Four: Climbing to the Second Peak

Creative Stage

- *Major Tasks for Self-Esteem:* Creating, caring, and nurturing.
- *Time into Marriage:* Approximately 7 to 15 years.
- *Major Relationship Challenges at This Stage:* (1) Creating and caring for something larger than yourselves. (2) Holding on to the intimacy you have achieved.

Now that you are well rested, it's time to start climbing again. But be warned! On this part of Marriage Mountain, the path narrows and becomes considerably steeper. You are going to have to proceed one step at a time, and tie a line to your partner so you don't lose each other.

This is truly one of the most interesting and exciting stages of married life, and the personal growth this stage affords will often move a marriage to the next level on *The Relationship Pathway* (e.g., from Lifeboat to Apprentice, Apprentice to Partner, etc.). The seeds of your dreams and goals — which were planted in the Honeymoon Stage, germinated in Conflict and Negotiation, and rooted in New Patterns — now burst out of the ground and into the sunlight. This is the *Creative Stage*, the time in your marriage when you begin to create something larger than yourselves. This is the time in your lives when you start that family, build that home, further your education, launch the business you've been dreaming about, and follow through on at least one million other wonderful things.

Assuming you have taken the time to learn the lessons and resolve the challenges of each previous stage, the Creative Stage is like a public proclamation that the love you and your mate have for each other requires a larger package. You want to become more — to create *a world* together that reflects both your oneness *and* your uniqueness. Children will be an important part of that world, as might be building a home that meets the needs of the people living in your world, and doing work that serves the dreams and dignity of all of those living in your world. This is most certainly the experience of Partners and Romantic Peers. These couples are especially adept at building one another's dreams while increasing the depth of the intimacy in their marriages. Early on in their marriage, in the Honeymoon Stage, they created and protected the rituals of connection that allowed them to have regular times to work, play, talk, and pray on both a daily and weekly basis. These rituals of connection allow couples the *time* they need to process life experiences, adapt to changes, and continue to discover new ways to be loving to each other, using all the things they go through as an opportunity to grow in intimacy and understanding.

Apprenticeship couples fare pretty well at this stage, too, though the ride is a bit bumpier because they often make the mistake of assuming they don't need rituals of connection until they start missing each other, whereupon they struggle to retrofit their marriage with some ways to stay connected. Usually, for a time, the Apprenticeship couple loses each other in all the commotion. The husband and wife become so busy attending to their own set of branches (work, kids, etc.) that they forget to nurture the tree (marriage) that is feeding their efforts. One day they notice that the leaves on their respective branches are wilting. They know that "something is missing," but they can't figure out what. This phenomenon has been popularly called "the seven-year itch" (although it has been known to occur as late as fifteen years into a marriage, depending on how long a couple postpones childbearing and other adventures). Sadly, this "itch" has been the cause of many affairs and divorces.

So what's the best way to deal with this "embarrassing itch"? Prevent it. Every day you must remind yourselves to step out of your own little worlds and meet to work on your marriage. The "Twenty-Five Ways to Make Love Stay — Every Day" exercise, in Chapter 7, will offer additional suggestions in this regard.

Special Considerations: Lifeboat Couples and the Creative Stage

For those of you who suspect you might be in Lifeboat Marriages, the Creative Stage may be the single most difficult crisis of your marital relationship. The difficulties presented by this stage have the potential to move you to an Apprenticeship Marriage, but only if you survive them — and many couples (especially Lifeboat Couples) don't. You'll need to pay special attention to the following if you hope to survive beyond the ten-year mark.

The problem is this: the requirements for your continued mental health may now be at cross-purposes with the foundation upon which you built your marriage. On the one hand, you have a normal and deeply personal longing to be more, to take risks, to expand your role in the world, and to test your limits. On the other hand, your marriage was built around maintaining security and guaranteeing the basics of life. At first glance, it would seem that you cannot have both. It is impossible to quit your job to start that business you've always dreamed of without threatening the financial security of your family. You can't demand more intimacy from your mate without increasing the conflict — and thereby jeopardizing the safety — in your marriage. You can't expand your role in the world without taking the risk that you might prefer another person to your mate or another circumstance to your marriage. These are all conflicts that the Lifeboat couple has tried to avoid for the last ten years but all of a sudden can't. These risks must be taken if the Lifeboat Marriage is to evolve into something more; but Lifeboat relationships, which are built to defend the status quo at all costs, don't *do* risk.

Until now, that is. There are only three possible "solutions" to the problem of a conflict between the needs of a marriage and the needs of the individuals in that marriage. Only one of those options is healthy.

Some couples try to sacrifice their personal needs for the sake of the marriage, which often leads to depression, anxiety disorders, infidelity, and a host of other problems. Clearly not a great choice.

Other couples may simply throw away the marriage, believing that they cannot grow as long as they stay with their spouse. Unfortunately, what these couples (and the poorly informed therapists who support them) forget is that making a marriage work is a major developmental milestone that is necessary for both mental and physical health. In fact, research shows that divorce impacts both mental and physical health in very dramatic ways. People who divorce continue to be at higher risk for heart disease, hypertension, cancer, and inflammatory diseases, as well as depression and anxiety disorders, even if they remarry (Hughes and Waite, 2009). Jettisoning a marriage often feels like a ticket to freedom and personal development, but there are so many unexpected consequences of divorce, the estranged couple usually spends so much time just trying to put their lives back together and keep themselves solvent (mentally and emotionally, as well as financially) that they don't have time to grow as they thought they would. This is especially true when children are involved.

This leaves the third option — and really, the only healthy choice — what we like to call, "*The Both-And Solution*." Since you *must* grow, *and* since your optimal growth *requires* you to maintain intimacy, why not learn to do both at the same time? [To borrow the tag line from an old TV series, "We have the technology...."] *Why not make your marriage into something that allows for both intimacy and personal growth?* ["We can rebuild it...."] This will take persistence, strength, and courage — all qualities you want more of anyway — but your efforts will be rewarded. (Presenting ... the Six-Million-Dollar Marriage!) To successfully accomplish this, you and your partner must revisit the "Creating Shared Meaning" exercise at the end of Chapter 2.

Whether your marriage is Romantic Peer, Partnership, Apprenticeship, or Lifeboat, the tasks of the Creative Stage remain the same: creating something larger than yourselves and holding on to the intimacy you have already achieved. To accomplish both of these goals is to allow your marriage to evolve into something more intimate, more enduring, and more vital, giving you much joy and satisfaction in the years to come.

Stage Five: The Second Plateau

Homecoming Stage

- *Major Tasks for Self-Esteem:* Clarifying priorities; finding a balance.
- *Time into Marriage:* Approximately 14 to 25 years.
- *Major Relationship Challenges at This Stage:* (1) Simplifying. (2) Reasserting the priority of marriage and family. (3) Preparing the marriage to withstand the empty-nest syndrome.

"I thought it would be good, but I never knew it would be like this," you say, as you gaze up at the stars from your camp on the second plateau of Marriage Mountain. Every muscle in your body hurts. You and your partner even slipped a couple of times on the last part of the climb. And when you encountered that stampede of mountain goats, you thought you were goners for sure. But you can chuckle about it now from the relative safety of your camp. Before settling in tonight, you and your partner are going to check your lines to make sure they're secure. You are also going to go through your backpacks and get rid of some of the things you picked up along the way. Those herbs and berries can stay, but the rock that reminded you of your great-aunt Hildegard is a little less fascinating now that you see the cliff you are going to have to scale tomorrow.

In the *Homecoming Stage,* you will continue to maintain the projects you began in the previous chapter of your marriage — but you have less to prove. You have demonstrated your ability to be successful in the world at large, and you have shown yourself to be a capable parent, all while holding your marriage together. *Congratulations!* Even so, doing all of those things takes a lot of energy, and you are starting to wonder if you need to stay as busy as you have been the last few years. The kids are getting older, and you begin to feel that "time is going by so fast." Your heart is calling you to simplify.

It is perfectly natural to go through a period of anxiety as you start to pull away from some of the less necessary commitments of your life. You are nervous that such and such will not be able to function without you, or perhaps you are concerned that not working those extra hours will hurt you financially. Soon, howcvcr, your anxicty givcs way to thc pcacc that comes from having your life in order. Accomplishments are nice, but love is better, and you find yourself becoming more relaxed and able to enjoy what time the kids still have left at home.

Which brings us to your second task: preparing your marriage for the fact that one day in the not-too-distant future the kids will be leaving the nest. Even though this is a few years off, it is important to anticipate this change now because too many couples blow through this stage without even taking a minute to consider life without kids. When it happens, they find themselves having to cope with two major crises: saying good-bye to the little ragamuffins (who aren't so little anymore) and getting to know each other again. It will be important for you and your mate to take this time to celebrate your marriage and all you are accomplishing together. Start talking about what you would like to do with yourself and the marriage when the children are gone. Make new plans, dream new dreams — but, most of all, reconnect with your mate, because the next stage can be a shock even to the best of marriages.

Stages Six and Seven: The Third Peak and the Third Plateau

Launching Stage and Second Honeymoon Stage

- *Major Tasks for Self-Esteem:* Developing new goals; maintaining intimacy.
- *Time into Marriage:* Approximately 20 to 45 years.
- *Major Relationship Challenges at This Stage:* (1) Getting the kids out into the world. (2) Answering the question "Now what?"

You are climbing up what appears to be a perpendicular wall of rock. The footholds and handholds are about as wide as your bootlace. Between gasps for air, your partner calls down to you: "This is the part of the climb that separates the big dogs from the porch puppies." You just grit your teeth and smile. Your mind can't decide whether this is the biggest thrill of your life or the dumbest thing you have ever done. You hope it's the former. Better keep climbing and find out.

You've come a long way, baby. Little Gunther, the last of your 14 children (you had two sets of quints, plus four others) is off to study computer-assisted animal husbandry at the University of Wherever ("One of the top ten schools for computer-assisted animal husbandry" — you proudly tell your coworkers). You and your mate unpack Gunther's belongings in his dorm room and bid a tearful goodbye as you say, "See you over Christmas break."

The ride home is quiet. But one question is going through both of your minds: "Now what?"

You are smack dab in the middle of midlife, and it is a time for a mini-reckoning. Is your life going the way you thought it would? Has your marriage been what you hoped it would be? What — if anything — stands between you and the sense that your life has had meaning? What must yet be done for you to feel as if you have fulfilled the purpose of your life?

If you have been conscientiously attending to your marriage — and especially conscientious about maintaining those rituals of connection that give you regular time to work, play, talk, and pray together — throughout the last 20 years or so, this could be the beginning of a wonderful time in your lives. You and your mate will begin making plans for that second honeymoon, and upon your return, the two of you will get down to those projects that you just didn't feel right about pursuing while you still had the little ones around. The *Launching Stage* will smoothly evolve into the *Second Honeymoon Stage,* in which you and your beloved rediscover the joys of working side by side on fulfilling what remains of your most personal dreams.

If, on the other hand, you have been a little careless about your marriage — and depending on how careless you have been — this stage of your journey could include anything from mild crises to major catastrophes. What can compound the difficulties of this stage is that you begin to realize that (Wait! Are you sitting down?) you are not going to live forever. The major disease of this phase is the "midlife crisis." If you feel that your life and marriage have basically been on track, then this will not be cause for too much concern; after all, you did and are doing what you were put here to do. But if you have been neglecting your marriage, or have been cavalier about figuring out who you wanted to be when you grew up, you are in for a wild ride that could include affairs, divorce, cosmetic surgery, psychotherapy, remarriage, and starting all over again with the Honeymoon Stage — probably in that order.

The best way to prevent the collapse of your identity and marriage at midlife is to keep both in the forefront of your mind today. Socrates said, "The unexamined life is not worth living." But too many people would rather just go where life leads them. It sounds so-o-o-o romantic, but what happens at midlife is that these same people break into a cold sweat upon realizing they are nowhere near where they hoped their romantic road would lead. They then wreck a lot of lives in their crazed frenzy to get where they think they should be.

But you have nothing to fear as long as you have built your marriage around fulfilling your identities in Christ and daily working for each other's good. All of this enables your marriage to survive and thrive through the Launching Stage and into your Second Honeymoon years. You will remain passionate friends and lovers long into your dotage — eating your oatmeal out of heart-shaped bowls.

Stage Eight: The Summit

"Happily Ever After"

- *Major Task for Self-Esteem:* "Ego integrity."
- *Time into Marriage:* Approximately 45 or more years.
- *Major Relationship Challenges at This Stage:* (1) Supporting each other through retirement and beyond. (2) Financial issues related to retirement. (3) Fostering "oneness." (4) Confronting mortality.

The sun is just beginning to set as you reach the summit of Marriage Mountain. You are tired, and you are a bit low on supplies, but any worries are secondary to the scene that greets you. As you look around you, you understand what all the work was about, and you think about how the two of you worked together to get here. You take your partner in your arms, saying, "We made it." You both still have concerns about the future and are aware of the challenges that face you as you make your way down the mountain again, but you are looking forward to being able to share your wisdom with those who will climb after you. For now, it is enough to be here. Together. You thank God for your partner because you see that you never would have made it without him or her.

You have survived the most serious threats to your marriage. You have protected both your intimacy and your autonomy throughout the course of your life. God willing, you have quite a few years to go (as many as 20 to 30 years, depending upon when you got married). There will be some hurdles along the way, but most of the challenges to be faced are of a more personal nature. You will encounter such issues as how to spend your retirement years, asserting your continued relevance even though you are no longer working, confronting physical problems, mourning the death of friends, and eventually facing your own and/or your mate's passing.

But throughout all of this, assuming you have faithfully attended to all the tasks along the way, you are at peace with yourself and your marriage. You begin to exhibit what is called "ego integrity" — that is, when you review the years of your life you are filled with a deep sense of rightness. Regrets? Perhaps a few. (But, then again, too few to mention). You are satisfied with the choices you have made, and somehow, all the insanity of life makes sense to you. You may know things now that you wish you had known when you were younger; but life has been good, and you expect it to continue that way for the foreseeable future. You and your partner will spend this phase of your lives exploring new depths of the phrase "soul mates." You will take on new challenges, continue to enjoy each other's company, and seek opportunities to pass on your wisdom. As a bonus, your teenage grandkids *want* to be like you when they grow up.

There are some who will suggest that we are being overly optimistic about this stage of life. We are not blind to the realities of this stage of life. Many older couples do not achieve ego integrity. Too many couples consistently make poor choices, lead tragic lives, and meet tragic ends. But this book is not about them. We are writing about the couples *you want to be like* when you "grow up," the genuinely happy couples — they really do exist — who are both satisfied with their lives and their relationships well into the twilight years. Armed with what we hope are the good directions contained in these pages, some persistence, and a prayer or two, there is no reason you should not achieve "happily ever after" status. Prince and Princess Charming are alive and well and living in a neighborhood near you. *Maybe they can be you.*

The biggest challenge couples in this stage encounter is facing mortality. Some married people arrive at this point in life, only to despair at the futility of it all, lamenting, "We've been through so much together. Only to have it end like this." Very few sorrows can compare to the loss of a spouse. But rather than undermining the meaning of marriage, preparing for death *is* the meaning of a Christian marriage: In life and death we belong to God (Rom 14:8). Our marriages are supposed to be a testament to the belief that we have a better chance of becoming all God created us to be with our mates than without them. This last stage of married life demonstrates the fruit of such a partnership more than any other stage. It can be a powerful witness.

When Greg's grandmother died, he knelt over her coffin to offer a prayer for her soul. As he looked at the body of this woman, he noticed the wedding ring on her hand. What struck him most about it was how thin and worn it had become over the years. His first reaction was to see this as just another metaphor of our mortality. But then, right in mid-prayer, a beautiful and hopeful thought pierced his sadness. The ring, he realized, hadn't worn thin because it was corrupted by time and labor; it had worn thin because through the years the gold rubbed against her hand and, slowly, it was absorbed by her body. At some point in her life, his grandmother no longer simply *wore* his grandfather's wedding ring — she *became* his grandfather's wedding ring. What an amazing and beautiful symbol of how, through a lifetime of partnership, two people really do become one. In that moment, you could almost hear the Lord saying to her, "Well done, my good and faithful servant" (Mt 25:21, NABRE).

For the Christian married couple, death is "graduation day." It is the beginning of everything we have been working for. The entire point of a Christian marriage is spending one's life preparing one's mate for the heavenly banquet. The couple that understands this will certainly suffer the pain of loss, but will not be crushed by it.

In his book *Spiritual Passages,* Father Benedict Groeschel recounts the story of Frank Sheed and Maisie Ward, a powerhouse Catholic couple of the last century who were internationally respected publishers, speakers, and founders of the Catholic Evidence Guild. For years, the two lived and worked together, rarely leaving each other's side. When Maisie passed away, Father Groeschel went to visit Frank and pay his respects. He expected Frank to be agonizing over the loss of his dearest friend and lover. Frank responded to Father Groeschel's condolences with a comment reflecting that peace which goes beyond all understanding: "On the contrary, I feel closer to her now than ever."

When we grow up, we want to be that couple, true examples of Catholic Romantic Peerdom.

As you consider the eight stages of your love life, remember that the difference between a happy couple and a miserable couple is not the difficulties each couple faces along the way. Most people's lot in life is basically the same. What really makes the difference between happy and unhappy couples is that the former never stop expecting the best from themselves and their mates. They never give up, never stop striving for the good of one another. No matter what life throws at them, whether they *feel* like it or not, daily they choose to love. "Better and worse, richer and poorer, sickness and health" aren't just poetic words whispered in front of the altar. These words are reality. Good and bad times, wealth and poverty, sickness and health have absolutely nothing to do with our responsibility *to* love or our capacity *for* love. In fact, it is because we humans are so often sick, poor, and sad that we *need* marriage. A happy marriage is not an escape from reality; rather, it is a celebration of that reality and a promise to love each other "into Real" — even if that means enduring some popped stitches, worn velveteen, and sagging stuffing along the way.

The View from the Peak: Nine Tasks of Marriage

Throughout this chapter, we have attempted to give you a crystal ball with which to see the future of your marriage. As you are now aware, each stage of your journey involves new challenges that you must face if you are ever to arrive at "happily ever after." When people talk about marriage being hard work, it is mostly the challenges described in this chapter they are talking about. While we have done our best to spell out the tasks each marriage must accomplish, the following might serve as both a summary and a second opinion. Think of it as a view from the peak of Marriage Mountain. Taken from the book *The Good Marriage*, here are the nine tasks Dr. Wallerstein's research identified as necessary for a marriage's healthy growth and development. They are not listed in any order, and each is as important as the last:

- To separate emotionally from the family of one's childhood so as to invest fully in the marriage and, at the same time, to redefine the lines of connection with both families of origin.
- To build togetherness by creating the intimacy that supports it while carving out each partner's autonomy.
- To embrace the daunting roles of parents and to absorb the impact of Her Majesty the Baby's dramatic entrance. At the same time, the spouses must work to protect their privacy.
- To maintain the bond in the face of adversity.
- To create a safe haven for the expression of differences, anger, and conflict.
- To establish a rich and pleasurable sexual relationship and to protect it from the incursions of the workplace and family obligations.
- To use laughter and humor to keep things in perspective and to avoid boredom by sharing fun, interests, and friends.
- To provide nurturance and comfort to each other, satisfying each partner's needs for dependency, and offering continuing encouragement and support.
- To keep alive early, idealized images of falling in love while facing the sober realities of the changes wrought by time.

If you would like assistance with any of these tasks, or help overcoming the challenges you may encounter on your climb up marriage mountain, check out *When Divorce Is Not an Option: How to Heal Your Marriage and Nurture Lasting Love*, or contact the Pastoral Solutions Institute to learn about our Catholic telecounseling practice by calling 740-266-6461 or online at www.ExceptionalMarriages.com.

At the close of Part Two, you should have a pretty good idea of what it takes to build a happy marriage and overcome the challenges that stand between you and becoming the couple God is calling you to be. In Part Three, you will uncover how to celebrate a joyful, intimate, grace-filled love that fills your days (and nights!) with the passion that helps you wake up every morning thanking God for another day with your beloved!

PART 3

The Road to Intimacy

Do you know what it takes to create an uncommonly joyful, passionate, peaceful, and soul-satisfying relationship? Wherever you find yourself on *The Relationship Pathway*, and whatever stage of Marriage Mountain you're climbing, there are certain habits that every couple needs to cultivate to get the most out of their relationship. This section examines the true source of lifelong love. Discover the four qualities that create deep marital intimacy, and find out how you can make certain that you have enough of each. Explore what it takes to stay in love every day of your lives together! Plus, we'll reveal the surprising habits that allow Exceptional couples to draw closer together *because* of their arguments, rather than *in spite* of them. Finally, *For Better ... FOREVER* will expose the secrets to celebrating a *toe-curling, eye-popping, mind-blowing* (and yes, *profoundly* spiritual) *sexuality*. Go figure!

CHAPTER 7

What You Can Do to Maintain the Woo!

The Secrets of Lifelong Love Exposed

"Love is a selfless surrender of everything one has and is for the sake of another. There is the expectation in this selfless gift that the other ... will make a similar gift in return. Human beings love because they are made in God's own image. Without love, human existence is meaningless."

R. Hogan and J. LeVoir, *Covenant of Love*

One of the saddest things we hear in the course of our work with couples is "I don't know if I love him anymore. In fact, I don't really know if I ever did."

How can you make certain that you never become the person making such a tragic statement? Or, if you already identify with this sentiment, how can you find your way back?

Love Defined

The secret to lifelong love starts with having a solid understanding of what love really is. Some people say that we love a person because he or she makes us feel good about ourselves. Others say that love is a mystery; it comes and goes with the wind, and the best we can do is enjoy it while it lasts. Still others don't make distinctions between romance, sex, and love, believing that as long as passion lives, love exists.

The problem with all of these definitions is that they are limited, at best. Of course, love should uplift our spirits. But if love is simply one person's ability to make another person feel good, then what happens to love when stress, illness, depression, or other serious but common problems cause a person to resist even our best efforts to help that person feel better? As for the second definition, love is most certainly a mystery; but if it is completely incomprehensible and transient as the tide, how can we ever hope to find the safety and security that we crave from a so-called "stable relationship"? Lastly, sex and romance are an important part of married love, but most of us are too familiar with examples of sex without love — and romance without substance — to still believe that sex, romance, and love are the same thing.

Recipe for True Love

So, what is love, and how do you really know if you are in it?

The happiest couples know a simple recipe for creating "true love": According to taste, mix seven to eight cups of companionate love with two to three cups of romantic love. Bake slowly over a lifetime.

Do you have enough of both ingredients in your cupboard? Let's find out.

The First Ingredient: Companionate Love

The psychologist, Harry Stack Sullivan, wrote that "when the satisfaction or security of another person becomes as significant to one as is one's own satisfaction and security, then the state of love exists." Happily, this is one area in which psychologists and theologians agree. According to Cardinal Donald W. Wuerl, Ronald Lawler, O.F.M. Cap., Thomas Comerford Lawler, and Kris D. Stubna, the editors of *The Teaching of Christ*: "Love is ... the free and firm commitment of each to pursue the good of the other, for the other's sake."

Both of the above are excellent definitions of the first and most important ingredient in married love: companionate love. Companionate love is the active commitment you make to fulfill each other's dreams, goals, and values — your identities in Christ. At its most essential and important level, to love is to will and work for the good of another. You know that someone loves you if he or she both *desires* your well-being and *is willing to work for it daily*. Both conditions are absolutely necessary for companionate love to exist. You've probably known plenty of people who have wished you well as they slammed the door in your face: "Keep warm, and eat well" (Jas 2:16, NABRE). Is this love? Of course not. Even though they said the right words, they didn't *do* anything to help you achieve your well-being. This seems obvious enough, and yet, we encounter so many people who say, "My husband [wife] cheats on me [beats me, doesn't tell me his/her work schedule, lies, calls me names, doesn't come home, calls me "silly" or "stupid"]; but he/she *says* he/she loves me, so it must be true." Once, on our radio program, a caller said, "My husband doesn't treat me real well, but he was going into surgery last month, and when he was under anesthesia he told me he loved me. People don't lie when they're under anesthesia, so I know it's true!"

True companionate love requires more than saying "I love you" (with or without the help of anesthetics). It even requires more than a deep sense of longing or attraction for your mate. The words and feelings must be backed up with *action.* If your partner truly loves you, then every day he or she will make decisions with your needs in mind, make plans with your interests in mind, and prepare his or her schedule with you as the most important thing on his or her mind. To paraphrase that preeminent social philosopher Forrest Gump, "Love is as love does."

By the same token, you love your mate if your *daily actions and choices reflect an obvious concern for your spouse's happiness and fulfillment.* One way of understanding the importance of companionate love would be to say that couples should be each other's best friends, except that many people who have an immature understanding of love also tend to trivialize what "best friendship" really entails. Many people think of friendship as "being with someone I feel good around," "having fun with somebody," or "having someone to drink [or hunt, go to church, go to the club, etc.] with." We once heard someone define a friend as "someone who fosters your illusions about yourself." Obviously, marital friendship is a call to something significantly deeper. The following excerpts capture the essence of marital friendship:

> Friendship is — in a sense not at all derogatory to it — the least natural of all loves; the least instinctive.... [Friendship] alone, of all the loves, seemed to raise you to the level of gods or angels. (C. S. Lewis, *The Four Loves*)

> "Friendship" may seem to some a weak word for so close a union [as marriage]: but "friendship" is in fact a rich concept. Friendship is the most perfect form of love: Christ calls those bound most intensely to Him by divine love His friends.... For friendship, in its most authentic form, is an unselfish and mutual love persons have for each other, as each knows he or she is loved by the other. (*The Teaching of Christ*, fifth edition)

Companionate love has the power to separate us from our illusions while leading us to a reality that is more wonderful and fulfilling than anything we could have imagined. Its importance cannot be overemphasized. The essence of a good marriage is the couple's commitment to pursue the good of each other. Unfortunately, couples frequently come to marriage counseling saying, "I know I care about my husband [wife]. I mean, I love him [her] — it's just that I don't know if I'm *in* love with him [her]." Whether they realize it or not, what these couples are saying is actually very encouraging. They are saying that there is at least a basic friendship in their marriage, though they are lacking a certain "specialness," or passion. To use a medical analogy, this couple is describing the difference between being heart-dead and brain-dead. You wouldn't *want* to be either, but you can — in many cases — get a heart pumping again. Likewise, it is possible to get the romantic "heart" of a marriage pumping again, but only if there is some "brain activity" — that is, a basic *friendship* that manifests a desire and willingness to work for the good of the other. As long as there is love (i.e., companionate love) the potential for being *in* love (i.e., romantic love) exists.

Which brings us to an excellent point. As vital and indispensable as companionate love is, it really can't make up the whole of married love because it is missing one important quality: passion. Any emotion that accompanies companionate love is best described as "regard" or "caring." Passion, excitement, and "warm fuzzies" are the domains of romantic love, the second ingredient in true love. In fact, without a healthy dose of romance, companionate love can feel downright familial. Even so, companionate love must be the more plentiful ingredient in the recipe for a happy marriage because, as any mature married person knows, romantic feelings tend to come and go — and come again — thousands of times over the life of a marriage. As essential as romantic love is, it is not stable enough to be the foundation of a marriage. We'll explore romantic love further in a minute; first, answer the following questions to find out if you have a healthy amount of companionate love in your relationship.

QUIZ: *The Marital Friendship*

Directions: You and your spouse should each take the following quiz separately. Give yourself one point for each statement you mark as true (T). Do not add your scores together. The purpose of this quiz is to discover how strong *each of you* thinks your marital friendship is.

T F You have a hard time identifying what is important to your partner.

T F You think that some of the things that are important to your partner are silly, unreasonable, or beneath you.

T F You are not sure how you can be a part of helping your mate fulfill his dreams, goals, or values.

T F You are uncomfortable with how much your partner expects of you.

T F You feel love for your mate, but you are constantly being pulled away from him by other pressing matters.

T F Having your partner along is okay, but you really prefer doing the things you enjoy on your own or with your other friends.

T F Your partner discourages, belittles or ignores your input.

T F Your partner disregards you when you tell him he hurts your feelings.

T F Your partner gives you the distinct impression that you are really not welcome to participate in his interests or activities (he may not say it — but he doesn't have to).

T F Your partner says he loves you, but he seems to disregard your needs when he makes decisions, schedules activities, or makes plans.

Scoring

0–2 Most likely, you have a healthy amount of companionate love in your relationship.

3–5 Your companionate love is probably closer to 50 or 60 percent (instead of 70 to 80 percent). Talk about ways you and your mate will actively improve this. Be specific. Make a commitment to your plan. Be sure to work through the exercises in Part Three of this book.

6+ You need to do some serious work on your capacity to be friends to each other. Be sure to work through the exercises in Part Three of this book. You may wish to seek the help of a faithful counselor. Learn more about the

Pastoral Solutions telecounseling services at www.ExceptionalMarriages.com or call 740-266-6461.

Discussion

Remember, companionate love is defined as your desire and commitment to work for the good of your partner. It doesn't just apply to what you think you ought to do (i.e., pay the bills or raise the kids); it really applies to the daily efforts you make to help your partner achieve the happiness and fulfillment that comes from pursuing the path he has discerned God leading him down.

Ideally, companionate love should contribute about 70 to 80 percent to the marital mix. To find out if your relationship has enough companionate love, answer and discuss the following questions with your partner.

PART ONE

How Well Do You Love Your Spouse?

(Answer and discuss the following.)

1a. List up to five things that you believe are most important to your mate.

1b. Describe the specific efforts you make on a daily basis to help your mate receive more fulfillment and/or enjoyment from the items you listed in 1a.

1c. Do you enjoy involving your partner in the activities and ideas that excite you, or are you a person who prefers people to stay out of your way?

1d. Do you work to develop an interest in the things that give your partner joy, or are there some activities that you wish she would drop out of, or at least stop talking to you about?

PART TWO

How Well Does Your Spouse Love You?

(Answer and discuss the following.)

2a. Does your spouse actively solicit your opinions, encourage your growth, and work to further your interest and values? List specific examples.

2b. Does your partner look for ways to include you in her activities and interests, or does she seem to view your involvement as a burden?

2c. In your opinion alone, does your mate make decisions with your needs in mind, plans with your interests in mind, and prepare her schedule with you as the most important thing on her mind? Share specific examples of each with your partner.

Companionate love is the first part of the recipe for a healthy love life. Now that we've discussed the cake, let's get to the frosting.

The Second Ingredient: Romantic Love

Romantic love is the snugly, cuddly, warm-fuzzy-makin', toe-curlin', make-me-feel-special, *woo! woo!* kind of love. It includes both sexuality and sentiment (i.e., romantic gestures), from love notes to pillow talk and everything in between. In Chapter 11, we'll take a closer look at the sexual aspects of romantic love. For now, it is important to remember that whatever form romantic love happens to be taking (sex or sentiment), the function of romantic love is to add a quality of "specialness" to a relationship. This is romantic love in the broadest sense.

Many Christians tend to write off romantic love as something those in "the worldly media" have invented for the purposes of titillating and leading us to hell. These folks are missing the bigger picture. The fact is, romantic love is a very important part of a Christian marriage. God himself uses the metaphor of romantic love as one way to explain how he loves us. The Old Testament's Song of Songs — a completely scandalous book to many early Scripture scholars — made the cut in the canon of Scripture specifically because it was considered to be a beautiful example of love, not only between a husband and wife, but also between God and his chosen people. Part of loving our mates as God loves us means manifesting the potent, stirring, intoxicating romantic love found in the Song of Songs. If your mate isn't worth a couple of flowers, a love letter, a well-deserved compliment, and some generous physical affection from you, how do you ever expect her to enjoy the immense bounty of love God has prepared for her in his heavenly kingdom? We can only imagine that appearing before God after spending a lifetime in a romantically empty marriage would be like a diver who surfaced too fast and contracted the bends. Come to think of it, that is not a bad analogy for purgatory.

As we explained earlier, companionate love is a very noble and divine love. It is *the* essential foundation of true marital love. However, emotionally speaking, it is fairly tame. The thing is, married love is supposed to be a physical icon of the love that comes from God's own heart, and there is nothing tame about God's love for us. He is a passionate lover, a "jealous God," a God who longs for us to turn ourselves completely over to him — body, mind, and spirit. He wants us to experience the *petit mort* that comes from dying to ourselves and surrendering all to him. It was not for nothing that the great mystics referred to standing in the presence of God as being in "ecstasy." When God comes to us and we are profoundly touched by his love, we shiver, quake, cry, melt, feel special, feel humbled, feel awestruck, and fall truly, madly, deeply in love with him who constantly works for our good. If God is not ashamed to love us this way, we must not be ashamed of, or be inept at, loving our mates this way.

Having convinced you (hopefully) of the importance of romantic love, in a healthy relationship it usually doesn't make up more than 20 to 30 percent of the recipe for true love. For romantic love to be healthy, it has to flow *from* the friendship, not stand in place of it. This is the difference between wanting to be with your spouse because you become better people when you are together, and wanting to be with your spouse because of the feeling you manufacture when together. The latter reduces the relationship to a drug every bit as powerful as cocaine or heroin. In fact, it is because of such relationships that romance and/or sex addiction groups have little trouble keeping up their census. In her book *The Good Marriage*, Dr. Judith Wallerstein states that when a relationship is too dependent on romantic love, it "has the tragic potential for freezing the husband and wife into a self-absorbed, childlike preoccupation with each other, turning its back on the rest of the world, including the children." Wallerstein's findings seem to mirror St. John Paul II's definition of a healthy unity between husbands and wives when he says that "rather than closing them up in themselves, [true unity] opens them up towards ... a new person [or persons, i.e., children]" (*Letter to Families*, 8).

Even so, in good measure, romantic love is a wonderful thing and it is a logical outcome of companionate love. In this sense, romantic love is simply one more way you are working for the good of your mate. It prevents a marriage from devolving into a brother/sister relationship or a strictly utilitarian arrangement centered on raising kids and paying bills. It adds zest to life, can be an important contributor to self-esteem (remember Rudolph the Red-Nosed Reindeer flying through the air exclaiming, "She thinks I'm cu-u-u-u-ute"?), and even enhances spiritual growth by allowing us to have a tangible reference point for God's passionate love for each of us. Considering the importance of romantic love, every couple needs to know a few things about why it comes and goes, and how to make sure it always comes back again.

Everybody Do the Wave

As we suggested at the beginning of this chapter, many people believe that romantic love is a magical thing with a will of its own. People think, "I have no control over it. When I feel romantic, I do romantic things." Besides being a recipe for romantic disaster, this statement isn't entirely true. The following illustration will help you understand our point.

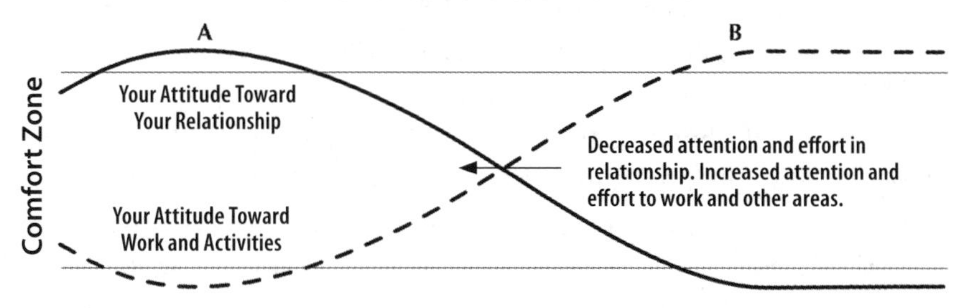

"Everybody Do the Wave" shows the romantic cycle in all its glory. Let's imagine that you and your spouse are experiencing a very close time in your relationship (point *A*). For the time being, you are able to put work and other pressures on the back burner and simply concentrate on each other, doing the things you do when you feel in love. After a bit, though, the world starts knocking at your door. Work is piling up at the office, and other commitments that you have been neglecting must be attended to. As you begin to focus on these other areas of your life, your attention turns away from doing the things that made you feel so close to your mate. The dinner meeting with a client takes the place of your Wednesday night walk with your partner. Finishing that important proposal — or in my case that book ("Sorry I can't spend time with you tonight, honey; I'm writing that chapter on being attentive to your spouse") — makes it impossible to take your spouse to a movie tonight. It isn't that you wouldn't rather be with your mate; it's just that you only have so much time and energy to divide between so many areas of your life.

Soon, you are on top of everything at work, but you begin to feel the effects of your lack of attentiveness to your relationship (point *B*). All of a sudden, you and your partner begin sniping at each other, forgetting to perform even the simplest gestures of affection and consideration, just because you are too busy to think about doing them.

At this point, there are two courses of action from which you may choose. Which of the following scenarios comes closest to what you would do under similar circumstances in your relationship?

A. You tell yourself that if your mate really cared he or she would make time for you. You yourself don't take any action to improve the circumstances because you don't feel like it. After all, in return for your hard work, don't you deserve a little "caring for" now and then? You wait and hope that either your partner will stop being so insensitive, or these "blah" feelings will change and your motivation will return.

B. You think about the things you and your partner need to do to get things clicking again. You start doing some of them on your own. On top of this, one evening you tell your partner how much you've missed him or her lately. You and your spouse then get your schedules and the two of you make specific plans to take some time together.

If you chose *A,* then your romantic love will probably bottom out until such time as you and your mate have a big argument, during which each of you will accuse the other of being neglectful and unappreciative. This will result in the begrudging offer of a "date night" or "pity sex" that pacifies you for the moment but doesn't lead to any significant change over the long term. The relationship may continue having these little quasi-romantic hiccups for years, until one or both of you decide that the crust of bread you get isn't worth all the trouble. At this point, romantic love goes on life support, and you and your mate console yourselves with the old chestnut: "It's only natural for the fire to die out when you've been married as long as we have."

If you chose *B*, then ("survey says ...") you are absolutely right! ("Bob, tell our happy couple what they've won!")

You and your mate understand that romance is not some mystical thing that lies beyond your control. You understand — quite correctly — that behavior, not the Fates, drives romance. When you *do* romantic things for each other, you begin to *feel* romantic toward each other. Choosing answer *B* says that you understand what the *Exceptional Seven Percent* know about romantic love. Specifically, it isn't something you sit around waiting for your partner to do for you, becoming resentful or whiny when she doesn't do it. Romantic love is a gift you give your partner — in a way that is meaningful to her. It is a gift she will return as a loving response to your loving efforts. Perfecting your ability to give this gift to your spouse allows you and your mate to fall into a gentle rhythm of love in which the highs are celebrated and the lows — because you never allow them to get too low — are accepted as a natural, even welcome, respite. The happiest spouses take great joy in knowing that they don't have to be "on" for each other at all times. This ebb and flow of romantic love actually contributes to the peace and security of the relationship, giving you a feeling not unlike the one you might have while gently floating on a raft just off the beach of some tropical island. Warm, safe, luxurious, and sensual.

Hopefully, you see that *B* is the more desirable choice. Sitting around waiting for romance to happen gives you nothing but a one-way ticket to the doldrums or, worse yet, Divorceville. Couples who make up the *Exceptional Seven Percent* understand that when they don't feel particularly romantic, it is probably because they haven't *done* anything particularly romantic for a while. Recognizing this, they don't whine to their partner, "When are you going to make time for me?" They take action into their own hands. Couples in Exceptional Marriages become more romantic toward their mates in the hopes of *inspiring* a loving response (as opposed to whining for one). For example, instead of sitting around feeling justifiably neglected, one spouse may go to her mate's office with a surprise picnic lunch. Or she may kidnap him for a weekend getaway. Or even do simpler things like leave loving self-stick notes pasted all over the windshield of the spouse's car, or chocolate candy hidden in places where the spouse will keep finding the candy all day, or a million other possibilities any fertile, loving mind might concoct. If such interventions aren't enough to get the romance curve swinging upward, then the neglected spouse sits down with her mate and — without accusing him of anything — calmly asserts, "I really miss doing *X*, *Y*, and *Z*. Get your schedule and let's make some time for each other."

In sum, the best way to resolve the number one threat to romantic love is to remember Newton's (not Isaac, uh, the other one ...) First Law of Romantic Dynamics: "When you want to *feel* romantic again, *do* something romantic again."

KISS — Keep It Simple, Silly

This "law" leads us to examine the second misconception people have about romance. Namely, that it has to be a *big thing*. Yes, romance is weekends in the country at your favorite bed-and-breakfast, or buying that terribly expensive whatsit when your spouse least expects it; but at its core, romance is mostly about making your partner feel special by attending to her in the course of everyday life. Romance is looking into your partner's eyes when she speaks to you (instead of continuing to text your friend or surf the Internet), kissing her when you enter and leave a room, sitting on the same piece of furniture together, going to bed at the same time (even "just for sleeping"), remembering to say "I love you" a thousand times a day, taking time to pick up her favorite ice cream on your way home, and countless other "little things." Couples who save all their romance for that "One Big Night" are inevitably disappointed. Who could communicate all the love a person has for his or her partner in one night? Who needs that kind of pressure? No, the happiest couples actively work to develop their repertoire of both simple and grand romantic gestures. The following exercise will help you do just that.

EXERCISE: Twenty-Five Ways to Make Love Stay — Every Day

STEP ONE: *Make a List*

Successful marriages are nurtured every day in the little exchanges between two people. Major efforts (weekends away, extra-special surprises, etc.) are important, but tend to become less frequent as time goes by. Real romance is played out in the simple consideration, playfulness, and attentiveness that a couple exhibits every day to each other. When you complete the list below, think small. What are the simple, daily things that your mate does — or that you would like him or her to do more of — that demonstrates regard for you and makes you feel cherished? If you get stuck, try recalling the things people do that help you feel listened to, cared for, or appreciated. In short, what simple things make you feel special when someone does them?

Keep it positive (this is a *love* list, not a complaint list) and don't be afraid to break things down. For instance, "I feel loved when you're affectionate" could be restated as several items such as, "Hold my hand when we're walking together." "Kiss me when I walk into the room." "Sit on the couch with me instead of sitting across the room." What things will you come up with?

1. ______________________________
2. ______________________________
3. ______________________________
4. ______________________________
5. ______________________________
6. ______________________________
7. ______________________________
8. ______________________________
9. ______________________________
10. ______________________________
11. ______________________________
12. ______________________________
13. ______________________________
14. ______________________________
15. ______________________________
16. ______________________________
17. ______________________________
18. ______________________________
19. ______________________________
20. ______________________________
21. ______________________________
22. ______________________________
23. ______________________________
24. ______________________________
25. ______________________________

STEP TWO: *Trade Lists with Your Spouse*

Assuming your mate hasn't asked you to do something that is objectively immoral, be generous. See the list as God's invitation, written on your mate's heart, to grow in ways you'd never think of growing if you were left to your own devices. Challenge yourself to do at least two easier things and one somewhat more challenging thing for your spouse every day. Be patient with each other as you try to become more comfortable with those love-list items that are outside your normal comfort zone, but don't forget that self-donation, the key to a happy, grace-filled marriage, requires you to love your spouse more than your comfort zone!

STEP THREE: ***Discuss Each Day***

Each evening, spend a little time talking about the ways you tried to take care of each other that day. Make a point of thanking your spouse for the things that you noticed that he or she did. Don't be afraid to tell your spouse about some of the things you did for him or her. Ask what difference the things you did made in your spouse's day. Ask if there is anything that you could to for your mate tomorrow to make his or her day a little easier or more pleasant. Also, take note of any new requests your spouse makes of you. Add these items to the list. Oh! And don't be afraid to think up new ways to cherish your spouse based on the ideas he or she has given you, and ask if those things would be meaningful to your mate.

Discussing your love lists even briefly each day helps you do a better, more mindful job of attending to each other and prioritizing your marriage, even when life gets busy.

Making Romantic Love Stay, and Finding Your Balance

Remember, when you feel less warmth toward your mate it probably means that you and/or your partner have stopped doing some of the things you listed in the exercise — or are doing them less than you ought to. Referring to this list often and discussing the simple ways you attempt to care for each other daily will help you level out the highs and lows in your romantic life, and help love stay — every day. Tape your love lists to the dashboard of your car, the mirror in your bathroom, the fridge, or any other place where you will be constantly reminded to work for your lover's good. Use your love list as a gauge of the degree to which you are succeeding at prioritizing your marriage and cherishing your spouse. Think of your love lists as a kind of "marital examination of conscience" that reminds you of the importance of valuing your mate and attending to your romantic friendship daily. The payoff is more good times, fewer and less-threatening lows, warmer feelings for each other in general, and a relationship that feels secure no matter what life throws at it.

In the book *Love Letters*, Count Gabriel Riquetti writes to his beloved, Sophia: "You alone have succeeded in combining … the most luscious fruits of friendship with the most fragrant flowers of love." What a beautiful sentiment. This is exactly our wish for you: to be able, in your marriage, to combine all the support of a deep companionate friendship with the flames of an eternal passion that springs from God's own heart.

Putting It All Together

Earlier, we indicated that the recipe for true love is to "mix seven to eight cups of companionate love with two to three cups of romantic love." Now that we've looked at both types of love, the following example might help explain the healthy interplay between the two.

Imagine you are building a house. Unless you are building this house in Aruba (in which case, can we come to live with you?), you are going to want to heat your home. You have to decide whether you are going to do this with a fireplace, a gas furnace, or perhaps electric heat.

Obviously, fireplaces are very romantic. They provide a great deal of atmosphere, are nice to cuddle by, and can throw off a lot of heat. On the downside, they tend to burn a lot of fuel very quickly and take a great deal of effort to maintain — all that hauling and chopping, not to mention cleaning out the ashes and the chimney. To be perfectly honest, sometimes you just don't have the energy or the time to do all the work involved in maintaining a good fire. On those days, it would be nice to know that at least you won't freeze to death because your trusty gas furnace is chugging away in the basement. No, it's not romantic — no one writes songs about "chestnuts roasting on a pilot light" — but in a pinch, it gets the job done. Nine days out of ten, it will be your main source of warmth.

The same holds true for the relationship between romantic and companionate love. Good feelings, sentimental gestures, and a passionate sex life are indispensable for a good marriage. But if you aren't building your lives around the fulfillment of each other's dreams, goals, and values, your love doesn't exist in the real world. A marriage without the greatest measure of companionate love gets very cold, very fast, when the couple's normal sexual-romantic tide is at low ebb. Just as the most welcoming home would have both a fireplace and a furnace, the best marriage will include both companionate and romantic loves.

With a little practice, romantic love flows very easily from companionate love. If you are already working for the good of your mate on a daily basis, then it is a small matter to do the "little things" you listed in the "Twenty-Five Ways to Make Love Stay — Every Day" exercise. Just remember, if you ever find your romantic love waning, don't accuse your partner of neglecting you (even if you think he or she is). You will only sound pathetic and cause him or her to resent you. We are constantly amazed at the people who consider themselves to be loving who, upon experiencing a little benign neglect from their spouses, begin whining, "When are you going to make time for me? Do you know *how long* it's been since you made love to me [or took me out, bought me flowers, rubbed my back, etc.]?"

So what should you do instead of whining? To paraphrase President John F. Kennedy, "Ask not what your mate can do for you. Ask what you can do for your mate." This is the secret to keeping the romantic flame burning. Instead of whining to your mate for attention — or even worse, dragging out your romantic repertoire when you want some attention from her — get in the habit of consulting your "Twenty-Five Ways to Make Love Stay — Every Day" list, and every day ask yourself, "What can I do to make her life easier or more pleasant today?"

Many of you will find at first that your mate will respond suspiciously, saying things like: "Why are you being so nice to me? What do you want?" This will be your biggest clue that you might not be quite the lover you thought yourself to be. When your mate says this to you, tell your spouse you're sorry for having taught him or her that you would only be loving on special occasions or when you wanted something. Tell your mate that you were hit on the head by a rock, as you deserved to be, and from now on you are going to work every day to cherish your spouse, because it is your job to help him or her learn how special he or she is to God. Your spouse will probably look at you as if you sprouted a third eye in the middle of your forehead. That's okay. You'll make a believer out of your spouse in time. Don't romance your mate because he or she deserves it. Don't romance your spouse because you want something. Romance your partner because he or she is special both to you and to God, and you want your beloved to know it.

Incidentally, this goes as much for wives as it does for husbands. For all the popular wisdom that says women are the fountains from which all relationship knowledge flows, we know too many wives who think that romance is something husbands are supposed to do for them. If you are a woman who happens to believe this, we have only this to say: "Wrongo-bongo, Miss Thang. Time to get off your gilded tuffet." Remember, *true* romance is not something that is done *to* you; rather, it is an atmosphere that you and your mate work to *create together.* It is a by-product of a husband's and wife's mutual service to each other. It is the logical outcome of your both working daily for each other's physical, emotional, spiritual, and relational well-being. Husbands and wives, you know your mission. What are you waiting for?

In Love for a Lifetime

Earlier, we suggested that couples could guarantee that their love — both kinds — would last a lifetime. This is a shocking thing to think in a world of people who claim that their love "just died."

You might hear someone say, "I don't know what went wrong. It just happened. We grew apart." Or "What can you do? If the love just isn't there anymore...."

Love doesn't ever "just die." You have to kill it. Sometimes people poison it slowly with years of mutual neglect and playing Marital Chicken. Sometimes people take it out and shoot it. But it never "just dies."

Life is complicated — actually, chaotic is more like it. There isn't much in this world you can control. Fortunately, everything you need to guarantee the success of your love and marriage is completely within your grasp. It all comes down to your freedom to make choices. Every time you speak, *you* choose whether to support your partner or tear him or her down. Every time you encounter a problem, *you* choose whether to let the stress ruin your marriage or to view your marriage as a refuge from the stress. Every time your partner says he needs more of your love, your time, your support, *you* choose whether to offer yourself generously or to ignore him and watch as he slowly starves. *Your* marriage, *your* choices, *your* control over *your* success.

This concept can be a little overwhelming for most people. After all, it's one thing to say you have the power, but it's quite another thing to say that you know what to do with it. In moments such as these it can be helpful to sit at the feet of the masters, the married couples who have already discovered how to make choices that lead to uncommonly satisfying relationships. Over the years, we have learned a great deal from such couples. The following represents some of those lessons.

Twelve Things Happy Couples Know About Love

1. Love Assumes a Positive Intention

It is inevitable that your spouse will slight, offend, neglect, or otherwise step on your toes at some point. When this happens, you will be tempted to go into "fight mode" — as if your partner sat up in bed last night thinking of *Twenty-Five Ways to Make My Mate's Life a Living Hell.* You may respond with comments such as:

- "You're such a jerk! I can't believe you did [said] that!"
- "If you loved me, I shouldn't *have* to remind you!"
- "You don't give a damn about me, do you?"

In each of the examples above, you assumed it was your mate's intention to be offensive. Exceptional couples have a very different way of dealing with this. When an Exceptional spouse encounters a slight, she gives her mate the benefit of the doubt. She assumes that her partner didn't mean to hurt her. After all, they didn't get married to hurt each other. Something *must* be amiss. Perhaps the spouse wasn't thinking, or wasn't feeling well, or was having an especially bad day. The Exceptional spouse's response to an offensive comment or behavior sounds more like one of the following examples:

- (*Concerned*) "You're usually so considerate. What's going on?"
- (*Helpful*) "You seem really upset. What can I do to help you through this?"
- (*Firm but loving*) "Look, I love you too much to let you make an ass of yourself at my expense. What are you *really* trying to tell me?"

Couples in Exceptional Marriages aren't always syrupy-sweet, but they do assume that each spouse is trying his or her best *and*, with a little help from the other, can perhaps achieve such a goal. Love gives the benefit of the doubt (more on this in Chapter 10).

2. Love Is Always Present

Couples in the best marriages know that love is always present, even when it *feels* dormant at times. Healthy couples know that getting those special feelings back is simply a matter of a little time and effort. They do not respond to emotional down times with accusations of neglect. Nor do they become "St. Woe-Is-Me the First, spouse and martyr." If love was only implied yesterday, both husband and wife accept their responsibility to make love explicit today.

3. Love Catches Its Lover Being Good

Outstanding couples know that they have a daily obligation to express their love for each other. They make a point to not just criticize and complain, but to *catch each other being good*. They say, "Thank you for *X*" and "I really appreciate your taking care of *Y*," even when thanks aren't expected, necessary, or seem redundant. Exceptional couples are liberal with compliments and generous with affection. One major study showed that couples in good marriages have *20 time*s more positive interactions than negative ones during normal interactions and *5 times* more positive exchanges than negative ones in conflict (we'll discuss this more in the chapter on problem solving). In the same study, a significant number of those couples who consistently dropped below this 5:1 ratio were divorced within five years (Gottman, 1995). Don't let your love become a statistic. Be generous with your praise, affection, and gratitude. Your love lists will be a huge help in this regard.

4. Love Is a Full-Time Job

Some people mistakenly believe that marriage is a part-time job. Such spouses may be more committed to making their moms and dads happy or playing savior to friends and employers than they are to having a successful home life. You're not a bad person if you do this — you're just lousy marriage material.

Couples in the happiest marriages understand that promising to "forsake all others" means just that — *all* others. And that includes not only romantic interests, but also parents, friends, club memberships, and certain job placements — *if* these threaten the primacy of the marriage. This is what Greg calls the skill of "exceptional fidelity" in *The Exceptional Seven Percent: Nine Secrets of the World's Happiest Couples*. This is not to say that if you love someone you may never leave the house. But it does mean that if you want an Exceptional Marriage, you have to require your family of origin — as well as your friends, work, and various activities

— to play a supportive (and secondary) role to your relationship. Not the other way around.

5. Love Is Willing to Make Itself Uncomfortable

Research shows that loving couples are benevolent. That is, they are willing to sacrifice their comfort zones for the sake of cherishing the other (Mayer, Davis, and Schoorman, 1995). Love stretches you. It requires you to do things you never imagined yourself doing, to grow in ways that can be scary at times. When you married, you promised to allow yourself to be pulled, stretched, opened up, and "loved into Real." Don't hide out behind such selfish comments as "I would never do *X*, go to *Y*, or try *Z*. That just isn't me!" Challenge yourself a little. God will reward your efforts with a richer life and a more satisfying marriage.

6. Love Takes Care of Itself

Love knows how to meet its own needs. It does not *expect* you to clean up its emotional or literal messes (though help is always appreciated). It does not expect you to be its parent or mind reader. It would sooner die one thousand deaths than ever say, "If you really loved me, you would just know."

7. Love Is Tactfully Honest

Love doesn't stuff feelings. It says what it needs to say. And yet, if love doesn't *hide* the truth, it doesn't beat you about the head with it either. People who say cruel things under the guise of "just being honest" are fooling themselves. There is no virtue in verbal evisceration. Love says what it needs to say, lovingly.

8. Love Is Safe

Love behaves itself. It does not demean, humiliate, or intentionally embarrass. Love earnestly defends the dignity of the beloved. Love encourages the beloved to do more, to say more, to be more.

9. Love Is Willing to "Fake It Till It Makes It"

You won't always feel loving or feel inspired to do loving things. But the best couples know that it is important to do loving things, especially when they don't feel like it. In the first place, their Christian dignity demands it. In the second place, sometimes you've got to prime the pump to get the water flowing again. Less mature couples say, "I can't be loving if I don't feel it. That's dishonest." That's rubbish. Love is not a feeling. It is a commitment to work for the good of your mate whether you feel like it or not. And unconditional love is the willingness to do this unconditionally. Therapists remind their clients that feelings are always the last thing to change. First comes behavioral change, then comes thinking change, then comes emotional change. Sometimes, to get a desired state of feeling back, you've got to start by acting as if you already are feeling that state. That's not being dishonest. That's being hopeful.

10. Love Is Generous

Loving people do not say, "I'm a loving person," and then go on to complain about how empty their marriages are. You cannot simply give as much as you are comfortable giving and then call yourself a "loving person." This is self-serving at best. If you are in a healthy relationship and want to be loved more, you've got to love your mate more, and *you've got to love in a way that is meaningful to your beloved*. Exceptional lovers know that it doesn't matter whether they think they are being loving. All that matters is that their spouse is receiving the message. And how do they accomplish this? By working hard to see the truth, goodness, and beauty in the things their spouse finds true, good, and beautiful and doing those things with a willing and happy heart — not necessarily because they "get it" but because their spouse loves it.

11. Love Laughs

Love is playful. Love enjoys itself. Love isn't afraid of being silly. It never intentionally makes fun of the beloved, but it can help the beloved find the fun. Love has a funny bone.

12. Did We Mention, "Love Is Not a Feeling"?

It bears repeating. Love is action. Love is a choice. Love is hard work. Love is daily making personal choices with the good of your partner in mind. There are many other good things that are feelings. Affection is a feeling. Romance is a feeling. Attraction is a feeling. Passion is a feeling. But "love for love's sake," as the poet, Elizabeth Barrett Browning put it, is *not* a feeling.

Love Lasts Forever but, Mercifully, This Chapter Doesn't

It is our hope that after reading this chapter you will find love to be a little less mysterious but no less wondrous. In this very busy world, there are many things that compete for our attention. Many of these things are, in fact, hostile to marriage and family life. Despite these many distractions, it is our most deeply held conviction that there is no work more important than the work of loving. If we stopped doing marriage ministry, our clients would quickly find someone else to work with (not as good as us, mind you, but still . . .). If we stopped writing, someone else would publish in our place. If we dropped dead this minute, all traces of us would be wiped out tomorrow — unless we have loved. We could never be replaced as spouses or parents. Some other bodies could fill our shoes, sleep in our bed, eat our food, but they could never remove the influence we have had on the people we have loved, if indeed we have loved well. You will never doubt the meaning and purpose of your life — if you love first.

When you finish this chapter, put down this book for a minute (just for a minute, now). Find a way to let your partner know that he or she is on your mind — right now. Call your spouse. Write a note. Go to the store on your way home and pick up his or her favorite whatever, or walk into the next room and kiss your spouse— just because. Celebrate the purpose of your life by bringing some love into hers. Do it now. Fill this moment — in fact, fill each moment — with the love you long to experience.

Love is patient and kind;
love is not jealous or boastful;
it is not arrogant or rude.
Love does not insist on its own way;
it is not irritable or resentful;
it does not rejoice at wrong,
but rejoices in the right.
Love bears all things,
believes all things,
hopes all things,
endures all things.
St. Paul (1 Cor 13:4-7, RSV-CE)

CHAPTER 8

The Road Trip

(or "Der Intimacy Ist Goot, Ja?"*)*

Let's take a road trip! (As if mountain climbing weren't enough adventure for one book.) Pack your bags — we're taking a road trip to "Intimacy."

Imagine that Intimacy is an actual place. For the sake of argument, let's say it's located somewhere in Pennsylvania Dutch country, just northwest of Intercourse, Pennsylvania.

To get to Intimacy, you are going to need a car (good communication skills), fuel (a willingness to be vulnerable), a map (romance), and plenty of road signs (a playful, healthy physical relationship). Successfully arriving at your destination requires all of the above to be present, plentiful, and in good working order. For example, without a map or road signs (romance and sexuality), a couple will frequently feel lost ("Just where do I stand with you, anyway?"). With everything but the car (good communication), spouses can do little over time except take their fuel and set themselves on fire.

The chapters that follow are concerned with seeing that your relationship will not only be loving, but also intimate.

Now Just a Cotton-Pickin' Minute!

No doubt some of you will be confused at this point. You might think that we already covered intimacy in the previous chapter on love, but there is an important difference between love and intimacy. Simply put, intimacy is the *measure* of love. If love were a tree, then intimacy would tell us how much fruit the tree could yield. If love were a body of water, intimacy would tell us how deep it was.

In his book, *The Seven Levels of Intimacy*, Matthew Kelly argues that there are seven increasingly intimate levels of connection that people cultivate in relationships. These include (in order):

1. *Clichés:* Simple social exchanges that we use to be polite (e.g., "How are you?" "Doing fine, thanks.").
2. *Facts:* Sharing easily observable truths and current events (e.g., "What did you do today?" "I went to the store. They had a sale!").
3. *Opinions:* Offering others a first glimpse of what you think, your priorities, and what you value (e.g., "I think politician *X* has some really good ideas.").
4. *Hopes and Dreams:* Discussing future plans and wishes for one's self and the relationship (e.g., "I'd love to have my own business some day.").
5. *Feelings:* Not the same as emotional outbursts. This is intentional, mutual sharing about how your life and relationships are contributing to your overall sense of well-being (e.g., "It really makes me happy that we've been taking regular time to pray together each night. I feel closer to you than ever.").
6. *Fears, Faults, and Failures:* Honest sharing about the parts of yourself you would like to heal or improve upon (e.g., "I'd like to stop beating up on myself so much. I have to learn to take compliments better.").
7. *Needs:* Not "I need milk from the store." But honest mutual sharing about how your relationship can specifically help you become everything God created you to be in this life and help each other get to heaven in the next (e.g., "I could really use your help being more patient with the kids.").

In our experience, the happiest couples make a point of using their *rituals of connection* — their regularly scheduled appointments for working, playing, talking, and praying together — to make sure they have the time to share on each of these seven levels. Rituals of connection help to safeguard the intimate core of the marriage and help the couple make sure they have the basic time they need to relate on a deeper level.

Notice that each of Kelly's intimacy levels requires a deeper degree of vulnerability. Taken together, Kelly's levels demonstrate that intimacy is a measure, not just of whether love is present, but the depth and the degree of the love that is present.

In Chapter 6, we drilled a well — metaphorically speaking — to find out if there was any water (i.e., love) on your land. We also tested that water to make certain it wasn't too "hard" or "soft" (i.e., had the right mix of companionate and romantic loves). Now, by examining your capacity for vulnerability, communication, physical affection, and romance we are going to find out how much water your well is producing. Better still, if it turns out to be a puddle, then Part Three of *For Better ... FOREVER* will show you how to go deeper and find an ocean. To begin, let us take a look at the first and most frightening of the four pillars of intimacy: healthy vulnerability.

The "V-Word"

Vulnerability is seriously misunderstood and undervalued, but without vulnerability, people can too easily become self-righteous, self-absorbed bullies whose marriages are not so much relationships as they are extensions of their own infantile egos. Most people equate vulnerability with weakness. In fact, the word does mean "capable of being wounded." And we agree that this does not sound at all desirable. Shouldn't people get married to protect each other from harm? Well, of course, if you mean protected from indignity, humiliation, physical injury, and emotional wounding, you are absolutely right. A marriage that involves any of those is not vulnerable — it is *codependent.* Remember point 8 from the "Twelve Things Happy Couples Know About Love" is that *love must be safe.*

But there is one kind of pain from which no person should be exempt: the pain that is a necessary part of our growth as human beings. Even if we have a good sense of what our Christian identities are, we don't always live up to them. Worse still, sometimes we think we are living up to our values when in fact we are not. At such times, our vulnerability — our willingness to listen to some hard truths from a trusted friend — will determine whether or not we are put right again. And that's where you come in as a spouse. If your marriage is to be a true partnership in fulfilling your Christian destiny, there will be times when you will need to gently wound, and be gently wounded by, your spouse in order to remain faithful to God's plan for your life.

Doctor, Doctor, Give Me the News

Imagine that you fall down the stairs and break your leg, except you don't know it is broken because it is only a hairline fracture and you decide you don't need to go the doctor to have it checked out. Time goes by and there is little improvement. Weeks later you are still limping and your leg hurts almost as much as the day you fell. One morning you wake up and say, "Enough is enough," and you make appointments with two different doctors. (If you are going to do this, you might as well do it right.)

Doctor A says that while he sympathizes with you, you are really doing just fine. He proposes to give you some painkillers and sends you on your way. Doctor B, however, says that he would prefer to fix your leg. There is, of course, a small hitch. Since you waited so long to receive treatment, the bone has knitted itself back together incorrectly — and to fix it, he is going to have to break it again. The leg is going to hurt for a while, but after you heal, you will be better than new. "Well, what do you think?" asks Doctor B.

While most of us might be tempted to go with Doctor A, most of us would choose Doctor B. We *want* to be better than new, even if we might have to undergo some pain to get there. People do not relish pain, but we can endure it if necessary. In a sense, we are all like that patient with the broken leg. We are all limping along in pursuit of our God-given dreams, goals, and values; but we will never get there at the rate we are going. Some spouses, like Doctor A, just give each other painkillers: "Will I ever become the person God wants me to be?" "Oh, yes, dear. I'm sure you will" (plod, plod, plod). Other, healthier, spouses are like Doctor B: "Will I ever become the person God wants me to be?" "Honey, you know I believe in you, but I think I see how you might be getting in your own way a bit. Do you mind talking about it?"

There have been plenty of times in our marriage when we thought we were living up to our values. Times when we thought our actions were loving and our intentions sincere — but, in reality, we were being anything but loving to each other. In these times, we rely on our healthy sense of vulnerability (our willingness to be wounded, if necessary) and our practiced ability to *gently* break that malformed, misinformed part and get each other back on course again. No matter how lovingly the words are said, they always sting — sometimes a lot. But to our minds, it is more compassionate for a spouse to do this than to simply leave one's mate to his or her delusions and become more resentful over time. In short, our vulnerability allows us to be lovingly challenged to become the people God wants us to be when we grow up.

I Love You Just the Way You Are?

A healthy sense of vulnerability allows marriages to do the work they were ordained to do. It enables couples to move up *The Relationship Pathway* toward greater competence, fulfillment, security, and participation in marital grace. But in our experience, there are two erroneous beliefs that stand between individuals and their ability to appreciate the need for vulnerability in a marriage. The first is represented by the following statement:

1. "Isn't marriage supposed to be the place where you can just be yourself? You know, where you can stop pretending to be some goody-goody and just let the real you out?"

In a word, no. There are so many things wrong with this statement that it is difficult to know where to begin. In the first place, this belief usually assumes that the "real you" is the most vile, disgusting, and disagreeable version of yourself. This is clearly not the Christian view. For the Christian, the "real you" is not the person you see when you look in the mirror, but rather the person *God* sees when he looks at you. The "real you" is the person you may hope *to become* by spending a lifetime cooperating with God's grace. *Becoming who we are* — whom God created us to be — takes real work, and for the most part, there is no better place to do this work than in our homes with our spouses and children.

While we will grant that love calls husbands and wives to be more tolerant of occasional breaches of good taste and behavior, there are entirely too many people who make the mistake of thinking that being ignorant toward, or neglectful of, their mates is somehow a *proof* of love. As C. S. Lewis writes in *The Four Loves*, "[A person] knows that Affection takes liberties. He is taking liberties. Therefore (he concludes) he is being affectionate." I hope you can see the absurdity of this notion.

In Christian marriage, we are given the grace to work with our mates to *become* ourselves. Most of us are not there yet. Once we *become* the person God created us to be, then, by all means, we should sit around the house being *that* all day. Until then, we have way too much work to do on ourselves to take advantage of too many "liberties." This leads us to the second misconception about relationships, namely:

2. "I've always thought you shouldn't try to change your mate. Shouldn't a husband and wife accept each other for who they are?"

The best answer to this question is "yes and no." Your partner should never try to change you simply to meet *his or her own* expectations — and vice versa. However, when you marry someone, you *are* swearing that person to help you stay true to *your own expectations for yourself* (this is why it is important to have some). Remember, the best marriages — the *Exceptional Seven Percent* — are built around both the husband and wife being able to say, "I married you because between now and the day I die, I have a better chance, with you than without you, of becoming the person God created me to be."

Think of the thousands of times you have disappointed yourself — much less anyone else. You do not really want to be accepted for *that*, do you? The healthy person may want to be loved through such things, or handled delicately in these areas, or even accepted as a "work in progress," but no one has the right to be let off the hook for disappointing himself or God. Pacifying — or expecting to be pacified — in the name of compassion is cowardice at best and enabling at worst. For the Christian, everything is an opportunity to grow in love; everything can be a spiritual exercise, from formal prayer, to kissing our spouses when we leave and enter a room, to getting off the couch when we are too tired to play with our children or wash the dishes. Every time we stretch ourselves to love, honor, and serve more than we happen to want to at the moment, we become a little more like Christ.

The renowned family therapist Cloe Madanes has said that the institution of marriage is the best kind of group therapy going. This goes double for marriage's potential for spiritual therapy. When husbands and wives celebrate their vulnerability to one another, they embrace the spiritual and therapeutic nature of all good, loving Christian marriages. They allow their marriages to help them become the people God created them to be.

A Word to Those Who Wound Others

Having heard all this, keep in mind that the obligation to help your partner remain true to himself or herself is not a license to kill. Remember St. Paul's admonition to the Corinthians: Love keeps no score of wrongs; it does not gloat over another's sins (1 Cor 13:6). Under no circumstances do you have permission to lord your partner's faults over her, be constantly critical, or even mildly cruel in the delivery of any feedback. In fact, nine times out of ten, it will be better for you to keep your mouth shut and simply listen as your partner tells you of her struggles. Does this seem contradictory? We do not mean it to be. While you and your partner must be willing to say the hard words when necessary, it must not be the main activity of your marriage — far from it. Dr. John Gottman's 20:1 rule applies here (see "Twelve Things Happy Couples Know About Love," in Chapter 7). For *each* criticism you deliver you must give *20 times* as many sincere compliments and perform *20 times* as many loving acts if you are to be seen by your mate as anything more than a nag, a control freak, or worse. Maintaining this ratio is critical to marital growth and well-being. Spouses must challenge each other to be more loving and more faithful to their own values, but they must challenge each other gently and with love. The four tips below will help you approach your partner's soft spots respectfully.

1. Don't Volunteer "Constructive Criticisms": Wait for Your Spouse to Ask

Nobody likes a "buttinsky." Ideally, you should wait for your partner to ask for your input before you give it. If your mate tends to be slower than you would like in asking your opinion on how she should conduct her affairs, the solution is not to begin volunteering criticism. The *solution* is to practice your patience and build your credibility (see number 3 below). Wait to be invited to the party before offering to bring the potato salad.

2. What to Do When Your Usually Mature Spouse Doesn't Ask for Help and You Can't Bear to Suffer — er, We Mean, See Your Spouse Suffer — Any Longer

We all have blind spots. Sometimes we do not ask for assistance even when we really need it. If your spouse looks as if she is spinning her wheels and you genuinely want to help (not merely criticize for the fun of it), say something like, "I notice that you seem to be frustrated with such and such. Would you like to talk about it?" If she denies any problem, you can press a bit further with, "Well, it's just that I've noticed you pulling out clumps of hair [eyeing the gun cabinet, sticking straight pins in Barbie dolls, or other stress-behaviors]. What's that about?"

This line of questioning allows you to secure an invitation to offer assistance. It has the added bonus of earning you "brownie points" for having been so sensitive as to notice your mate's stressed-out behavior. All of this will increase the chances that any feedback you offer will be perceived as charitable and loving. At any rate, it sure beats yelling, "What the hell's the matter with you?"

3. Build Credibility with the "Lord, Change Me" Strategy

What if number 1 and number 2 don't work? Try the following.

Let's say your mate isn't being as loving, attentive, successful, thoughtful, holy, whatever, as you think she could and should be. Moreover (stubborn person that your mate is), she is not asking for your help in solving this particular problem. Let us also say that you are like me, insofar as patience is not exactly your strong suit, and on several occasions you have broken down and, both gently and not so gently, explained the (you think) obvious solution to your mate's "problem." Again, if you are like me, you probably expected undying gratitude and an immediate change in your mate's behavior as a result of your wise intervention. But do you get so much as a "thank you" for all your efforts? Heck, no! (The ingrate!) What to do?

Both personally and professionally, we have found that when our mates ignore our — ahem — wise counsel, and other — ahem — well-intentioned attempts to help them become better people, it is usually because, despite what we may like to think, we are not such hot stuff ourselves. In other words, we lack credibility. For example, we may ask our mates to love us the way we want to be loved, but very often we remain blind to the billion or so ways we are disappointing them. As our Lord pointed out, we see the speck in our neighbor's eye and not the beam in our own (Lk 6:42). In such a case, it is hard to imagine why our mates should *not* ignore us — expert lovers that we ourselves are.

No matter how high an opinion we may have of our own talents for holiness, love, romance, wisdom, success, etc., nine out of ten times our mates' ignoring our divinely inspired wisdom on how they can improve their lives is a clear sign that we need to work on our own credibility.

To truly call our mates on, rather than whine at them or nag them to change, we must become more loving *to them* and more faithful to *our own* values. Otherwise we end up playing Marital Chicken, as is evident in comments like "I would be more *X* if you would just be *Y*." If we want to lead our mates to the Lord, then we need to become someone worthy of following. We must ask the Lord to help *us* become more loving, faithful, *credible* spouses. When, and only when, our mates experience our loving them without a chip on our shoulder and without expecting some kind of payment in return — when they see us living up to our God-given values, dreams, and goals on a consistent basis — only then can we expect them to look at us and say, "You have it so together and you are so loving and generous to me. How can I be more like that?"

Congratulations! You have now been invited to the party. Pick up your potato salad and proceed in all haste to number 4, immediately following.

4. When Asked, Be Gentle

This should be so obvious as to be undeserving of mention, but our experience tells us otherwise. Be gentle when offering help, even after being invited. The best way to do this is to merely talk about your observations and be prepared to be told that your observations are incorrect: "*I could be wrong*, but I seem to have noticed such and such. What do you think?"

Repeat the formula as necessary. This approach allows you to assert what you believe to be true without overstepping your bounds. Compare the above to "Y'know what your problem is?" or the ever-popular "Why do you have to be such a jerk?" and you will understand what I am getting at.

Sacrificial Love? Or Codependence?

Vulnerability, as exhibited by our willingness to be "broken" for the sake of our identities in Christ, and our willingness to be loving to our mates even when they don't deserve it, falls under the heading of "sacrificial love" — and good marriages have plenty of this. Unfortunately, for many, the phrase "sacrificial love" has an even worse ring to it than vulnerability. It is easy to see why. Some people confuse sacrificial love with being spineless or codependent. But true sacrificial love, like true vulnerability, requires that one does not surrender unless one's values and/or personal dignity require them to do so. Compare this to the codependent person who throws down his or her arms for any reason at the first sign of conflict. If codependency is sensitivity in the *absence* of personal strength, then true vulnerability and sacrificial love demonstrate the *balance* between sensitivity and personal strength. The following quiz can help you see if you have what it takes to be healthily vulnerable.

QUIZ: Are You Vulnerable — In a Healthy Way?

PART A

Personal Strength

Directions: Write T for "true" next to each statement that applies. Answer according to how each statement applies to the way you act *in your marriage.*

1. ___ My life reflects a clear set of values — i.e., "I don't have to say, 'I believe such and such.' You can tell by looking at my life."
2. ___ I am capable of providing for my own needs, whether emotional and/or financial.
3. ___ I enjoy being by myself.
4. ___ I have strong opinions.
5. ___ I am comfortable in conflict (though I don't look for fights).
6. ___ I am not easily intimidated.
7. ___ I do not take criticism personally.
8. ___ My own satisfaction or fulfillment is important to me.
9. ___ Certain things are worth fighting for.
10. ___ I speak my mind.

Score Part A: Personal Strength _____

PART B

Sensitivity

1. ___ I am careful not to offend others with my speech or actions.
2. ___ I am quick to notice another person's pain.
3. ___ I go out of my way to help others in need.

4. ___ I am a good listener.
5. ___ People tell me I'm easy to talk to. (Or, "Everybody seems eager to talk to me.")
6. ___ Being considerate is very important to me.
7. ___ I am concerned about the happiness of others.
8. ___ I believe that the people I know are basically good-hearted.
9. ___ It would be very painful for me to lose a friend.
10. ___ I am comfortable talking about my feelings.

Score Part B: Sensitivity _____

Scoring

Compare your scores for both parts of the quiz.

- A score of *six or more in both* personal strength *and* sensitivity suggests that you probably have the skills to be vulnerable in the healthiest sense of the word.
- Scoring *less than six in both* personal strength *and* sensitivity suggests that you are neither remarkably sensitive nor do you have much strength of character. You probably don't care enough about anything — including your own personal growth — to make vulnerability seem worthwhile to you. You need to develop some passions and a greater concern for others if you want more than a perpetually stagnant life and marriage.
- A *high score* (six or more) in personal strength combined with a *low score* (five or less) in sensitivity suggests that vulnerability does not come easy to you. Depending upon the disparity between the two scores, you may tend to come across as a bully. Work on your awareness of other's feelings and perceptions of you. Being right all of the time is no fun if it eventually causes you to be alone all of the time.
- A *low score* (five or less) in personal strength combined with a *high score* (six or more) in sensitivity suggests that you may have a tendency toward being a doormat instead of vulnerable in a healthy way. Depending on the disparity between these two scores, you may also have some *codependent* tendencies. Find something to believe in — starting with yourself — and stand up for it.

Vulnerability: You've Got the Power

As we explained earlier, vulnerability enables your marriage to become a truly spiritual endeavor. It allows you to stand in awe of the transformative power of God's love working through you and your mate.

When your mate has earned your trust by demonstrating his credibility and you grant him the right to rummage through the closets and cobwebbed basements of your soul, inevitably he will come across some gunk-encrusted thing, a behavior of which you are ashamed, or a belief that is unhealthy or destructive. In a good marriage, the finder will not recoil with disgust; instead, he will help you uncover and reclaim that part of yourself.

Because secrets melt in the heat of true vulnerability, you will constantly be discovering new facets of your mate and yourself. You will never have to fear becoming bored with each other because every day another defense will melt away, another part of yourself will be healed and transformed in the spiritual fire of your love for each other. As you grow in trust, love, and vulnerability, you and your mate will fling open the doors to each other's secret chambers. Light and air will pour into the once dank and dreary corners of your soul. Each day a new piece of your heart will be captured until there is no part of you that is left untouched; until your partner has dwelt in every part of your body, soul, and consciousness — and you in his. Practicing this kind of vulnerability is the only way you will ever know what it means for two to become one. No thrill will ever come close to the fear, anticipation, and sweet release that are experienced in the presence of true vulnerability. It is a thrill that will last a lifetime.

As you might well imagine, vulnerability lends itself to an uncommonly rewarding sex life. Most of the books on sex are dead wrong. You don't have to dress up like Batman and Catwoman to add spice to your marriage. If you want a thrill befitting a "Real Man" or a "Real Woman," try exposing every aspect of your being to your mate over a lifetime. It is no great mystery that spiritual people have more intense orgasms. Studies show that while others are mere technicians, spiritual people "pay more attention to the mystic and symbolic aspects of . . . sexuality" (Janus, 1995). No prop, costume, or role-play could ever compare to the soulfully orgasmic, transcendent ecstasy that accompanies offering one's whole self as a free, unrestrained gift to one's beloved.

The following will help you increase the healthy vulnerability in your own life and inspire the same in your mate.

DISCUSSION: Surrendering to Love

1. Make a point of living out the "Twelve Things Happy Couples Know About Love" (Chapter 7). Pay special attention to numbers 1, 3, 5, 7, and 8.
2. Maintain the 20:1 ratio of positivity to negativity by checking your "Twenty-Five Ways to Make Love Stay — Every Day" list at least once a week. Are you living up to your value of being a loving person?
3. Discuss the following.
   (a) What are the ways you sabotage your own progress toward your fulfillment? For example, where do you experience fear, shame, or self-doubt? When your partner sees you stumbling on the road, how could he or she be helpful — without stepping on your toes?
   (b) What shortcomings do you have about which you are especially sensitive? While acknowledging your primary responsibility for correcting these faults, what can your partner do to assist you in this transformation?
   (c) When your partner disappoints or frustrates you, how would your partner like to be approached with this information? That is, what does your partner think would be a considerate and respectful way to let him or her know of your hurt?

Conclusion

Having covered vulnerability (There, now, that wasn't so bad, was it?), we can move on to the second pillar of intimacy: the secrets of exceptional communication. As a bonus, you'll also find out the *shocking true story* behind the courtship of the Princess and the Frog Prince. Go to the next chapter — if you dare!

CHAPTER 9

The Princess, the Frog Prince, and Freud

Once upon a time …

There was a beautiful but lonely princess. She sought her Prince Charming among the royalty of the neighboring kingdoms — with no success. She sought her one true love in the cities and villages of the world; but again, she met with no success. One day, weary and exhausted from her travels, the Princess found a sun-dappled knoll in the middle of a forest. She lay down and fell fast asleep.

She awoke to the sound of tiny voices and laughter. A short distance from her, she saw a small gathering of children sitting around a weathered, stooped old man. "A bard!" thought the princess to herself. She crept closer so that she could hear the old man's tale.

She couldn't make out everything he said, standing as far back as she was, but she heard enough to know that his story was about a princess, like herself, who, having found a frog wearing a crown, convinced him of her love, whereupon the frog was transformed into a handsome prince with whom she lived happily ever after.

The Princess could scarcely contain her excitement. After the story was completed and the children dismissed, she approached the storyteller. "O wise bard, I am a lonely princess, but I am encouraged by your remarkable story. I am sure that your tale was intended for my ears and that you, at long last, can help me find my prince. Will you help me?"

The old man considered her request; then, waving her to follow him, the bard took her to some wetlands. Sure enough, looking decidedly uncomfortable among the other amphibians was a singularly distinctive frog, wearing a singularly distinctive — crown.

The Princess' heart leapt. Her search was over! The bard looked at her and smiled. "I have done what I can for you. Now you must convince him of your love. If you can do this, you and your prince will live 'happily ever after.' " With that, he left her.

The Princess immediately began thinking of ways she could convey her love to him. "This should be easy," she thought. "I'll simply do the things I would want my beloved to do for me." So she sat down and composed a beautiful love song with a profound lyric and gentle, stirring melody. With the sweetest voice in all heaven and earth, the Princess sang of her love with such feeling that the birds swooned and remained silent, as they could not compete with her song. When she was finished, she looked to the Frog Prince with great anticipation.

He began to stir, then twitch. All of a sudden, much to her astonishment — his tongue flew out of his mouth and zapped a fly that had invaded his airspace. "BZZRRT!"

She was crushed. How could the frog not be convinced of her love? She regained her composure and said to the frog, "Wait right here." With that, she walked to the field on the other side of the road. She picked a bouquet of flowers whose fragrance was so rich and intoxicating that the royal perfumers still seek to copy the scent of that loving gift. She carried the flowers to the frog and, laying them before him, said, "My love for you is twice as sweet as the most fragrant buds in this bouquet."

That got him. The frog's heart quickened. The Princess stood, arms outstretched, eagerly awaiting the man of her dreams. What would he say to her?

"RRRBBBBBTTT!"

That did it. She picked up the frog and his crown and ran to the village. There, she found the bard in the local pub. She grabbed the old man in a most unladylike way and screamed, "You gave me a defective frog! I sing him songs, I give him gifts, but nothing! He still isn't convinced of my love. You old fool!"

The bard was stunned. "My child," he said, "did you not hear the story? You must kiss the frog with the passion of a thousand lovers on a midsummer's night."

The Princess froze. "Kiss him?" she thought. She fully intended to do that — and a whole lot more — after he became a prince, but kiss the frog? Ugh. That was weird. Gross, even. She looked at the bard as if to ask, "Isn't there some other way? He's slimy and that tongue.... Ugh!" A shiver traveled from her feet to the tips of her strawberry-blond locks, but the bard only smiled and shook his head, "No."

"Oh well." She sighed. She closed her eyes, puckered her lips and after taking a good, deep breath, she let the frog have it right on the kisser. "Hmmm. This isn't so bad," she thought. Imagine her surprise when she opened her eyes in mid-kiss to see before her the most handsome and charming prince in the world. Knowing when she had a good thing, the Princess immediately carried the Prince to the village church and before he could say, "Excuse me, Miss, I'd like some ketchup with my flies," they were married — and they lived happily ever after.

The moral of the story is ...

It is not enough to love. You must love in a way that is meaningful to the beloved.

The end.

A Love of Another Kind

In the last chapter, we looked at the first pillar of intimacy: the willingness to be vulnerable. The second pillar of intimacy is good communication. In this chapter, we'll explore how you and your spouse can communicate your love more effectively for each other.

Every person prefers to give and receive love differently. Many believe these differences are basically gender-related. The popular line is that men prefer physical — and especially sexual — displays of affection, while women prefer emotional and more romantic displays. But this is an oversimplification. Research shows us that gender does not account for such differences in *at least* 20 percent of both men and women. This is an important statistic because many of us, coming home from the bookstore with one of the more popular relationship tomes, think that we have it all figured out: Wives will do *X* for their men, husbands will do *Y* for their women, and everyone will live "happily ever after." But a large number of husbands and wives simply don't fit the stereotypes. So, if gender isn't the primary determining factor in affection styles, what is? Believe it or not, it's neurology.

Getting Schooled in Your Love Style

There are three major *love styles* — that is, three different ways people prefer to give and receive affection (Cameron-Bandler, 1985). People with a *visual love style* need to see signs of love. People with an *auditory love style* need to talk, share, and discuss their love for each other. People with a *kinesthetic love style* demonstrate their love through affection, service, and just being together. These styles are based on our primary senses (sight, hearing, touch) — specifically, which of our primary senses is most highly developed in any given person. To best explain how this works, we need to take you back to grade school for a minute.

Kids all learn differently, and teachers spend a great deal of time trying to figure out their students' "learning styles." For example, children who learn better by reading, taking notes, and visual aids — such as pictures, diagrams, and videos — are said to have a *visual learning style*. Students who learn best through lectures, songs, and being "talked through" tasks have an *auditory learning style*. Finally, kids who learn best by doing hands-on projects and activities have a *kinesthetic learning style*. These styles can change over time, but they never go away completely because they are *neurologically based* — that is, they are dependent upon the senses that are most highly developed in a particular student. When we grow up, our learning styles become our *communication styles* — or in intimate relationships, the three major love styles.

Fast-forward to adulthood. You are married. Imagine that your mate displays a visual love style while you have a more auditory love style. You will *tell* him, "I love you," about a million times a day. This will be very meaningful to you (auditory people love to hear themselves — and everyone else — talk), but *your mate* (visual person that he is) will probably think, "Ho-hum. That's nice, dear."

You see, if you *really* want a visually attuned person to understand the depth of your love, you must *show* him you love him — literally. Get that person a silly card and write a poem that he can *read* over and over. Leave love notes for him. Get him a present and wrap it in beautiful paper. Cook a fancy dinner and (this is the important part) light candles, set the table, use your best china, and the good silver, and dress up. For visual people, atmosphere counts — a lot.

Likewise, if you are "in the mood" and want to make sure your visual mate is similarly inclined, wear something sexy. Better still, make love to him with the lights on. He wants to *see* how much you love him. If you do any or all of these things for your visual spouse, then he will really understand your love in a meaningful way. Why? Because you are speaking your partner's visual love style. Cognitively, he *understood* what you meant when you (in your auditory way) *said*, "I love you"; but he *experienced* it when you *showed* him.

You, however, as a person with an auditory love style, would consider many of the things that mean so much to your visual spouse irrelevant and distracting at best or completely stupid at worst. Let's take this same example and flip it around. Because your mate has a visual love style, he is going to bring you flowers, cards, or other tokens to *show* you how much he loves you. But, after the novelty of this wears off, because you have a primarily auditory love style, you will probably think, "Ho-hum. That's nice and all, but why don't you *tell* me you love me more often? I love *hearing* you *say* it."

More than getting flowers, cards, or notes, you would probably rather stay up all night with your mate talking about your feelings, or your plans for the future or, for that matter, about nothing at all. You will want him to sing you songs, call you pet names in a silly tone of voice, leave you cute messages on the answering machine, or read you love poems. When you are in the mood to make love you will want him to *tell* you what he is thinking and how wonderfully you are making him feel. In and out of bed, you want to *hear* how much he loves you. If he's not talking to you, he's not being loving to you.

As time goes by, if neither of you learns to understand the reasons behind the way you communicate love to each other, one of you is going to accuse the other of neglect. For the sake of argument, let's say it's you.

"You don't ever *tell* me you love me unless I *say* it first. What's wrong with you?"

Your partner will probably be insulted and become defensive at your accusation. He will probably say that since *your* gums never stop flapping, he doesn't have half a chance to "say it first." Next, he will point out all the things he does to *show* you that he loves you, bringing up such things as the cards, flowers, candy, and love notes he's given you over a period of time. Depending upon how bad a day he is having, he may even "diagnose" you as being "insecure" because he has to *tell* you how much he loves you so often: "You should know I love you by now. Why do I have to tell you all the time?"

You will eventually become disgusted with your spouse and decide he just doesn't get it. More than likely you will have a big argument, or a series of big arguments, in which you will accuse each other of being "insensitive." (Little will either of you know how literally true this is. Keep in mind that love styles are neurologically based on the five *senses*.) As a result of these arguments, you will probably come to one of two conclusions:

1. You were never meant for each other and should proceed, posthaste, to divorce court.
2. You decide that each of you loves the other "in his or her own way," and even though it is basically meaningless to you, you'll try to choke down your disappointment and get on with it. "Nothing's perfect. Right?"

Well, very little is perfect, but love can be. For the Christian, it must be, since Jesus said: "Be perfect, therefore, as your heavenly Father is perfect" (Mt 5:48). That is, perfect in love. In order to perfect our ability to love our mates, we must learn how to love them in a way that, literally, makes *sense* to them (i.e., appeals to the *physical sense* to which they are most attuned).

The problem is, in the above example, it would never have dawned on you that some of the loving expressions your mate values would be valued by anybody. You just think he's a big, dumb idiot. In our example, you were *literally* not wired (neurologically) to think the way he does. Furthermore, when a person with a different love style than your own expresses his preferences, you will be apt to forget what he said, not because you are inconsiderate, or don't love him enough, but because your brain simply isn't wired to understand what he is telling you.

It is like the first day in an immersion Japanese-language class. You nod politely, act as if you understand the instructor, but you really won't get it until she has repeated herself a hundred (or maybe a bazillion) times and your brain has *literally* acquired the neurological connections it needs to make *sense* of her message. You may think we are overstating this. You may prefer to believe that your mate is insensitive. He is. Just not the way you mean. If you identify with anything you are reading so far, your partner may literally be "out of sense" with you. It takes real work to make the neurological connections necessary for translating across a couple's conflicting sensory styles (i.e., love styles), but it can be done. Neuroplasticity is the term for how the brain learns to rewire itself because of the experiences we have. There are now hundreds of studies demonstrating that when a person changes his or her behavior, communicative ability, and life experiences, he or she actually causes structural changes in the brain and nervous system. When spouses talk about "struggling to make a connection" with each other, they don't realize they are describing a neurological reality. Understanding and loving your mate in a meaningful way *is* hard work, because it often requires rewiring the way your brain processes messages, loving messages (both giving and receiving). As challenging as that might sound, St. John Paul the Great's Theology of the Body reminds us that, at our core, our bodies were created by God to master the art of loving fully and loving well. God gives Christian married couples the grace they need to be up to the task.

So far, we have described visual and auditory love styles. Let's take a minute to explain the third major love style: *kinesthetic* (i.e., pertaining to touch). Stereotypically, this is the style most often attributed to "guys." However, *at least* 20 percent of women exhibit this style as well.

Spouses with a more *kinesthetic love style* tend to be very physical. They can never get enough touching, holding, hugging, kissing, cuddling, and/or lovemaking. They need to "be in touch" with their partners to "feel connected." People who have a primarily kinesthetic love style tend to love quiet times together, just sitting and being, and when they feel *really* ambitious, sitting, being, *and* holding. That's not to say that kinesthetics are lazy (quite the contrary, they are often very hard workers); they just aren't super-showy about their love. They tend not to say much or be very talented at the things many people would consider to be romance. For the kinesthetic, romance is best demonstrated either by being affectionate or by faithfully carrying out the common duties of daily life. The best kinesthetics are usually very good at quiet, humble service. (Contrast this with auditory people who tend to ask for feedback about everything they do, or visual people who want to make sure you saw their gesture.) Most often, to demonstrate their affection for you, kinesthetics will *do* things to make your life easier. They will get you coffee, wash your car, clean the house, and pay the bills. Visual and auditory spouses often hate this. They are usually very critical of their kinesthetic partners for trying to get relationship points for "doing stuff they would just have to do anyway." Visual and auditory people tend to believe love is something you have to make a fuss about. Kinesthetic spouses, on the other hand, tend to view love as something they live, feel, and are, commenting, "Why do we have to try so hard all the time to analyze everything? Can't we just *be* together?"

When stressed, the purest kinesthetics tend to withdraw into themselves, immerse themselves in work, or exercise vigorously. Kinesthetics tend to come across as stoic and aloof until you get to know them. They are the people who like to hang on the edge of a crowd and remain quiet until they *feel* comfortable with their surroundings. Kinesthetics are often criticized as being unemotional, but nothing could be further from the truth. In fact, because their sense of touch is so acute, they tend to *feel* emotions in their body more strongly and deeply than either visual people (who tend to live in their heads) or auditory people (whose feelings change with the subject they are discussing). The problem is, the purest kinesthetics don't *show* their emotions or *talk* about them. They just *feel* them. In arguments that exceed their comfort level, they are easily overwhelmed and may either agree with their partners just to shut them up, or react explosively when they can't keep it in anymore. Kinesthetics tend to be impulsive, making decisions based on how they *feel* at the moment. They tend to have an intense dislike of conflict (it just feels too stressful); they also tend to abhor schedules insofar as they hate committing themselves to anything they might not *feel* like doing later. Again, contrast this with auditory people who love to debate everything, and visual people who would post their morning shower routine on a schedule (in triplicate) if they could — because if they can *see* it, they know it will be done correctly.

Do you see the potential for problems here? Obviously, mismatched love styles can become a serious problem. But, believe it or not, of all the marriage problems we encounter in our counseling practice, differences in love styles are the easiest to fix. There are three steps:

1. Determining your style.
2. Separating who you *are* from how you're *wired.*
3. Rewiring.

Loving in Style: Step One

Determining Your Love Style

When a husband and wife have different love styles, they may know they are loved by their partner — in their own way — but a wife won't really experience the fullness of that love unless her husband takes the trouble to learn her love style and vice versa. So far, we have taken a cursory look at the three major love styles (visual, auditory, and kinesthetic). Some of you may wonder why — if they are truly based on the five senses — there are only three love styles. Elementary, dear reader. The other two senses (taste and smell) are not usually dominant enough for either one to be a person's primary love style. (We suppose you *could* smell how much you love your mate — but, frankly, we don't want to know about it.) At best, our senses of taste and smell add spice and freshness to our experience of the three primary love styles: visual, auditory, and kinesthetic.

The first step to overcoming the communication barriers between you and your mate is to identify the specific ways in which you are different. The following exercise describes the behaviors, speech patterns, and preferences of each love style. See if you can identify your love style and that of your partner.

EXERCISE: Identify Your Love Styles

Directions: Chances are you use all of your five senses, but you will *favor* one or two of them when it comes to giving and receiving love. The following are some of the most prominent characteristics, speech patterns, and preferences associated with each love style. Write *M* for "me" next to each quality that describes you. Write *P* for "partner" next to each quality that describes your mate. You will probably check some in each category. You are looking for the category you check the *most* items in. This will be your primary love style.

The Visual (Seeing) Love Style

Check the statements that describe how you are *most* of the time.

___ "*Show* me that you love me."
___ Flowers, love notes, cards, etc., *most* meaningful (not just liked).
___ "Presentation" important (i.e., presents wrapped nicely, meals arranged decoratively on a well-set table, etc.). Think "Martha Stewart."
___ Lighting important to mood.
___ "Turned on" by candlelight, lingerie that looks sexy even though it may be horribly uncomfortable, other visual stimuli.
___ Clothes important. *Looking good* more important than comfort or practicality.
___ Desktops and visible surfaces neat as a pin. Desk drawers and closets, however, may be a disaster. Out of *sight*, out of mind.
___ Always making plans. Very productive. Tracks a hundred projects at once.
___ Good at decorating or other visual arts (photography, painting, etc.).
___ Good at matching unusual colors and patterns in attractive ways (clothes, house decorations, etc.).
___ A house that "looks clean" more important than a house that *is* clean.
___ Unconsciously makes neat piles out of anything that happens to be in front of you.
___ Mess *causes* stress.
___ Thinks more clearly when house is neat.
___ Cleans or tidies up *when* stressed.
___ Daydreams a lot.
___ Speaks quickly. Uses a lot of words.
___ Tends to be "anal retentive" (i.e., uptight, proper, or detail oriented).
___ Enjoys books with vivid descriptions and/or pictures.
___ Loves to keep journals, make plans, and write lists.
___ Charts, graphs, or other visual aids helpful. "Learns by watching."
___ Uses visual metaphors in speech like, "I've got to focus," "Imagine that," "It seems vague," "It seems clear," "I can see right through you," "I'm seeing things in a new light," "I'm drawing a blank," "See my point?"

Visual love style scores: "Me" _____ "Partner" _____

Auditory (Hearing) Love Style

Check the statements that describe how you are *most* of the time.

___ "*Tell* me that you love me."
___ Talks constantly about everything.

___ Has an opinion on every subject. Sometimes told, "You analyze and/or think too much."
___ Likes hearing and saying "I love you" a million times a day.
___ Loves to have extended conversations about anything.
___ Important to "talk things out."
___ "If you talk to me, that means you love me."
___ No such thing as a "rhetorical question"; he or she answers everything.
___ Likes music, poetry, etc.
___ Speaks with a certain rhythm or variations in tone.
___ Very sensitive to other's tone of voice.
___ Hums, whistles, talks to self, perhaps constantly.
___ Radio or TV on at all times, "Just for the noise."
___ Sounds (music, tone of voice) affect mood.
___ "Turned on" by romantic, emotional, and/or sexual *conversations*.
___ When arguing, doesn't know when to stop. May follow other person from room to room talking, whether or not the other is listening.
___ When moderately stressed, tries to talk about it. When maximally stressed, needs quiet to restore calm.
___ Phone permanently connected to head.
___ Always gets the last word.
___ Always late because he or she "just stopped to talk for a minute."
___ Would rather die than be quiet.
___ Uses auditory comments, "Hear me out," "I could tell by your tone," "I need some feedback," "We need to talk," "Just *listen* to me," "It made me want to scream," and other auditory metaphors in speech.

Auditory love style scores: "Me" ____ "Partner" ____

Kinesthetic (Touch) Love Style

Check the statements that describe how you are *most* of the time.

___ "You love me if you're touching me."
___ "I love when we're both quiet and we can just *be* together."
___ "Why do we have to talk all the time and/or work so hard on our relationship?"
___ Likes touching and hugging more than any other expression of affection.
___ Dresses for comfort. Appearance secondary if considered at all.
___ Tends to withdraw or shut down in arguments fairly quickly.
___ Easily overwhelmed in verbal conflict. Often feels picked on. "I never know what to say...."

___ Has a hard time making decisions. Tends not to reason things out. Gives "gut reactions" to things.
___ Poor organizer. Lots of unorganized piles. "Don't touch my mess. I'll never find anything."
___ Gestures, grunts, and shrugs more than talks.
___ Works off stress physically. Either by exercising and/or "working it off," or by taking "spa time" (i.e., hot bath, pampering one's body, naps).
___ Talks slowly. Has trouble finding the right words.
___ "Turned on" by touching, hugging, kissing, massage, other physical contact. May have a hard time not "going all the way" when physical affection started.
___ Tends to have a hard time delaying gratification. Sexually, may rush through "preliminaries" to get to "the good stuff."
___ After arguments, looks for physical reassurance (hugs or sex) to make sure "we're still okay."
___ Loves sports or other physical activity.
___ Hates making plans. "I don't know what I'll *feel* like doing that day."
___ Tends to be impulsive or spontaneous.
___ Sometimes hard to get motivated. Can't get past how he or she *feels right now*, in that particular moment.
___ Learns by doing. Often a slower learner in school.
___ Doesn't like to read, or prefers books and movies with "action."
___ Tends to be a slob. Doesn't see mess unless he or she trips over it.
___ Says things like, "Get a grip," "I'll handle it," "Take it easy," "We're really connected," "I just feel that way, that's why," and similar physically attuned metaphors in speech.

Kinesthetic love style scores: "Me" ____ "Partner" ____

Scoring

- In which category did you mark the *most* checks?
  "Me" ______________ "Partner" ______________
  These are your primary love styles.
- Which category had the second-most checks?
  "Me" ______________ "Partner" ______________
  These are your secondary love styles.
- Which category had the least number of checks?
  "Me" ______________ "Partner" ______________

These are your tertiary love styles.

Love-Speak Continued

As you can see, there are significant differences between each style. But don't be too surprised if you checked some items in each category. Most of us have five senses and use them all to one degree or another; it's just that, because of neuroplasticity, our life experiences have wired some of those senses in a way that makes them more acute than the others. In the exercise, you identified your primary, secondary, and tertiary love styles. Even if you and your mate's primary love styles are different, you will probably share a highly developed secondary "style" together. If you didn't, it would have been hard to understand each other well enough to get together in the first place. For most couples, wanting to increase proficiency in a secondary or tertiary love style springs from the desire to develop even greater intimacy than already exists. As such, differences in love styles tend to be a greater concern for Apprentices and Partners. Still, differences between spouses in their primary love styles can be fairly problematic.

Early in our marriage, we struggled with this very issue. Greg tends to be highly visual (his primary love style). But he is also very auditory (my secondary love style). Lisa, on the other hand is highly kinesthetic (primary love style) *and* highly auditory (secondary love style). We really connected when it came to our love of long conversations, saying, "I love you" a million times per day, and all that auditory stuff. But when it came to other areas, we kept missing the boat. Greg would bring home cards and flowers and Lisa would say, "Thank you, honey," and leave them sitting on the table for a week. "How insensitive," Greg thought. "Such things should be displayed prominently on the mantle so that all the world could *see* how much I loved her. How dare she just let them sit there!"

Meanwhile, Lisa would sit on the couch and say to me, "Come and hold me. Why do we have to always be running somewhere? Let's just sit together."

Greg is much different than he used to be, but back then his definition of hell was "sitting still." It wasn't that he didn't *want* to cuddle together; it was just that everywhere he looked, he *saw* something else that had to be done.

Until we started learning about love styles, we just felt that the other person was being an intractable idiot:

Greg: "I wish you would get *me* some flowers or a card sometime, just as I do for you."
Lisa: "Anybody can do that. Come here; let me hold you."
Greg: "Hold you? Gee, a whole lot of thought goes into that!"

Greg: "Let's make plans for Saturday." (Visual people can't *stand* to look out into the future and see a blank space on their mental calendar.)
Lisa: "Can't we just see how we *feel* when we get up?" (Kinesthetic people can't *stand* to be committed to something they might not feel like doing later.)
Greg: "I don't understand. Why can't we plan something for a change?"
Lisa: "Why do you have to be so compulsive?"

No matter how many times we tried to explain our positions to each other, they never made *sense*. It was getting to the point where we began thinking that the other was thoughtless, inconsiderate, "just didn't love me enough to remember what was important to me," or worse. Once we learned what our love styles were, we began to understand that the reason we weren't being loving in as meaningful a way as possible (i.e., working hard, not smart) wasn't that we didn't love each other enough — we were simply wired differently. And once we learned how to do it, we could "rewire" ourselves to increase our understanding of the true depth of love that existed between us.

This brings us to step two.

Loving In Style: Step Two

Separating Who You Are from How You're Wired

It is at this point that most couples say, "So, that's it? We're wired differently? You mean, we're doomed?" *Au contraire, mes amis.*

Remember what you read earlier? You and your mate must understand each other on some level or you never would have gotten together at all. If you and yours don't speak the same primary love style, chances are you at least share a highly developed secondary or tertiary one. What we are really addressing here is the fact that at some point most couples hit a wall where there will be no more growth in their intimacy unless they develop their proficiency in a second or third love style. This wall will take the form of a minor crisis. That is one of the many times spouses look at each other over the course of a marriage and say, "Uh, now what?"

The second step to successfully bridging the differences between you and your spouse is realizing that your love style is not who you *are*. It is not who God created you to *be*. It is simply how you are *wired*. While you may only be *proficient* with one or two of your senses, God *gave* you five senses and he expects you to learn to use them to the fullest extent possible. As we are told in the New Testament: "To whom much has been given, much will be required" (Lk 12:48). Why would God want you to do this? Because God reveals himself to us through the created world almost as much as he does through Scripture. As St. Thomas Aquinas put it, there are two "books" of revelation: the Bible and nature.

God wants to share his "natural" revelation with all of us, but we will be completely unable to receive it unless we open up all the channels he has given us (our senses). Limiting yourself to your preferred sense (or senses) while attempting to understand how God is appearing to you, speaking to you, and reaching out to you through his world is as absurd as trying to appreciate a painting by one of the great masters while wearing sunglasses, listening to one of Beethoven's symphonies while wearing earmuffs, or running your fingers over the *Pietà* while wearing gloves. St. John Paul II, in his Theology of the Body, encourages us to prayerfully contemplate our bodies as a way of understanding God's plan for us and the world. Learning to first identify and then rewire the neurological circuits that control our love style preferences helps us do just that. By doing this work, God doesn't just improve our marriage; he brings about a healing in the deepest parts of ourselves, so that we can experience more of his grace though our senses and cooperate more effectively with that grace by being able to feel, see, and hear him more clearly.

Before we met each other, we were perfectly content to live in our own visual and kinesthetic worlds, respectively. Greg appreciated the arts, especially good music. He dressed as well as his budget would allow. He was creative and productive. He lived life to what he thought was the fullest. But after we got married, he discovered a whole new world that God created that he knew little, perhaps, about. This was a kinesthetic world where people could just sit and not do anything (good grief!) except maybe, if they were really ambitious, hold hands. This was a world in which people were quiet (heaven forbid!), and closed their eyes (scandalous!), and just *felt* the breeze on their skin. This was a cozy, comfortable world where sometimes it was enough to just "be."

In the same way, prior to our marriage, Lisa was perfectly content in her kinesthetic world. She enjoyed sports, and relished spending time with people she loved, just being together and soaking up the energy of companionship. She enjoyed taking naps and reflecting and doing things for people she cared about — and not sweating the small stuff. When we got married, her eyes were opened to another world as well. A world where little things matter, where structure and feelings work together to make poetry out of life instead of mere prose. A world where creating beauty and order is a joyful experience. We've benefitted immensely because of each other's influence; but neither of us could have gotten to such places on our own. Because of our unsanctified, *insensitive* neurology, we didn't even know God created such places. God is using our marriage to open our eyes, ears, nose, mouth, and hands to all the wonderful worlds he has created, and we are better able to praise him because of it.

Husbands and wives, we need to stop hiding out behind phrases such as "That's just not who I am" or "That isn't the way people are *supposed* to relax [or communicate, make love, wash dishes, express affection, clean the house, etc.]." We need to humble ourselves and learn to benefit from our partners' unique experiences, preferences, and styles — especially the ones that don't readily "make sense" to us. By doing this, we become more well-rounded individuals and have happier relationships.

Let's do some rewiring.

Loving in Style: Step Three

Rewiring

Now that you know *how* you and your mate are different, *why* you and your mate are different, and *what* your motivation is for challenging those differences, it's time to get to work.

As we briefly mentioned, neuroplasticity enables us to be "wired" by our experiences. It also enables us to "rewire" ourselves by participating in experiences that, to this point, you have not yet taken advantage of. As you read earlier, the last thing Greg, as a visual/auditory, busy, productive, noisy, hyperactive person, wanted to do was sit still and hold Lisa for more than 2.5 seconds. The last thing Lisa wanted to do was clean and straighten when she and Greg were stressed. But because we understood these kinds of things *would demonstrate our love* for each other in a more meaningful way than all the notes Greg could write or all the hugs Lisa could give, we forced ourselves to do them.

No doubt there are those of you who think that love should just "come naturally." Well, it does to a degree, but sometimes even the most natural of loves requires a bit of heroic effort to help it along. It was important to us that each was loved in a way that the other could really feel; so Greg *sat there* and controlled his urge to get up and adjust the crooked picture frame. He resisted the impulse to start gabbing about nothing, or making plans for what we were going to do after we were done sitting there. He sat, and he held, and you know something? He learned to really like it! Pretty soon he wanted to do more of this "sitting and being quiet thing." Next, he started noticing some kinesthetics creeping into other areas of his life. He became less compulsive, more able to tolerate petty concerns and offenses. He could relax more easily. He used to be the kind of guy who wore a jacket and tie to bed, and now he found himself (*quelle horreur!*) wearing sweaters and open-collared shirts — to work!

Similarly, Lisa pushed herself to take time with Greg to straighten up a bit before sitting down to relax. She made herself pay attention to the little things: how the table was set, how to make the home homier. She made an extra effort to dress nicely when what she really wanted to do was put on a pair of sweats or comfy, ratty pj's. And again, an amazing thing happened. She learned to enjoy it! She liked being able to contribute to making their home a warm and welcoming place. She enjoyed the confidence she gained when she caught herself in the mirror and felt put-together. She had fun putting together new outfits and paging through home decorating and gardening and cooking magazines with Greg to see new ways they could make their home a sanctuary, not just for them, but for friends and family too. It was nice to not have to be nervous about people just dropping by. It was even fun to anticipate doing something interesting together on the weekend, even if she wasn't exactly sure how she might feel when she got up that day.

This probably sounds pretty silly to you, but we're trying to make a point. In order to grow both as people and with regard to the intimacy we enjoyed as a couple, we had to stop saying, "I am not the kind of person who...." We had to humble ourselves, remind ourselves that maybe each of us really did have something to offer that the other didn't immediately understand, and then we had to try it. Not just once, but over and over until we developed an appreciation for it as well. Maybe not as great an appreciation as the other had, but an appreciation nonetheless. We had to try these new experiences until they literally wore a new groove in our brains through which our respective visual and kinesthetic senses could develop as fully as God would allow.

This is actually the definition of true respect. Ultimately, respect isn't just about being polite to each other. It is about valuing the other person enough to suspend your doubts and work to see the truth, goodness, and beauty in all the things your spouse finds true, good, and beautiful! When you truly respect people, you want to see the world though their eyes, experience it as they do, and learn from what they have to offer.

When we were first married, our old rule was, "I don't do anything that makes me uncomfortable." Now our rule is, "As long as it isn't morally offensive or objectively demeaning, we're game." This newer rule encourages us to be more well-rounded people, better lovers (in and out of bed), and more flexible, effective servants of God.

To derive similar benefits in your life, complete the following exercise with your mate.

EXERCISE AND DISCUSSION: Rewiring

PART ONE

1. What real differences in preference *come between* you and you mate? What activities and/or interests does your mate enjoy that you simply can't relate to, or couldn't care less about (in fact, you'd be happy if she never did — or asked you to do — *X*, *Y*, or *Z* again)?
2. Excluding anything that violates your personal dignity or morality, what expressions of affection has your mate asked you to give or show her, but you have resisted because it's "just not you" or "I just don't want to, that's why"?

PART TWO

1. Over the next week, what steps will you take to begin challenging your shallowness, trying to develop at least a moderate understanding (or

respect, interest, etc.) of the things that are important to your mate but, until now, have not been important to you? (Refer to your answers to question 1 of Part One for the starting point.)

2. Of all the expressions of affection that may be important to your mate but seem unimportant or "stupid" to you, which of them could you bring yourself to do or show if you were genuinely conscientious about it? Be honest. Remember, you are not going to do these things because your spouse necessarily deserves them; you are going to do these things because your Christian dignity demands that you be loving in a meaningful way — especially to your mate.

Write your answers to questions 1 and 2, and then carefully review the "Twenty-Five Ways to Make Love Stay — Every Day" list in Chapter 7. Check this list weekly — at least — to see how you are measuring up to your own goal of becoming a more loving servant to both God and your spouse.

PART THREE

The following are some suggestions for activities that demonstrate love in either a visual, auditory, or kinesthetic way. Review and discuss them with your mate. Which would your spouse like you to do more of? Which would you like her to do more of for you? What are some of your own ideas for novel visual, auditory, or kinesthetic expressions of love?

How to Increase Your Visual Love Style

If your mate has a primarily visual love style and you want to *show* your mate you love him or her, see if he or she would like any of the following.

___ Write love notes.
___ Buy or make an "I love you" card. Just because.
___ Have a glamorous, professional photo taken and give it to your mate.
___ Take lots of "ussies" to post to social media. Show the world how much fun you are together!
___ Learn to tie bows and wrap gifts decoratively and/or neatly.
___ Keep all clutter out of sight. Concentrate on making your home "look clean" even if it really isn't.
___ Leave love messages on Post-it notes and stick them all over your home and your mate's car.
___ Read books together.
___ Have a candlelit meal. Use the good china and silver. Even if the meal is just hot dogs.

___ Get a blanket. Lie out under the stars at night and count constellations or make up your own.
___ Wear lingerie or attractive pajamas to bed.
___ Make love with the lights on.
___ When making love, spend lots of time on foreplay.
___ Keep the bedroom free of laundry and clutter.
___ Look into each other's eyes and don't say anything for a whole minute.
___ Send love texts throughout the day.
___ Have lots of candles in your bedroom, bathroom, or on your mantel.
___ Go to a movie together.
___ Make a silly video of you and your beloved making snow angels, building sand castles, baking a cake, or whatever. Make popcorn and watch it later.
___ Make a sign that says "I Love You, (name)!" and hang it from the door.
___ Dress up in your best clothes for a date with your mate, even if you are just going to the mall. Don't worry about overdressing; just look good for *your partner.*
___ Buy your spouse flowers regularly. They don't have to be expensive. Anything pretty and thoughtful will do.
___ Write your own card at one of those "create-a-card" websites.
___ When you look at your mate, smile.
___ (Other) ____
____.
___ (Other) ____
____.
___ (Other) ____
____.

How to Increase Your Auditory Love Style

If your mate has a primarily auditory love style and you want to express your love more effectively, ask your spouse if he or she would like any of the following.

___ Say, "I love you" a million times a day. Say it in a genuinely loving tone.
___ Call your partner from work as often as you can just to say, "Hi."
___ Regularly compliment the things your spouse does and the way he or she looks.
___ Read aloud to each other.
___ When making love, talk about how your spouse is making you feel. Tell your beloved what you like. Make noise.

___ Make a recorded "love note." Put it in your mate's car stereo so that it automatically clicks on when he or she is driving to work.
___ Leave cute messages on your mate's voicemail.
___ Buy your spouse some CDs of his or her favorite music and favorite groups.
___ Compliment your spouse publicly. *Don't ever* criticize him or her in public.
___ *Tell* your mate often how glad you are that you married him or her. Be prepared to answer why you think this way.
___ Ask your partner's opinions. Listen respectfully. Contribute to the conversation.
___ Make a habit of remembering jokes and stories from your day. Share them with your beloved.
___ Talk about current events.
___ Whisper "sweet nothings" in your spouse's ear.
___ Give him or her a "pet name." Use a silly voice when you say it.
___ Be very careful of your tone of voice.
___ On stressful days, be available to talk but keep noise to a minimum.
___ Buy your mate a sound machine (with the sounds of waves, woods, etc.) to relax by.
___ Write a song and sing it to your spouse. Write a love letter or poem and read it to your beloved.
___ Hum your mate's favorite love songs when you are around him or her.
___ Auditory people remember every single word that comes out of your mouth. Learn to choose yours carefully.
___ (Other) ____
____.
___ (Other) ____
____.
___ (Other) ____
____.

How to Increase Kinesthetic Love Style

If your partner has a primarily kinesthetic love style and you want to demonstrate your love for him or her more effectively, do the following.
___ Hold your mate's hand.
___ Sit on the same piece of furniture with your beloved (instead of across the room).
___ Kiss and hug your spouse a million times a day.
___ Do the chores your spouse likes the least without being asked.
___ Spend a quiet evening just sitting with him or her watching the tube.

Don't talk. Give your spouse the remote control, and don't complain about what he or she picks!

___ Snuggle.

___ Give your mate massages.

___ Do things to make your spouse's burden a little lighter each day.

___ Scratch his or her back. Rub your beloved's neck.

___ Keep your hands on him or her at all times. (Please be discreet in public!)

___ When at home, or if you're *sure* no one is looking, pinch your mate's butt.

___ Nibble his or her ears.

___ Work with your mate side by side on household projects or other activities.

___ Don't talk while making love. Don't tell your beloved what you want him or her to do; just take your spouse's hands and passionately demonstrate what you like.

___ Be sexually assertive.

___ Skip foreplay once in a while and "go right to the good stuff."

___ Wear nothing to bed. Turn off the lights. Make your partner feel his or her way around.

___ Cuddle under the blankets with your spouse.

___ Give him or her a "spa day" to be alone (soak in the tub, exercise, whatever your beloved needs to recharge his or her body).

___ If your mate likes to watch or play sports, learn to love watching or playing them too.

___ Go to a bath-and-body store. Stock up on massage lotion, bubble bath, and other comfy stuff.

___ Don't pick on your mate when he or she wears that ratty and old but very comfortable whatever-it-is.

___ (Other) ____
____.

___ (Other) ____
____.

___ (Other) ____
____.

Some General Tips

1. If your partner has indicated that he or she likes something on the above lists, do it for him or her.

It doesn't matter if it makes sense to you or not. It doesn't matter whether you happen to like it or not. It doesn't even matter if you think your spouse deserves it or not. You *claim* to love her. Love means working for your mate's good. Now that you know what she thinks is good, get to work.

2. Don't *ever* criticize your mate for behaviors and preferences related to her love style. If you do, you might as well smack her in the head with a board while you are at it. Since love styles are so personal, criticizing your partner will be taken very personally. Don't criticize; instead, compliment.

3. Challenge your comfort level. If a particular request is not offensive to your dignity or your value system, then *fulfill that request.* We have to love our mates even when it makes us uncomfortable. "That's just not me" or "I'm not comfortable with such and such" isn't good enough. Stop whining. You'll never *get* comfortable sitting on the edge of the pool; you've got to stick your toe in — at least.

4. There comes a time in every couple's life when the spouses are getting as much intimacy as they are going to get from their lives unless they really shake things up. Becoming fluent in a second and third love style is a great way to do this. It stretches you to go beyond a merely "comfortable intimacy"; it also empowers you to develop an intimacy based on actualization, becoming who God created you to be. An intimacy that has this kind of power is to be envied. It is this latter form of intimacy that separates Partnership and Romantic Peer couples from Conventional/Apprenticeship couples.

Solving the "Something's Missing" Problem

Frequently a client comes to counseling, saying, "Something's missing in my marriage, but I don't know what. I know he [she] loves me. Everything just feels so dry and dull."

Very often, what's missing is a particular love style, and the person is suffering from a kind of *marital sensory deprivation*. For example, if you are a primarily kinesthetic lover, your nervous system will literally crave touch. If you are primarily a visual lover, your nervous system craves visible demonstrations of love. If you are primarily an auditory lover, your nervous system aches to hear the words "I love you" and similar messages. If you don't receive enough loving input through your most acute senses, you will *physically* feel dried up and dull when with your spouse. Why wouldn't you? The neural pathways that carry loving signals to your brain are dried up and dulled. They are literally atrophying from a lack of stimulation. If this continues over a long period of time, you may become depressed, possibly seriously so. For many individuals, love styles aren't just a cute thing they read about in some book. Love styles can actually mean the difference between mental health and mental anguish. As a husband or wife, you get from God an immense amount of power to affect the health of your mate's body, mind, and spirit. Will you love your spouse the way she *needs* to be loved, the way God wants you to love her? Your marriage. Your choice.

For his part, Christ reaches out to each one of us through every channel we leave open to him. We are called to be Christ to one another, but we can't do that unless we, too, are actively seeking to love our mates through whatever channels they leave open to us. Sometimes this causes us to be uncomfortable, and we become reluctant to give of ourselves in our marriages. But God is not too proud to put himself out for the sake of loving us. Scripture tells us that Jesus emptied himself and became a slave (Phil 2:7). How much more uncomfortable can you get? We all know this, but admittedly it's a tough act to follow.

Father Brian Cavanaugh, author of the *Sower's Seeds* series of books, tells the story of a teenager who lived in the early 1900s. This young man had an accident on his bicycle and sliced open a vein on a piece of glass. He lost a lot of blood and would have died if the family doctor hadn't been familiar with what was then a brand-new medical treatment called a "blood transfusion."

The doctor tested the other family members. The only person with a similar blood type to that of the teen was his four-year-old brother. The doctor asked the little boy if he would be willing to give blood to his brother. The four-year-old thought for a minute, swallowed hard, and nodded his head. Using a hypodermic needle, the doctor took blood out of the little boy's arm and injected it into his brother. Over and over. Finally, the procedure was complete and the injured brother was resting comfortably.

Though he had been so brave and not even flinched during the procedure, suddenly the four-year-old burst into tears. His father scooped up the boy and asked if he was hurting. "No," the child sniffled. "But my blood is gone, and I'll miss you when I'm dead."

With each vial of blood the doctor took, the little boy thought he was losing his life.

Becoming fluent in another love style sometimes requires us to give more of ourselves than we want to give. Too often, we experience the littlest pricks of love's needle and immediately panic.

"I'm losing myself!"

"This hurts!"

"How dare you ask me to do that!"

"You know that's just not *me*!"

We think and act as if we are going to die, but in reality, it's such a small thing. Jesus did the hardest part of loving. He emptied himself and all of his veins so that we wouldn't have to. He just asks us to give a few drops of our blood to our spouses when they need it.

Of course, it hurts. But if you don't do it, who will?

CHAPTER 10

The Secrets of Red-Hot Loving

(or How to Be Loving When Conflict Heats Things Up)

"Lord and Savior, you have told us that we, too, must accept crucifixion if we are to accept resurrection with you. Help us to rejoice in the sufferings that come with the fulfillment of our daily duties, seeing them as the royal road of the cross to the Resurrection."

THE WAY OF THE CROSS (PRAYER AT THE ELEVENTH STATION: "JESUS IS NAILED TO THE CROSS")

So far, in our look at what it takes to cultivate true intimacy, we've explored the willingness to be vulnerable and the need to know how to communicate your love for each other. In this chapter, we'll continue our look at the second pillar of intimacy — good communication — by exploring the secrets of "Red-Hot Loving." That is, how can we fulfill our call to love even when conflict heats things up? Needless to say, this can be very tricky; but mastering this skill is one thing every Christian must do. After all, doesn't the Lord tell us: "Love your enemies, do good to those who hate you" (Lk 6:27)? How can we resolve problems, maintain our integrity, be loving, *and* not be a doormat, all at the same time?

"Problem Solving" vs. "Fair Fighting"

First, it's important to note that there is a huge difference between what we will call "problem solving" and what some people call "fair fighting."

Just as war is the failure of diplomacy, fighting is the failure of problem solving. We don't mean to suggest that couples should experience the kind of bliss usually reserved for deodorant commercials every time they have an argument. Far from it. Problem solving can and does become heated at times. But while problem solving is mainly concerned with finding solutions, fighting — even so-called fair fighting — is mostly about getting one up on your sparring partner and winning at any cost. In reality, once you and your mate are actually fighting, it's probably way beyond fair already, and whether you box with fists or gloves, someone's still going to get hurt.

We all need to stop thinking about marital arguments as boxing matches and start thinking about them as business meetings where you and your mate solve problems as a team. Stop chuckling and think for a minute.

When a problem arises at the office, do you pout, threaten, stamp your feet, pretend it doesn't exist, put on a big crying show, call your boss evil names, or just walk out the door if you don't get your way, and then expect to have a job when you get back? Probably not. (If you do, you need more help than *this* book can give you.) Most likely, you take a breath, think before you speak, outline your position, write a couple of notes, argue back and forth a bit with coworkers, go out with your team for a coffee break, table discussions when they get too hot, and keep coming back until the problem is solved. After all, the wheels of commerce must grind smoothly, no?

Effective *marital* problem solving is very much like this. Why? Because pouting, threatening, whining, grandstanding, and/or running away doesn't solve problems at the office, and such "options" won't work at home, either. Moreover, don't try to bring up that "Let it all hang out at home" excuse, because we already dealt with that in Chapter 8. If you want a fight, take a karate class, buy an exercise dummy, or better still, call the IRS tax helpline. But if you want to be married, you are going to have to give up fighting — even fair fighting — and start to learn the very different skill of problem solving.

Massaging Your Marriage

The *Exceptional Seven Percent* have a lot to teach us about conflict management. While couples in more-or-less Conventional Marriages often leave arguments feeling beaten up, a little distant, and worn out,

Exceptional couples actually grow in intimacy *because* of their arguments. In the words of one Exceptional husband, "Our arguments are like a deep muscle massage. It hurts a little while you're going through it, but you always feel better in the end, and your relationship seems looser and more comfortable than when you started."

To master the art of marital massage, you need to know a little about what separates healthy arguing styles from unhealthy ones.

The Three Arguing Styles

There are three major arguing styles. Each of them could be healthy or unhealthy, depending upon whether or not each meets certain criteria. You'll learn about those criteria in a minute, but first I need to describe the three major arguing styles. They are: *Validating*, *Volatile*, *and Avoidant* (Gottman, 1995).

The *Validating* style is the most civilized of the three and the one that therapists — as opposed to normal people — like to promote. The Validating style is typified by such behaviors as taking turns, not getting too emotional, making sure everybody understands each other, solving one problem at a time, etc. At its best, the Validating style is a very caring and efficient way to get things done. At its worst, people can get so concerned with "validating" each other, smoothing over emotions, and playing armchair analyst, that they never solve any problems.

Alternatively, the *Volatile* arguing style is the style therapists tend to like the least. It is loud. It yells. Sometimes it even calls names, slams doors, and pounds fists (although it is *never* physically abusive — no remotely healthy arguing style ever is). At its best, it would be better to say that the Volatile style is a "passionate" style, demonstrated by a person who is *even more passionately demonstrative* of his or her positive emotions (affection, love, praise, etc.). If you will forgive the stereotype, the image that a healthy Volatile style calls to my mind is that of a few large Italian families we knew growing up, who at one moment were shaking the rafters with their yelling and screaming and the next moment were hugging, kissing, crying, and swearing eternal fealty to one another (this went for the women as well as the men).

Jesus himself had a fairly Volatile arguing style. The phrase "Get behind me, Satan!" (Mt 16:23 and Mk 8:33) was not exactly in the warm-fuzzy category. Nor, for that matter, was, "Woe to you, … hypocrites!" (Mt 23:13). And the idea for turning over the money changers' tables didn't come from a Dale Carnegie "How to Win Friends and Influence People" course either. In certain contexts, with certain people, the Volatile style can be a perfectly acceptable way of arguing. On the other hand, at its worst and decidedly *least* Christian, the Volatile style can be just plain mean.

Finally, there is the *Avoidant* style. Its name says it all. These folks really hate arguing and avoid conflict as much as possible. At its best, the Avoidant style prevents a couple from having a whole bunch of genuinely unnecessary arguments. At worst, it stops spouses from dealing with issues that really need to be addressed until they have swallowed so much anger that it nearly causes an aneurysm.

There are pluses and minuses to each arguing type. But particular style notwithstanding, the thing that makes an argument healthy or unhealthy is its ability to meet three criteria:

1. A mutually satisfying solution results from the argument.
2. There are certain lines the couple just doesn't cross, no matter how heated things get. The spouses have explicit or implicit "rules of engagement."
3. There is a 20:1 ratio of positive to negative interaction in the overall relationship and a 5:1 ratio of positive to negative interactions *during the couple's disagreements* (Gottman and Gottman, 2011)!

Why are these things necessary? The first point is self-explanatory. If an argument never reaches a solution, either the spouses just like beating up on each other or they lack the skills they need to solve their problems. Either way, it's unhealthy.

With regard to the second point, every person has hot buttons, topics, words, or actions that — if you love the person — you just won't bring up, say, or do in an argument. This is true even of Volatile couples. For example, a Volatile husband might not think twice about his Volatile wife calling him stupid. But she would never, ever say that he reminded her of his abusive, alcoholic father who abandoned the family when he was a child. Healthy Volatile couples are very savvy. Their arguments are like fireworks. That is, the families who make them are proud of them, the explosions are loud and amazing to watch; but, somehow, no one ever really gets hurt.

Finally, maintaining a ratio of 20:1 positive to negative interactions in the day-to-day relationship and a 5:1 ratio of positive to negative interactions during disagreements is critical. First of all, it builds credibility (see Chapter 8). Second, when spouses are arguing, they need to be able to remember that things were not always so unpleasant. In order to do that, a couple must have ready access to an overwhelming bank of positive experiences to draw from. This enables the couple to give each other the benefit of the doubt, so that even in the midst of an argument, they will be able to say to themselves, "Generally speaking (at least 38 times out of 40), I am absolutely sure my spouse is on my side and working for my good, and even now my mate is working really hard to show me that he [she] loves me (eight times out of ten) despite the fact we don't see eye-to-eye. Even though I might feel otherwise right now, the law of averages says he [she] is probably not out to get me. Maybe I should try a little harder to understand his [her] point."

The idea of maintaining these ratios can be a little intimidating to couples. Don't sweat it. "Positive interactions" include little things like a smile; a light, affectionate brush of the arm; an encouraging word; looking in each other's eyes, etc. If you are remotely trying to keep up with your love lists, you are probably at least in the ballpark of a 20:1 ratio in your day-to-day relationship, and the rest of this chapter will help you carry that caretaking attitude into your disputes as well.

Learning how to have arguments that meet these three criteria is the basis of healthy marital problem solving.

Christian Problem Solving

Now that you understand the three criteria for healthy arguing, we want to combine this with what our Lord teaches us about handling conflict. To understand how to solve problems in a way that is consistent with our Christian dignity, we need to meditate long and hard on the following words of Scripture (Lk 6:27-38):

> [Jesus said:] "But to you who hear I say, love your enemies, do good to those who hate you, bless those who curse you, pray for those who mistreat you. To the person who strikes you on one cheek, offer the other one as well, and from the person who takes your cloak, do not withhold even your tunic.... Do to others as you would have them do to you. For if you love those who love you, what credit is that to

> you? Even sinners love those who love them. And if you do good to those who do good to you, what credit is that to you? Even sinners do the same. If you lend money to those from whom you expect repayment, what credit [is] that to you? Even sinners lend to sinners.... But rather, love your enemies and do good.... Be merciful, just as [also] your Father is merciful.
>
> "Stop judging and you will not be judged. Stop condemning and you will not be condemned. Forgive and you will be forgiven. Give and gifts will be given to you.... For the measure with which you measure will in return be measured out to you." (NABRE)

That doesn't exactly leave a lot of wiggle room, does it? Christians are called to be loving no matter what our spouse/sparring partner throws at us. When we argue, no matter how "crazy" our mate gets, we must be able to say that we are proud of the way we conducted ourselves. Not because our mate deserves such displays of temperance, but because God demands it of us, and our Christian dignity requires us to respond to our Lord's call.

The following rules are some ways you might apply Jesus' words to your marital problem-solving sessions. Exceptional couples use many of them, and that is why their intimacy grows *because* of their arguments instead of in spite of them. You may initially be inclined to balk at some of the rules as being "not what normal people do" or simply "too hard." True enough, but to be frank, when you decided to live life as a Christian (especially a Catholic one) you gave up every chance you ever had of being anything close to normal. Christianity just isn't "normal," and neither is anyone who truly practices it. Had Adam and Eve not fallen, godliness (or righteousness) would be the most normal thing in the world. But they did, and it's not. And yet, with God's grace — and a lot of work on our part — it could be once again. In fact, if you and your mate master the skills outlined below, you might just come one step closer to becoming that new Adam and new Eve you are called to be.

THE FIFTEEN COMMANDMENTS OF RED-HOT LOVING

As you can see from the figure on the next page, the first six "commandments" are problem-solving habits that thou shalt practice regularly instead of fighting — fairly or otherwise.

I. Thou Shalt Know When to Hold 'em and Know When to Fold 'em

The *most* important thing to do before any argument is to decide whether or not it is really an argument worth having.

➤ *Red-Hot Loving Technique: Hold 'em or Fold 'em?*

Ask yourself the following questions to decide whether to hold an argument or fold it before it starts:

(a) Is the thing you are upset about a problem that is going to stop you from fulfilling your God-given dreams, goals, or values? Or is this just a petty offense to your comfort level?

- If this issue really is a challenge to your God-given dreams, goals, or values, skip to (c).
- If "you're just being petty," go to (b).

Fifteen Problem-Solving Commandments

The first six "commandments" *will help you and your mate solve problems as a team*

I. Thou Shalt Know When to Hold 'em and Know When to Fold 'em
II. Thou Shalt Begin with the End in Mind
III. Thou Shalt Get Thy Thinking Caps on Straight
IV. Thou Shalt Always Assume a Positive Intention or Need Behind Thy Spouse's Words, Actions, and Behaviors
V. Thou Shalt Use Respectful Deadlines Instead of Ultimatums or Nagging
VI. Thou Shalt Never Negotiate the "What" (But Always Negotiate the "How" and "When")

The remaining "commandments" *will help keep your problem-solving session healthy and productive even as things begin to heat up*

VII. Thou Shalt Take Thy Emotional Temperature
VIII. Thou Shalt Do Loving Things
IX. Thou Shalt Take Respectful Breaks
X. Thou Shalt Set Respectful Limits
XI. Thou Shalt Use "I" Statements Instead of "You Stink" Statements
XII. Thou Shalt Not Be Contemptuous
XIII. Thou Shalt Put It in Writing
XIV. Thou Shalt Not Go Crazy at the Same Time
XV. Thou Shalt Pray, Pray, Pray

(b) Don't give up. You might still get to argue. Even though this seems like a petty issue, ask yourself the following: Are you using this petty thing as a way to demonstrate your anger over another, more vital issue? What might that issue be?
  - If you can identify what you're really angry or upset about, go to (c).
  - If you really are just being petty, it's time to take a breath, swallow your pride, and spare yourself and your mate the unnecessary stress. This would be a good time to practice patience. Besides, every time you argue, you make a withdrawal from your emotional bank account. Spend wisely. "Offer up" your frustration for the intention of becoming a more accepting, loving, Christlike person. Hey, it worked for St. Thérèse of Lisieux, so it might work for you too.

(c) Well, it looks as if some problem solving is called for. Make some time to sit down with your mate (don't ambush him or her) and, after you read the rest of this chapter, you'll know exactly how to get your needs met every time. And, you'll be able to do it gracefully.

II. Thou Shalt Begin with the End in Mind

Would you ever start a business meeting without an agenda and expect to get anywhere? Of course not. In the same way, no couple begins an *effective* argument without a plan. Too many husbands and wives treat their marital problem-solving sessions like pointless, meandering bitch sessions. They have nothing more on their problem-solving agenda than "demonstrating my pain to you and proving what a pig you are." This is a recipe for disaster. Even if you were "successful" in proving your pain and demonstrating your mate's piggishness, then what? Can you really say that such a discussion would do anything except let off some steam? Would having such a "discussion" actually prevent the problem from ever happening again? Of course not. All you did was emotionally vomit all over each other.

Remember, your anger is God's gift to you, not anyone else. Anger is not a green light to start an argument. It is an invitation from God to take a step back and pray for the Holy Spirit to give you clarity about what, exactly, the problem is, and maybe even one or two ideas for what to do about it. Then, and only then, are you ready to start.

To have an effective argument, you must *begin with the end in mind* — that is, you must know the goal you want to achieve by initiating the discussion. Before you open your mouth and say something stupid, take a moment to pray and calm down enough to at least have some possible answers to the following questions:

1. What, exactly, am I really upset about?
2. What do I think needs to happen so that we can avoid this problem in the future?
3. What changes will I have to make to solve this problem?
4. How will I be willing to support my mate in making any changes she decides she needs to make? (That is, "What am I willing to do besides tell her what to do?")

Only when you have at least some general answers to these questions are you ready to begin an effective problem-solving session.

III. Thou Shalt Get Thy Thinking Caps on Straight

Greg's book *When Divorce Is Not an Option: How to Heal Your Marriage and Nurture Lasting Love* discusses the difference between the Solution-Focused Brain and the Misery-Making Mind-set. When we become stressed, a wash of chemicals flood our brain, engaging the fight, flight, or freeze response and shutting off our higher-level reasoning abilities. At that point, we begin to believe with all our might that our spouse is out to get us. Our threat response engaged, we become convinced that our spouse wakes up in the morning with their *Twenty-Five Ways to Make My Mate's Life a Living Hell* list fresh in mind. But this is simply not true.

In the first place, our mates love us, and because of this, under most circumstances, they would not hurt us *intentionally*. Most likely, any hurt we do encounter is the result of either a misunderstanding or their frustration at our own neglect or thickheadedness (that is, sometimes they do hurt us "on purpose," but only because we have not given them a more reasonable way to get through to us). We would do well to respond to such slights lovingly, as Christ himself does.

In the second place, even if we are questioning our mates' love for us, no living creature seeks to bring harm to itself. At their most selfish level, our spouses would not hurt us intentionally because they know or believe we would respond by hurting them in turn. When two people live in a house, if one of them isn't happy, ain't no one happy! Again, when we are emotionally wounded by our mate, chances are that the pain was inflicted unintentionally, or because he or she sincerely didn't know how else to get through to us. Think about it: Aren't those the only two reasons *you* ever cause another person pain? Why would it be any different for your spouse?

We *must* train ourselves out of thinking and responding as if our spouses were out to get us. Whenever we experience those negative thoughts such as "She is such a bitch," or "I can't believe that jerk would do that to me," or "He must not *really* love me," or anything even remotely similar, we must check ourselves, because reality tells us that *we are thinking irrationally*. What must we do instead? Pause and clarify.

➤ *Red-Hot Loving Technique: Clarify, Clarify, Clarify*

When your spouse offends you in word or in deed, give her the benefit of the doubt. (No, she doesn't deserve it, but do it anyway.) Assume *you* somehow misinterpreted her. Say, "I'm sorry. I didn't understand what you meant by that." Or "I really want to give you the benefit of the doubt. Could you please explain why you did that?" For example:

Your mate: "Sometimes you're such a jerk. You make me so angry."
You (*taking a calming breath*): "I'm not sure I understand what I could have done to make you feel that way. Could you please explain?"

Notice, nowhere in this example did you admit to, or apologize for, anything. How could you? You don't even know what she is upset about yet. In this example, you simply assume that your usually loving spouse would not say such an obnoxious thing if she didn't have a good reason for doing so. Because you love her and respect her opinion, you are going to find out what she meant by the comment instead of immediately jumping down her throat for being so blunt. You are going to make an effort to assume that she is not out to get you, but rather has some good information for you, which, unfortunately, she has expressed rather indelicately.

Responding to slights and offenses in this manner is rational, firm, loving, and efficient. It gives you a chance to find out what's really going on (instead of just mind reading what you *think* is going on). And it builds your credibility (reasonableness is always respected) and stops potentially explosive arguments from actually exploding. This technique is shored up by the next "commandment."

IV. Thou Shalt Always Assume a Positive Intention or Need Behind Thy Spouse's Words, Actions, and Behaviors

As we mentioned above, no living creature seeks to injure itself. Behind even the most idiotic and self-destructive behaviors is a positive intention or a need. Even people who attempt suicide don't think about it so much as a self-destructive act as they do a means of relieving their pain. When your mate does something you consider to be obnoxious, inconsiderate, or rude, you must operate under the assumption that he *does not actually intend to come across that way.* The ability to assume a positive intention behind another's disagreeable behavior is the essence of loving the sinner but hating the sin. There is no other way to do it. Jesus, hanging on the cross, practiced this concept. "Father, forgive them; for they do not know what they are doing" (Lk 23:34).

We are not attempting to excuse obnoxious or self-destructive behavior. Finding the positive intention behind an offensive behavior is *not an excuse* for the behavior; it is a respectful way to begin changing the behavior. For example, if you learn that the reason (intention) behind your spouse's temper is that it is the only way he knows to get you to take him seriously, you can suggest some more respectful and efficient alternatives. If you discover that the reason your spouse isn't "pulling his weight" around the house is that he is sitting up nights worrying about something, you can brainstorm solutions. Finding out the intention behind a problem behavior is the first step to changing it. It sure beats judging and alienating your spouse. Remember what Jesus has told us: "Stop judging.... For the measure with which you measure will in return be measured out to you" (Lk 6:37, 38, NABRE). Use the following technique to help your partner through an obnoxious relationship habit and toward a more respectful solution.

➤ *Red-Hot Loving Technique: Finding the Positive Intention*

Problem: Mate consistently does something that you consider to be obnoxious, thoughtless, or unloving.

What you used to say: "You are such a thoughtless pig!"
What you will do from now on:

1. Say to mate, "When you do [or say that obnoxious thing], what reaction are you hoping to get from me?"
2. After some initial confusion (he wasn't expecting the question) your mate explains how he wishes you would respond to him when he does or says *X*.
3. Say to mate, "Well, I could understand why you'd want that; but if that's what you really need, could you please do *A*, *B*, or *C* instead of what you're doing? I would like to give you what you're asking for, but I'll never be able to bring myself to doing that if you keep going about it the way you've been."

For example:

You: "When you refuse to speak to me after an argument, what reaction are you hoping to get from me?"

Mate: "I felt like you didn't care about what I had to say, so what's the sense in talking to you?"

You: (*taking a breath, not reacting, trying to understand*) "I'm still not sure I understand. What do you need from me?"

Mate: "I want you to stop trying to force your ideas down my throat and listen to me."

You: (*again not reacting*) "I never meant to give you that impression." (Aha! See? *Your* intention was misunderstood.) "It really *is* important to me that you know I care about what you have to say. Could you do me a favor?"

Mate: "What favor?"

You: "Since I don't know when I'm doing that, the next time could you just tell me, 'You're not listening'? It would sure help me change a lot faster than your pouting *after* an argument."

Mate: (*suspicious, but considering how well you've responded, he is willing to give you a chance*) "If you really think that'll work, I'm willing to try it."

You: "Great. I promise. I love you."

Mate: "I love you too."

Granted, this kind of maturity in problem solving is difficult to achieve, but it is something that must be done. You may have to repeat this several dozen times before the lesson really sinks in. Be patient and respectful. Look for the positive intention behind your spouse's offensive behavior, and invite your mate to find solutions so that it doesn't happen again.

V. Thou Shalt Use Respectful Deadlines Instead of Ultimatums or Nagging

Your well-meaning spouse doesn't want to disappoint you, so he tends to promise more than he can deliver. This leaves you disappointed and resentful. How to solve this problem?

➤ *Red-Hot Loving Technique: Don't Nag; Give Mate a Choice*

Instead of asking your spouse to do something for you and then becoming angry if he forgets or neglects your request, assume a positive intention to his oversight and have an alternative plan in mind.

What you used to do:

You: "Honey, can you do *X* for me?"
Mate: "Uh-huh." (Three weeks later, your request is still unfulfilled and you must either begin nagging, or give up on your spouse and assume that you will never get your needs met.)

What you will do from now on:

1. Set an *Arbitrary* Deadline

You: "Honey, I need to get such and such done. I'd really like your help, but I'd like to have it done by Tuesday. Can I count on you? Or should I call so-and-so to do it?"
Mate: "Huh? Oh, yeah. I'll take care of it."

Tuesday comes, and your spouse has forgotten. Don't remind him.

2. Call for Help
First thing Wednesday, call the plumber (or housekeeping service, auto mechanic, landscaper, etc.) and ask for the required service. Your

spouse will come home and find the task done. He will either be relieved or irritated. Either response is okay. If he is irritated, simply say in your most sincere, innocent voice, "I'm sorry, honey. When you didn't do it by the day you said you would, I just assumed you didn't have time. Rather than pester you, I thought I'd do you a favor and take care of it myself."

Granted, this technique may cause some short-term tension; but, let's face it, it solves the problem. It lets your mate know that: (a) you mean what you say, (b) you're not going to wait around forever for his help, and (c) it really is okay if he can't do something for you. You simply need him to be honest about it and help you figure out an alternative way to address your need.

Compare this option with the long-term tension and resentment that accompanies nagging (or whining, pestering, sulking) that not only doesn't solve the problem but also causes the heart of a marriage to rot. The fact is, if you need to have something done, the most you can rationally do is *invite* your mate to help. If he can't do it, simply come up with an alternate plan for getting it done. We've got to stop making every little thing be yet another test of our mate's devotion. Of course, your mate's help is a gift that should be given freely and generously. But like any gift, you can desire it, and you can be grateful when it is given to you, but you have no right to demand it and pout if it isn't forthcoming on your timetable.

VI. Thou Shalt Never Negotiate the "What" (But Always Negotiate the "How" and "When")

You are a spouse, not a parent. It is not your job to ever give or deny permission for your mate to do or have anything. It is merely your job to raise concerns about your mate's plans, taking care to do so supportively, and respectfully. Use the following rule: *Never negotiate the "What." Always negotiate the "How" and "When."*

In other words, you will never tell your grown-up spouse, who can think for herself, that something she wants (or needs) is stupid, silly, or cannot be had. You will simply state the conditions (the "how" and "when") under which you would be comfortable helping her get her "what."

For example:

Your mate: "Honey, I would like to start an ostrich farm."
What you used to say: "Are you nuts? Why would you want that?"
What you will say from now on: "Well, that's a really interesting idea. How could we do that and still [insert your concerns here]?"

Expressing your concerns and/or objections in this manner lets your mate know you care both about her and the big picture. Feel free to be very firm about requiring your concerns to be addressed even while supporting your mate in the pursuit of her goals. After all, for your marriage to become more intimate, you both must learn to respect each other's needs while pursuing your own dreams, goals, and values. This technique is the essence of a good partnership. In fact, mastery of this skill is one of the things that separates Partnership and Romantic Peer couples from more Conventional couples. *Don't* ever issue an edict that says your mate can't have or do something. *Do* raise your concerns and let *her* decide whether or not what she wants is worth the work it will take to get it. If she decides it's not worth it, then she has made up her own mind to drop the idea. On the other hand, if she does decide to figure out a way to address your concerns, she has you to thank for helping her fulfill her dreams, goals, and values in a way that is respectful of the entire family. Remember, never negotiate the "what." Always be willing to negotiate the "how" and the "when."

The remaining "commandments" will help keep your problem-solving sessions healthy and productive, even as things heat up.

VII. Thou Shalt Take Thy Emotional Temperature

Earlier, we mentioned that stress tends to shut down our Solutions-Focused Brain and engage our Misery-Making Mind-set. As stress increases, your body floods with stress chemicals like adrenaline and cortisol. Your rational brain begins to literally shut down (you can watch this happen on a brain scan, and your fight, flight, or freeze response becomes engaged). At that point, you can't solve anything; you can only react to it. Here is a play-by-play of how that happens.

On an emotional-temperature scale of 1 to 10 (with a 1 meaning that you are heavily sedated and a 10 meaning that you are climbing a clock tower with an AK-47 strapped to your back), no productive problem solving goes on above a 7. Here are some examples:

- At 1-3, you are perfectly calm, content, and relaxed.
- At 4-5, you and your mate are having a purposeful, respectful, and honest discussion.
- At 6, the stress-chemicals are beginning to drip into your bloodstream. You are beginning to become frustrated. You are starting to think some moderately unkind thoughts about your mate, but with some effort you are able to keep things under control and remain outwardly civil and cooperative.
- At 7, the stress chemicals are now affecting the non-verbal control centers of your brain. You are exhibiting behaviors that show your disgust (e.g., rolling your eyes, making dismissive hand gestures, shaking your head, and the like). Physiologically, your heart rate and blood pressure are beginning to increase. This is the outer limit of effective problem solving. You must either get control of yourself or take a break NOW. Beyond this point, there be dragons!
- At 8, Now the stress-chemicals are assaulting the verbal control centers of your brain. You are now officially angry, and you don't really care if anyone knows it. You aren't yelling or name calling, but you are defensive, lecturing, and blaming. If you are an avoider, you are shutting down or saying what you need to say to get your spouse to leave you alone. Either way, you aren't listening anymore. You are simply waiting for your spouse to shut up so you can say your piece in a tireless effort to convince your spouse that it really is all his/her fault after all.
- At 9, the verbal filters in your brain have completely fallen. You are now yelling, screaming, and calling names. If you are an avoider, you have probably gone mute.
- At 10, The physical filters in your brain are collapsing. This is when people storm out, throw things, slam doors, pound fists, and (in the extreme) become physically abusive.

You must learn to keep your arguments at a 7 or lower. If an argument rises to an 8 or above, there are few, if any, ways to stop it because, at that point, you are literally high on your own neurochemistry. The couple at that point is simply too far gone to think rationally. Past 7, the only choice you have is to ride the emotional roller coaster until one of you jumps off — or is pushed.

Some people tell me that they go from a 1 to a 10 in a second. This is a serious problem. It means that they probably live at a 6 but have just gotten used to it. They may struggle with poor emotional control, a long history of perceiving themselves to be victims, a high level of perfectionism, and/or a tendency to disregard others' feelings for the sake of being right. Please see Greg's book *When Divorce Is Not an Option: How to Heal Your Marriage and Nurture Lasting Love.* Counseling may also be needed.

Regardless of how quickly you ascend the emotional temperature scale, the following rules will help you maintain your problem-solving sessions within a healthy range.

VIII. Thou Shalt Do Loving Things

Scripture reminds us to be loving even in conflict (Lk 6:27-38). In fact, research shows that it is in conflict that such qualities are needed the most. Exceptional couples work hard to maintain a 5:1 ratio of positive to negative interactions even during disagreements. This isn't as hard as it might seem — as long as you practice containing your emotional temperature. When you suspect that either you or your partner is getting a little too close to a 6.5 on the emotional-temperature scale, *do something loving* to decrease the tension and increase the teamwork. Offer to get your mate a cup of coffee. Give him a smile or rub his shoulder consolingly. Actually look at her when she speaks. Thank him for hanging in there with you. Tell her you love her and appreciate her patience. Tell her that you are glad that she is your partner, both when things are easy and when things are hard. Ask if you can sit next to her, give him a hug, or hold her hand. Doing these things won't work so well once the argument has gotten past an 8 on the emotional-temperature scale (but then, why are you continuing past an 8?), but they do a great job of keeping things below a 7 if you use them early and often at the outset of a discussion.

Of course, if you view arguments as competitions in which the dirtiest fighter wins, then none of these things will make a bit of sense to you. If, however, you think of arguing as *problem solving* and your mate as your partner in solving the problem, such suggestions make all the sense in the world.

Just because you are angry with your spouse doesn't mean you can't be loving toward — that is, work for the good of — your spouse. This is the practical reality behind Judith Wallerstein's suggestion to "confront the realities of marriage while safe-guarding early romantic feelings." The more you do loving things and demonstrate affection even in conflict, the deeper your intimacy becomes, and the more your relationship will grow *because of* your arguments instead of in spite of them.

IX. Thou Shalt Take Respectful Breaks

Most people get this entirely wrong. If you or your mate is approaching a 7 on the emotional-temperature scale, take a short break. Go to the bathroom, get a drink (offer him one while you're at it), or cause some other short, polite interruption in the arguing process. At an emotional temperature of 6, all that is needed for a break to be successful is three to five minutes to pull yourselves together and remind yourselves that you are a team.

Some people think taking a break from arguing means storming out of the room and/or not speaking to one's mate for a couple of hours or days. This is not a respectful break; this is the running away that occurs at an 8 or 9 on the emotional-temperature scale. Doing loving things and taking plenty of short respectful breaks *while you are still at 4, 5, or 6* will keep you from ever getting to an 8 or 9 where you desperately feel that you must get away — *now!*

X. Thou Shalt Set Respectful Limits

Besides being able to be loving, and to be a generous servant in conflict, effective problem solving also requires you to be able to set respectful limits when you feel that the argument is getting out of control. Couples often disagree about what rules they should follow in their disagreements! One spouse is usually more comfortable with a little more heat than the other. Remember, respect requires you to be willing to see things from your spouse's point of view. If certain words or behaviors are too upsetting for your spouse, then they must be off-limits for you too, whether you think they should or not. Why? Because letting your mate know you respect him or her is Job #1 in effective problem solving, and you can't do that if you don't respect his or her boundaries. You must demonstrate that you love your spouse more than you love your agenda, and part of being loving — of working for your mate's good — means respecting his or her limits, even when those limits don't make sense to you.

➤ *Red-Hot Loving Technique: Setting Respectful Limits*

A respectful limit looks something like this:

Spouse says or does something that you consider out of bounds.

Say, "Honey, I love you, and I want to keep working on this, but I can't let you talk to me [or treat me] that way. Can you calm down and talk about this with me? Or should we take a break?"

Regardless of what your mate says, let her behavior speak her answer for her. If she makes a concentrated effort to cool down, continue the discussion. If she can't get a grip on herself, respectfully say, "Look, this is obviously getting too hot. I want to solve this, but we're not going to do it this way. I need a break. Let's pick it up at [insert specific time here]."

A respectful limit includes:

Step 1. A respectful "flag on the play" and an assessment of your mate's response.

Step 2. If the offensive behavior continues, remind your spouse that solving the problem is important to you *but*....

Step 3. If the offense still continues, a break is needed. *Period.* Insist on a break.

Step 4. As you are insisting on the break, be sure to suggest a specific time to pick things up again. This demonstrates that you really aren't trying to weasel out of the conversation altogether and makes it feel safe to take a break.

Setting limits according to the rules above is not always easy, but it sure beats storming out of the room, saying things you will regret later, "getting back" at your partner for hurting you, and other escalating behaviors that adversely affect the emotional-temperature scale. Setting limits this way teaches a couple that if finding a solution is important, then the solution must be sought while making a concerted effort to protect the dignity of all involved. This is one of the major skills required for having arguments that build intimacy instead of simply wounding the participants.

XI. Thou Shalt Use "I" Statements Instead of "You Stink" Statements

This old therapy chestnut really does work if you know why and how to use it. When conflict is heating things up, the last thing you want is someone telling you how *you* screwed up and what's wrong with *you* and what *you* need to do to fix it. Most likely, under such circumstances, you are going to start thinking, "Who the hell does he think he is?" — and you will feel obliged to direct a few rather pointed "*you*" statements at that person. Obviously, this just increases the tension. The people playing this game are more interested in determining who is at fault than discussing solutions to a problem.

Instead of diagnosing, analyzing, or blaming your partner, it is sufficient to describe your own thoughts and feelings. Perhaps the following example will help you understand the subtle but significant difference between "I" statements and "You stink" statements (or even "I think you stink" statements).

Imagine someone looking fiercely at you and saying, "You are so thoughtless, you make me angry [crazy, ready to kill, etc.]."

In response, you probably feel defensive or dismissive. You may be thinking something like, "Well, who do you think *you* are?" Or, "For heaven's sake, what's wrong *this* time?"

Now imagine that, instead, the same person looked at you and said, "I'm trying to hold it together, but I just feel so angry."

In response, you probably feel curious, or even slightly sympathetic. You may be thinking something like, "I wonder what happened?" Or "Is there anything I can do to help?"

A subtle word change made all the difference. Practice using "I" statements to describe your own insights and feelings about yourself, not your mate. Some other examples include:

- *Instead of*, "You need to get control of yourself," *say*, "I need a break."

- *Instead of,* "You are such an ass," *say,* "When you did that, I felt so hurt."
- *Instead of,* "You're nuts!" *say,* "I don't understand."

So many people think that "I" statements are silly, but when you start practicing them, you will begin to see that people respond to you more respectfully. Since you aren't threatening them, they have nothing to lose by listening to you. As the commercial used to say, "Try it. You'll like it."

XII. Thou Shalt Not Be Contemptuous

You need to avoid all contemptuous gestures, phrases, and actions in a problem-solving session because they just aren't helpful. Some examples include rolling your eyes at your partner, shaking your head in disbelief, agreeing with him so he'll shut up, walking out in anger, letting arguments become even moderately physical, stonewalling your spouse, calling him hurtful names, etc. One very well-respected longitudinal study demonstrated that a statistically significant number of couples who exhibited a high incidence of these behaviors divorced within five years. One of the worst examples of a contemptuous act is threatening divorce.

Although we're all tempted to engage in behaviors like this, anytime you feel like indulging in any of the above examples of contempt, especially threatening divorce, remember the acronym DUMM (*Don't Undermine My Marriage!*).

XIII. Thou Shalt Put It in Writing

Sometimes an issue is just too hot to talk about. Try as you might, you and your mate just can't be civil when discussing such and such. What to do?

Write to each other. Describe the problem as you see it, how that problem affects you, and your thoughts about solving the problem. Ideally, the husband and wife should both write their own letters and exchange them. Then they should respond to each other's letters by:

1. Restating what you understand your partner's biggest concerns to be.
2. Expressing your genuine empathy for those concerns. (If you're struggling, think of a concern that you are passionate about and how important it is for you to have your concerns respected).

3. Float a trial solution or two that incorporates your partner's concerns and your own. The point isn't necessarily to arrive at *the* perfect answer as much as it is to get a productive solution-focused discussion going.

Both Marriage Encounter and Retrouvaille have built their long histories and strong reputations on just such an intervention. Writing letters back and forth allows you to think about what you really need to say. When you get such a letter back from your mate, you are able to read it in small digestible pieces. You are able to react to it, calm down about it, and write a reasonable response back to your spouse. Writing problem-solving letters requires some discipline, but sometimes it is the only way to solve a problem when talking about it just doesn't work.

If you find that you are not able to even use this technique successfully, or genuinely struggle to empathize with your spouse's concerns, this is a strong sign that counseling is needed.

XIV. Thou Shalt Not Go Crazy at the Same Time

Perhaps the best advice we ever received before we got married was from an elderly husband who told us the secret of his good marriage, which was: "Don't ever go crazy at the same time."

If you've been working up a good lather all day, but your insensitive spouse (who has been "lathering up" all day as well) beats you to the screaming-lunatic role, do whatever it takes to bite your tongue, and wait your turn. In the meantime, use all the techniques you learn in this chapter to gently and lovingly help her through her tantrum. On the surface this might not seem fair, but there are some built-in benefits for you. Helping your mate get through her (nonviolent) tantrum increases your credibility and the likelihood that she will hear you out respectfully — and meet your needs more willingly — when you finally do get your turn to speak. Maintaining your cool under fire earns her respect (and makes her feel a little guilty to boot). All this translates into greater pride in yourself and, eventually, a more sympathetic audience from your mate.

Cooler heads will always prevail. Take turns going crazy.

Now, for the most important commandment.

XV. Thou Shalt Pray, Pray, Pray

Sometimes the only way through an argument is to pray your way through it. We cannot tell you the number of times we have had heated discussions that seemed impossible to solve at the time, but as soon as we prayed, sometimes together, sometimes alone, it was as if a switch clicked on and we knew exactly what we needed to do or say. This is more than pious wishful thinking. There is real power in prayer.

Your problem-solving prayer doesn't have to be fancy. Something like this will do in a pinch:

> Dear Lord,
>
> I am about to kill [insert name here]. Somehow I know that's not the right thing to do. But if you don't give me your wisdom right away, I know I'm going to do something stupid. Please, I'm desperate. Help!

That's not a particularly inspired prayer. It isn't very holy-sounding, but it is definitely sincere, and God has never failed to come to our aid when we pray it. When you get stuck and your own wisdom fails you, don't ask our Lord to change your mate; ask him to show *you* what to do. Call, and he will answer. "Knock, and the door will be opened for you" (Mt 7:7 and Lk 11:9).

While we can't study the power of grace, it is possible to examine its effects. One study found that simply instructing arguing couples to stop and think about how a neutral third person, who loved them both and desired the best for both of them, would advise them how to solve their problem, had a dramatic impact on the couple's ability to solve their problems and enjoy their marriage overall. What "third party" loves you more than God? How could reflecting on his will for the outcome of your arguments not give you the insight and grace you need to find godly solutions to your disputes?

But ... I Can't Remember All That!

You're probably asking yourself: "I'm supposed to remember all that? In an argument? Are you crazy?"

Relax. No one can apply all this at once. The best option is to choose *one* of the skills that you think would be most helpful to you, and practice it until you have mastered it. Then, if you feel the need, choose another arguing skill to master. Don't try to use them all at once — you'll only frustrate yourself. Take it one argument at a time. You've got the rest of your life to practice!

Everyone LOVEs a Shortcut

Besides this one-step-at-a-time approach, all you really need to remember to transform your fights into problem-solving sessions is to remember one word, an acronym really: LOVE.

L — *Look* for the positive intention.

O — *Omit* contemptuous phrases and actions.

V — *Verify* that what you think your spouse said is what he or she really meant to say.

E — *Encourage* each other through the conflict and toward a solution.

The Roman Missal tells us: "*Ubi caritas et amor, Deus ibi est*" ("Where there is charity and love, God is there"). Let God help you and your mate solve your problems respectfully, and as a team. Before you begin discussing a problem with your mate, talk it over with God. Ask him to show you how to present your concerns firmly, but with love and wisdom. Ask him to give you his words when addressing your mate, and when you open your mouth, make certain that only his words come out. We are supposed to be Christ to our mates. Would Christ say and do the things you say and do in an argument? I hope so. Besides this, every day pray that the Lord will make you better helpmates so that even in your arguments you will be grateful for a partner who is truly flesh of your flesh and bone of your bone.

The Selfish Person's Guide to Love

Many of you are probably like us. We know God wants us to be loving even when things get hot. But, sometimes, we just don't feel like it.

Knowing that we should do something often proves to be a less-than-effective motivator for actually doing it. Sometimes we need a more immediate, more "selfish" reason for doing the right thing. God, in his mercy, gives us not one, but two reasons to answer his call to love even when we would rather let it go to voicemail.

1. Choosing to Love Others Helps Us Feel God's Love More

When we bring a difficult situation in our marriage to the Lord, an odd thing happens. Somewhere in the middle of the prayer, a quiet voice stops us in our tracks.

"You know. Sometimes you do that to me."

"What are you talking about, Lord?" We say, irritated at having been interrupted mid-rant.

"That thing you're complaining about. Sometimes you do that to me."

It doesn't matter what it is. Invariably, God uses the circumstances of our anger to teach us about the latest way we have been putting him off, selling him short, or otherwise treating him with unintentional contempt. Moreover, where we might be tempted to whine, complain, or argue with each other to get what we want, God reminds us that he does none of these things when he wants us to change. He just loves us more persistently until we realize, "Hmm. Maybe I *should* trust him with more of my life."

When we ask God to help us in our marriage, he begins by leading us to see our own bouts of resistance to his love. When we confess them, seek his pardon, and ask for his grace, he not only fills our souls with a peace beyond words, he shows us that the answer to our current marital struggle is simple: We must love more, love better, and love now. Opening ourselves up to his love, we receive the courage to try and become the spouse he would be.

2. Choosing to Love Increases My Self-Esteem

There is a second reason we must choose to be loving even when we don't feel like it. Most of us don't like the people we become when we don't choose to love. St. John Paul II asserted that "the call to love is innate." If that's true, then to *not* love is to *not* be true to myself. When a person does things that are inconsistent with his or her nature, it has a horrible effect on that person's self-esteem. We see examples of this all day long when people tell us that they despise how they've let their marital problems turn them into "a bitch," "an abuser," "a miserable person," or worse. When we can help these people make more loving choices in their marriages (not because their spouses deserve it, but because their own dignity demands it), two remarkable things happen.

First, they begin to like themselves again. There is a great deal of satisfaction that comes from being able to say that at the end of each day, no matter how "crazy" your spouse was, you behaved in a way that you can be proud of.

Second, when the husband and wife respond to their calls to love, acting in a manner that is consistent with their personal dignity, nine times out of ten the marriage problems disappear; sometimes in a matter of weeks, sometimes overnight, but always faster than the couple would have ever dared dream was possible.

God rewards our choice to love with deeper submersion in his joy, greater self-satisfaction, and more-fulfilling relationships. The call to love is indeed the most invigorating and most important call we could ever answer. It is our beginning, our middle, and our end. To help you learn how to build intimacy because of your arguments instead of in spite of them, complete the following exercise.

EXERCISE: Becoming a Red-Hot Lover

COMMANDMENT QUIZ

Take the following quiz to see which of the skills in this chapter you need to work on the most. On a scale of 1 to 10 (1 is *completely false*, 10 is *completely true*) circle how much each of the following statements applies to you. The number of the statement corresponds with the same number "commandment" explained in this chapter (e.g., statement 1 applies to "commandment" 1, and so on).

1. My spouse and I often have arguments about "stupid things."
   COMPLETELY FALSE 1 2 3 4 5 6 7 8 9 10 COMPLETELY TRUE
2. Our arguments tend to wander all over the place and never solve anything.
   COMPLETELY FALSE 1 2 3 4 5 6 7 8 9 10 COMPLETELY TRUE

3. I frequently feel that my spouse is picking on me or is otherwise intentionally out to hurt my feelings.
   COMPLETELY FALSE 1 2 3 4 5 6 7 8 9 10 COMPLETELY TRUE

4. I have no idea why my spouse does the obnoxious things he or she does, or how to stop such behavior.
   COMPLETELY FALSE 1 2 3 4 5 6 7 8 9 10 COMPLETELY TRUE

5. I often have to pester or nag my mate to do things for me.
   COMPLETELY FALSE 1 2 3 4 5 6 7 8 9 10 COMPLETELY TRUE

6. I think my mate is controlling. *Or* my mate tells me that *I* am.
   COMPLETELY FALSE 1 2 3 4 5 6 7 8 9 10 COMPLETELY TRUE

7. Our arguments tend to get pretty hot, pretty quickly.
   COMPLETELY FALSE 1 2 3 4 5 6 7 8 9 10 COMPLETELY TRUE

8. In an argument, I often feel as if my mate is more an enemy than a partner.
   COMPLETELY FALSE 1 2 3 4 5 6 7 8 9 10 COMPLETELY TRUE

9. Our arguments usually end when one of us storms out of the room. *Or* when one of us stops talking to the other for a few hours or days.
   COMPLETELY FALSE 1 2 3 4 5 6 7 8 9 10 COMPLETELY TRUE

10. I often feel that my mate overwhelms or overpowers me in an argument.
    COMPLETELY FALSE 1 2 3 4 5 6 7 8 9 10 COMPLETELY TRUE

11. I pride myself on my insight into other people's lives, and I freely share these insights in my discussions with them.
    COMPLETELY FALSE 1 2 3 4 5 6 7 8 9 10 COMPLETELY TRUE

12. Either I or my mate or both of us tend to obviously show our disgust and/or frustration with each other in arguments (e.g., eye-rolling, threats, head-shaking, dismissive comments, etc.).
    COMPLETELY FALSE 1 2 3 4 5 6 7 8 9 10 COMPLETELY TRUE

13. My mate and I have at least one problem that is just too hot to ever talk all the way through without things getting out of control.
    COMPLETELY FALSE 1 2 3 4 5 6 7 8 9 10 COMPLETELY TRUE

14. My mate and I often try to one-up each other in arguments.
    COMPLETELY FALSE 1 2 3 4 5 6 7 8 9 10 COMPLETELY TRUE

15. I do not pray during arguments.
    COMPLETELY FALSE 1 2 3 4 5 6 7 8 9 10 COMPLETELY TRUE

Scoring

Which three statements did you indicate to be most true (i.e., circled the highest number of)? List them here.

Number ______, number ______, number ______.

Reread the problem-solving "commandments" with the corresponding numbers. For example, if you listed statements 2, 4, and 8, you will want to reread "commandments" 2, 4, and 8. Concentrate on mastering these skills first. Practice them regularly in your daily discussions and arguments with your mate and others as well. Add more skills as you master these.

EXERCISE: *Emotions-Temperature*

The goal of this exercise is to help you more closely identify your unique anger behaviors at the various points on the emotional-temperature scale, then to apply the things you've learned in this chapter to a particular argument in your marriage.

Pick a topic that you and your mate frequently argue about. Write it here:

____

____

When you are arguing about the above topic, identify the things you say or do at each point on the emotional-temperature scale. For example, "At a 6, I start 'organizing' whatever is in front of me. At a 7, I am usually rolling my eyes. At an 8, I start pacing," etc.

How do you act when you are at a:

1 ______________________________

2 ______________________________

3 ______________________________

4 ______________________________

5 ______________________________

6 ______________________________

7 ______________________________

Stop! What new behavior or skill will you use from now on to prevent yourself from going to an 8, a 9, or a 10? Write it here:

____

____

Now complete the scale to see what you are saving yourself from by interrupting your anger at a 7.

8 ____

9 ____

10 ____

Discuss and do the following.

1. What are those special "dirty tricks" or "gotcha's" you use in arguments that serve no purpose other than to irritate your mate and increase the tension?

1a. Which of the "commandments" will help you overcome this bad arguing habit? How will you remind yourself to practice this new skill? Is there anything your mate can do to support you in this change?

1b. Write a love note to your mate, apologizing for using those dirty tricks in the past. Explain how you plan to change. Be specific. Use examples from your life together.

2. How is God speaking to you through the things that irritate you about your mate? Do you do to God what you complain about your mate doing to you?

2a. How do you plan to address these shortcomings in your relationship with God? Can your mate support you in doing this? How? Or why not?

2b. Spend some time in prayer. Thank God for making use of even the difficult times in your marriage to facilitate your spiritual growth. Ask him to make you more sensitive to these insights and to your mate in the future. Meditate on the parable of the ungrateful servant (Mt 18:23-35).

For More Support

To discover even more about mastering the art of effective problem solving, we encourage you to check out Greg's book *When Divorce Is Not an Option: How to Heal Your Marriage and Nurture Lasting Love* or contact the Pastoral Solutions Institute to learn more about our Catholic telecounseling practice.

As this chapter draws to a close, we ask that you and your mate would take a moment to pray the following together:

Lord God,

You have called my mate and me to be partners — flesh of each other's flesh and bone of each other's bone. Let everything we do, especially the way we solve problems, reflect the intimate partnership to which you are calling us.

When we struggle through hardship, give us your wisdom, love, and grace, that we might speak only your words to each other and serve each other humbly and generously. Compel us to love even when it is difficult, even when we don't feel like it. For it is only through your holy love that we will conquer all.

Holy Family, pray for us.

Amen.

CHAPTER 11

"Holy Sex, Batman!"

(or Why Catholics Do It . . . Infallibly)

"Aslan," she said, ". . . there must be some mistake, . . . [the Witch] can't really mind the smell of those [magical] apples. . . . She ate one."

"Child," he replied, "that is why all the rest are now a horror to her. That is what happens to those who pluck and eat fruits at the wrong time and in the wrong way. The fruit is good, but they loathe it ever after."

C. S. Lewis, *The Magician's Nephew*

We've explored the first two pillars of intimacy in depth: a willingness to be vulnerable and good communication (understood both as effectively expressing your love for each other and problem-solving). Now it's time to reveal the third pillar, a passionate, joyful, grace-filled sexuality. (Insert record-scratching noise. "Wait, what? Passionate AND grace-filled? That can't be possible!")

Oh, but it is. And you have no idea what you've been missing out on.

Spiritual Sex: The Shocking Truth

Walk into any bookstore. Its shelves will be positively pregnant with texts on "Spiritual Sexuality." Of course, the "spirituality" they are hawking is usually some ancient Eastern thing that not even the "Easterners" practice anymore. For example, how many people do you know who actually practice *real* "Tantric Sex," in which the man is rarely, if ever, allowed to reach orgasm? If it's true that "there is a sucker born every minute," then, gentle reader, secular publishers think that sucker is you.

But does that mean there is no such thing as spiritual sex? Is there nowhere couples can turn to discover the secrets of a completely toe-curling, eye-popping, mind-blowing, *and profoundly spiritual* sexuality? Doesn't Christianity have *anything* to say about good sex? "Yeah," claim the cynics. "Christians say: 'Don't have it.' "

The cynics are wrong.

Sex, Lies, and the Church

Thanks to the popular press, most people believe that Catholicism takes a rather dim and ignorant view of sex. It seems that there are two prevailing schools of thought among Catholics. The first we call the "God Doesn't Care What I Do in My Bedroom School." This is the more Mediterranean *must-leave-morning-Mass-early-so-I-can-have-breakfast-with-my-mistress* laissez-faire relationship between faith and fornication. The thinking here is that God has more important things to do than keep score of my conquests. As long as I pray, donate to the Church, *and make sure my heart is in the right place*, everything is A-OK with the Big Guy. Needless to say, this is a very popular school, with a very impressive alumni mailing list.

The second group is the "Aunt McGillicuddy's Antique Urn School." This is the more Irish view, considered by many in America to be "the official Catholic position" on sex. This group grudgingly admits that sex is beautiful — in a somewhat grotesque Gothic sort of way — but more importantly, sex is *holy* (in the Old Testament "touch it and die" sense of holiness). Therefore sex must be approached *delicately, cautiously,* and — ideally — *infrequently,* like Aunt McGillicuddy's antique urn: "Don't ye be fussin' with that now, Missy! We only touch it if we have to dust it, and then only once a month er soo!"

You may be surprised to learn that neither of these schools of thought is Catholic. In fact, both reflect attitudes that have been *condemned by the Church as heresies* (a kind of low-church Gnosticism, and Jansenism, respectively). Because so many people — even some in the clergy — confuse these heresies with the truth of the Church, Catholicism has gotten an unjustly bad reputation for being "sexually oppressive."

The Truth Is Out There...

Greg likes to tell the following story about how he discovered the truth about Catholic sexuality while he was in, of all places, undergraduate seminary:

> I was a freshman in college planning an Easter Vigil Mass with a group of undergraduate seminarians and their spiritual director. We had gotten to the blessing of the baptismal waters when Father Cain, ever on the lookout for a teachable moment, smiled wryly and said, "Oh, that erotic rite."
>
> Eleven pairs of eighteen-year-old eyebrows shot up.
>
> Father Cain proceeded to explain that during the blessing, the Easter candle is plunged into the baptismal font as a symbol of Christ impregnating the womb of the Church, from which new children of God would be born in the coming year.
>
> His words stunned me. Until that moment I had believed the popular notion that "Catholics fear sex." Yet, here it was, a sexual act as the cornerstone of the chief Sacrament of Initiation — baptism. Clearly, not the action of an "erotophobic" faith.

The truth is, we Catholics do not fear sex — we esteem it. Sex is one of the greatest goods God has ever given us. The non-Catholic mind cannot even begin to imagine how much real Catholics honor, esteem, and *enjoy* sex. Sex to the true Catholic is like what relativity was to Einstein, the vaccination was to Pasteur, or the electric light was to Edison. We Catholics believe that great sex *belongs* to us. As far as we're concerned, everybody else is just playing children's games where sex is involved. As Greg reveals in his book *Holy Sex! The Catholic Guide to Toe-Curling, Mind-Blowing Infallible Loving*, the authentic, Catholic vision of sex is *completely* different from the world's understanding. In fact, what the world considers to be sex isn't even worthy of the name. Better to call it "eroticism" — a kind of glorified friction, in which two people rub against each other with varying degrees of pleasure, but this ultimately only alienates people from themselves and each other, fears life, makes people feel used, becomes stagnant with time, and causes pain, disease, and death.

By contrast, the Catholic vision of sex — what we like to call "holy sex" — is so powerfully spiritual, so eye-poppingly amazing, so wonderfully awe-inspiring, that most modern-day sexologists couldn't get their puny little minds around it even if they *would* put down their "sex toys" long enough to think about it. Just as Christ crucified was folly to the Gentiles of St. Paul's day, *truly Christian* sexuality is a stumbling block to the "Gentiles" of today.

Can *you* handle the truth?

The Five Powers of Holy Sex

Eroticism has no power except, perhaps, the power to alienate and destroy. By contrast, Catholics believe that holy sex has five amazing powers:

1. The Power to Make the Common Holy
2. The Power to be Sacramental and Redemptive
3. The Power to Be a Physical Sign of God's Own Love for Us.
4. The Power to Unite
5. The Power to Create

(For a comprehensive look at how you can experience each of these blessings more fully, check out *Holy Sex! A Catholic Guide to Toe-Curling, Mind-Blowing, Infallible Loving.*)

1. Holy Sex Has the Power to Make the Common Holy

"But wait," you might say "just a second ago you said people who think sex is holy are Aunt McGillicudy-ites!"

Not at all. Sex *is* holy, but not in the Old Testament "touch it and die" sense of holiness. It is holy in the sense that is given to us by the New Testament, through the Incarnation.

Before Jesus, holiness was something "out there." Holiness was something so beyond us that if we ever came in direct contact with "it," we would surely die. That's why the Israelites used to tie a rope around the high priest's waist when he entered the "Holy of Holies" once a year. This way, if he got zapped by the awesome presence of God, his assistants could drag out whatever was left of his toasted carcass for a decent burial.

But then along came Jesus, Word of God — true God, true man — the Christ. The "out there" came down here. *Elohim,* the utterly unknowable and transcendent God of the Old Testament becomes *Emmanuel,*

"God is with us." He emptied himself and became one of us, and in so doing, he shared his holiness with each and every one of us. His holiness became encoded in the spiritual DNA of all humanity, for all time. In fact, the Eastern Fathers of the Church were fond of saying that through the incredible mystery of the Incarnation, Christ "divinized our nature."

> The Word became flesh to be our model of holiness....
>
> The Word became flesh to make us "*partakers of the divine nature*" [2 Pet 1:4]: "For this is why the Word [that is, God] became man, and the Son of God became the Son of man: so that man, by entering into communion with the Word and thus receiving divine sonship, might become a son of God" [St. Irenaeus, *Adv. haeres.* 3, 19, 1: PG 7/1, 939]. "For the Son of God became man so that we might become God" [St. Athanasius, *De inc.*, 54, 3: PG 25, 192B]. "The only-begotten Son of God, wanting to make us sharers in his divinity, assumed our nature, so that he, made man, might make men gods" [St. Thomas Aquinas, *Opusc.* 57: 1-4]. (CCC 459, 460)

Talk about optimism!

So, sex is holy because it is the most profound way one "divinized nature" can give itself to another. Sex is holy because *you are holy*. God came to make it so: we are a chosen race, a royal priesthood, a holy nation, a people set apart. Once no people, now God's people! (cf. 1 Pt 2:9-10). Sexual intercourse is holy because it is the most complete way to share the gift that you are with another person. As St. John Paul II said, sex is a "self-gift." It is a sharing of all the holiness you are with all the holiness of another.

Holy sex is not glum sex, boring sex, or polite sex. It is godly sex. More than anything, "God is a lover" (*Our Sunday Visitor's Encyclopedia of Catholic Doctrine*). Even *The Imitation of Christ* refers to God as "Divine Lover." And make no mistake: God is no slouch as a lover either. Saints who experienced theophanies — powerful, personal, and very real encounters with the divine presence of God — didn't refer to the experience as "being in ecstasy" for nothing.

Bringing this concept of theophany a little closer to home, the Eucharist is overflowing with powerful imagery of God as our Divine Lover. To ransom his beloved (us, his Church), he suffered, died, and rose again by means of a love so strong that not even the gates of hell could prevail against it. Having won his prize, our salvation, he gives himself to us completely, body and blood, soul and divinity, through the Most Blessed Sacrament. We draw him close. He enters us. His flesh becomes one with our flesh. His blood courses through our veins. Fearful and eager at once to be completely vulnerable to him, we fall prey to his all-consuming love. Inspired by his passion, nourished by his loving embrace, and propelled by the power of his Holy Spirit alive within us, we enter the world again, refreshed, to do the great work of bringing new children to him through the waters of baptism.

Don't you see? For the Christian, there is nothing shameful or second-rate about holy sex. *Our Sunday Visitor's Encyclopedia of Catholic Doctrine* tells us: "God created the whole universe so that new beings might be able to share in the unimaginable riches of his being. He created human beings to share eternal bliss with him." To experience sacred sex is to experience the cataclysmic eruption of love that was the cosmological orgasm we call the "big bang," *through which* the entire universe was created and *from which* the entire universe continues to reel even today. Who wouldn't give his eyeteeth for a night like *that* with his beloved? When Christian married couples celebrate holy sex, it is just one more way they celebrate "the 'trinity' that the human being images" (*Our Sunday Visitor's Encyclopedia of Catholic Doctrine*).

2. Holy Sex Has Sacramental and Redemptive Power

The Church teaches that when married people make love, they are celebrating the Sacrament of Matrimony. But sacraments are chiefly concerned with salvation. What could sex possibly have to do with the achievement of eternal life? Well, besides participating in the mysteries we have already described, when we die, we are going to stand before the Almighty and all his glory — in all our glory (so to speak). Every blemish, wrinkle, crease, and bump of our physical and spiritual being will be — for all eternity — exposed to his penetrating gaze, completely vulnerable to his pervasive touch. Under such circumstances, for us to experience anything other than the sheer terror of hell, we must be able to stand confidently in the presence of that gaze, like Adam and Eve while they still enjoyed their original innocence. What better way for a husband and wife to prepare themselves for this awesome responsibility than to challenge whatever vulnerability or shame they may feel when they gaze on each other in their nakedness (both metaphorical and literal) and make love? It is this unique power of sexuality to challenge shame and expand vulnerability at the deepest level of our personhood that, in addition to its unitive and procreative aspects, makes lovemaking a spiritual exercise, first and foremost.

3. Holy Sex Has the Power to be a Physical Sign of God's Love for the Couple

The third power of holy sex is that it makes God's own passionate love for each of us physical, tangible, and real. Remember, in Ephesians 5:32, St. Paul tells us that marriage is a sign of Christ's union with his Bride, the Church. He calls this "a great mystery." St. Paul doesn't mean "mystery" in the sense that it is a big question mark, but in the sense that it reveals a "great and deep truth."

That sex is intended to be a physical sign of God's own passion for each lover is another sense in which sex is sacramental. Because we are bodily creatures, the sacraments always use physical stuff that appeals to our senses and actually makes present what it signifies. For instance, the water of baptism actually washes the soul clean of original sin. The words of absolution spoken in the sacrament of confession actually makes present the forgiveness of sin. The bread and wine actually become the Body and Blood of our Lord and Savior Jesus Christ, who becomes our soul's real food and real drink.

Likewise, man and woman — and more particularly, sex — are the actual stuff of the sacrament of marriage. If a couple is physically incapable of sex, they cannot complete a valid marriage in the eyes of the Church. The physical love between husband and wife makes present what it signifies; the passionate, healing, uniting, and life-giving power of God's love for each of them. Through the Sacrament of Matrimony, husband and wife are given the responsibility and the grace to be *alter Christi*, "other Christs," to each other. They are to be the physical sign of how much Christ himself loves each of them. On the days when the couple is so sad, frustrated, careworn, and depleted that they can't imagine that God loves them, the respectful, soulful, selfless lovemaking that rests at the heart of the sacrament of marriage is supposed to empower a husband and wife to look at one another and say, "My spouse loves me so well, I have no doubt of how much God loves me, because no one could love me that much on their own power — in or out of the bedroom."

The Theology of the Body tells us that sex — holy sex — manifests this sacramental sign most powerfully because of its unique capacity to make visible that which is invisible: that is, the passionate desire God has for each person and his longing to be intimately united with each person within a love that is free, faithful, fruitful, and forever. In the act of lovemaking, the couple bears witness in a way that is "a great mystery" — a profound truth— to the intimate, healing, fruitful, union that God desires with each person.

Keeping in mind that sex between a husband and wife is a sign of God's own passionate love for both of them, it is essential that husbands and wives be mindful that they are not just loving each other when they make love. Incredibly, they are the conduits through which God himself expresses his desire for passionate union with both husband and wife. This is both an amazing cause for celebration and an incredible responsibility. As much as possible, the husband and the wife must always approach each other with the same passion, joy, abandon, respect, friendship, and care with which God himself loves them. In other words, husband and wife may never use each other as things. Being representatives of God's passion to each other means that a husband and wife may never degrade each other, or demand sex as a personal right, duty, or obligation. Rather, they must always make certain that their lovemaking occurs in a larger context of mutual generosity, love, and respect.

4. Holy Sex Has the Power to Unite Two into One

Sex has the power to take two hearts and melt them into one: "And the two shall become one flesh" (Mt 19:5). We don't mean this in some schmaltzy, Hollywoody sort of way. When spouses build their marriage around helping each other fulfill their identities in Christ, intercourse becomes a celebration of the reality of that partnership. When couples make love the Christian way, it is as if they are saying, "How wonderful! We spend our days working toward the same ends, helping each other fulfill our God-given dreams, goals, and values. Look, even our bodies work for each other's good. Praise God!"

5. Holy Sex has the Power to Create Life

We treated this fairly thoroughly in Chapter 3. God is a lover, and because he is a great lover, he creates more creatures to love. So ... if you want to have great, godly sex, you've got to at least be *open* to life. It is true that the Church does not teach that couples must have as many children as their bodies can bear: during an in-flight press conference, following his 2015 visit to the Philippines, Pope Francis even stated that "some people believe that — pardon my language — in order to be good Catholics, we should be like rabbits. No."

Even so, an ongoing, prayerful, responsible openness to life is what transforms mere eroticism into holy sex: that is, sex in which the husband and wife are willing to receive everything each has to give the other, including their fertility, and which is empowered by God to take something invisible — the love of husband and wife — and make it visible, in the face of a child.

If you haven't yet experienced the true power and beauty of the creative power of holy sex but would like more information on how your intimate life can help you grow in love and spiritual maturity, then check out *Holy Sex! A Catholic Guide to Toe-Curling, Mind-Blowing, Infallible Loving* and learn more about Natural Family Planning by contacting your diocesan Family Life office. You won't be sorry. I promise. More importantly, the Church promises.

Summary of the Five Powers

Appreciating sex for all it is — holy (in the New Testament "hands on" incarnational sense), sacramental, physical sign of God's love, unitive, and procreative — allows Christian married couples to both experience the fullness of their sexuality and derive more joy from their lovemaking than couples belonging to any other group.

Recall that couples who live out their faith have more satisfying sex lives because they "pay more attention to the mystic and symbolic dimensions of ... sexuality" (Janus, 1993). God asks so little of us, and he gives so much in return. By giving our sexuality to him, he enables our enjoyment of it to increase by a hundredfold.

A Rose (or a Narnian Apple) by Any Other Name ... Stinks

"Wait a minute!" you say. "I know plenty of people who have had sex that was not holy, sacramental, unitive, or procreative, and they seemed to enjoy it well enough. Sex isn't all those things all the time. Nor does it have to be."

We see what you're getting at, but remember the important distinction we made at the start of this section. For the Christian, sex is *always* holy, sacramental, a physical sign of God's love, unitive, and procreative. If it isn't, then it isn't sex. It's eroticism. Eroticism comes in many forms (e.g., contraceptive sex, solo and mutual masturbation, fornication, adultery). But its hallmark is that it values your personal pleasure *over* either the dignity of the person, the dignity of the act, or both. Eroticism treats your God-given, holy body as a mere *thing* to be used as you please. It treats a person — even a married person — as a *thing* to be used to satisfy oneself (or a *thing to be resented* when the person refuses to be used).

Likewise, eroticism treats sex like a common street drug you take to make yourself feel better. Again, this turns lovemaking into an act that is more about meeting your own needs than about giving yourself to your mate. This very sentiment tends to breed resentment in a marriage. Further, contraceptive practices of eroticism reduce lovemaking to sexual bulimia, in which all the pleasurable sensations of sex are sought but any real spiritual or physical effect is disallowed. (Bulimia is the binge-purge eating disorder.)

Like all sin, eroticism is superficially very attractive — but it's fool's gold. It eventually causes sex to become boring. After the novelty of "eroticism as sex" wears off, those practicing this form of sex are either led to believe that "sex isn't all it's cracked up to be" (thus devaluing the gift real sex is — and fulfilling the C. S. Lewis quote that began this chapter) or they find they must practice even more extreme forms of eroticism ("swinging," S&M [sadomasochism], sex toys, pornography, etc.) to derive the same emotional benefits from their sexual drug.

The problem is that everyone thinks of eroticism as "naughty sex." But that couldn't be further from the truth. They are two completely different things. There is no more such a thing as "naughty sex" as there is a "putrid-smelling rose" or a "hot snow." A putrid-smelling rose isn't a rose — it's garbage. A "hot snow" isn't snow — it's rain (Duh!). Eroticism is to real sex what dumpster diving is to dinner at your favorite four-star restaurant. Sure, you *could* do either, but why in God's name would you want to?

Think about it. If you saw a Rockefeller, or Prince William, or a Kennedy climbing out of a dumpster, you'd be shocked! You'd say, "That poor guy. Someone should commit him." How much more shocking for a son or daughter of the Most High God to make his marriage bed a dumpster?

If Real Sex Is So Good, Why Is It So Hard?

The reason that real sex does not come easy to us, but eroticism does, is something called concupiscence (pronounced con-CUE-pih-sense). That's a technical term theologians use to describe the longing for the mud we have even after baptism washes away the stain of original sin. Perhaps a metaphor will help you understand this.

Imagine that you left your garden hose curled up every which way in the driveway. Moreover, imagine it took you a while to put it away and you ran over it with the car about a half-dozen times. (No, you're not the only one!) When you get around to it, you find that the hose cleans up well enough, and you can straighten it out just fine. But as you attempt to coil it back up, it starts fighting you. Why? It's a matter of simple physics. The hose physically "remembers" the distorted shape it was forced to lie in for weeks, and it will continue to "remember" that distorted shape (and vex you) every time you try to roll or unroll it for many years to come.

In the same way, while baptism "washes us clean" and straightens us out (so to speak), our humanity retains the "memory" of the distorted thing it was before our baptism (from the Fall to the Resurrection was a long time to lie in the driveway). Try as we might, when we aren't paying attention, we have a tendency to want to return to this distorted shape. (Our love of eroticism and our tendency to treat our bodies and the bodies of others as sex objects are two examples of this tendency.)

We Christians must learn to cooperate with God's grace so that we can overcome the natural longing our humanness has to return to its old former distorted shape. This way, when the Master wants to "use" us to water his garden, we won't vex him too much. Practicing real sex and abstaining from eroticism are two ways to overcome concupiscence, thereby continuing and furthering the process of sanctification that was begun and made possible at baptism, but whose actualization takes a lifetime.

And this brings us back to the original point. Just like the "old us" (i.e., who we were *before* our baptism in Christ) was so inferior to the "new us" (i.e., who we are now *because* of our baptism in Christ), eroticism is a sin because it is so *inferior* to "real sex." Real sex incorporates erotic elements; but, unlike *eroticism*, there is so much more to it (i.e., the five powers). Eroticism is sinful because it is copulation that is *not* holy, *not* sacramental, *not* an effective sign of God's love, *not* unitive, *nor* is it procreative. Real sex, however, is never sinful, because it is always *holy and sacramental, and signifies God's passion, and is unitive and procreative.* Married Christians are free to have real sex as much as they want, *and* they should enjoy it as much as their bodies, minds, and spirits are able.

Now that we've got that straightened out, we don't ever want to hear another person bashing Catholic sexuality. And, if *you* hear someone criticizing it, just look that person in the eye and say, "You should *be* so lucky, you poor, love-starved, ignorant neo-pagan."

Renew Your Vows

The Church teaches that every time Christian married couples make love, they are physically restating their marriage vows and recommitting themselves to all the promises they made at the altar. Every time Christian married couples make love, they promise — using a language that can only be spoken by one ensouled body to another — to love, honor, and cherish, in good times and bad, sickness and health, wealth and poverty, all the days of their life, till death do them part. So many couples look forward to their 25th anniversary when they, by popular tradition, get to stand up and renew their vows; but no married couple has to wait that long. You can renew your vows tonight — or right now — if your mate is available.

Because lovemaking is a reenactment of all the joys and promises of the wedding day, Christian married couples must *never* take their sexuality for granted. Think about it. Did you take your wedding day for granted? Did you *miss* the ceremony because you were tired or stressed out? (We were both, but it didn't stop us from coming down the aisle.) Did you say to the pastor witnessing your ceremony, "Can we move this along, Father? We've got a lot to do tomorrow, and we'd like to turn in early tonight." Of course you didn't. You had been looking forward to your wedding day your whole life and planning it since the Paleozoic Era (or did it just feel that way?). Tired as you may have been, you drew strength from your wedding day. You hung on every word, sign, and gesture. All married couples that understand the truth of Christian sexuality view their ongoing sexual relationship in the same way.

In today's work-centered (as opposed to love-centered) world, one of the fastest-growing sexual disorders is hypo-sexual desire disorder" (or HSDD). An entire library of books with titles like *The Sex-Starved Marriage* (Weiner-Davis, 2004) and *Wanting Sex Again: How to Rediscover Desire and Heal a Sexless Marriage* (Watson, 2012) has been published to help couples struggling with so-called "bed-death."

The chief cause of HSDD, according to research, is that most couples place their sex lives at the bottom of their priority list. In a world drunk on eroticism — the tendency to see sex as nothing more than recreation — couples' sex lives are, ironically, dying. They have so many other things to do that by the time they fall into bed at night, they barely have enough strength to acknowledge that there is someone else in the room, much less make love. But Christian married couples that understand their lovemaking as a restatement of their wedding vows rarely, if ever, fall prey to HSDD. How could they? Just as the first wedding ceremony is energizing and life-giving to spouses who should otherwise be dead on their feet from months of fighting with caterers, in-laws, musicians, and assorted other wedding nuisances, the Christian couple experiences each private "wedding celebration" as a beautiful, life-giving, energizing, desirable event. No matter how tired they are, the spouses can't wait to walk down the aisle to their bedroom (or any other room for that matter) and renew their vows on the altar that is their marriage bed (or sofa, or dining-room table, or stairway, etc.). To such couples, sex is not "just one more thing to do"; it is the fountain from which they drink to grow in love and celebrate the partnership that daily helps them become who God created them to be. Christian married couples with a deeply spiritual sexuality spend as much time and energy nurturing, planning, and rejoicing in the private, physical celebrations of their wedding day as they did nurturing, planning, and rejoicing in the public celebration of their first wedding day. They do this because they realize how beautiful and essential lovemaking is to the core of their married vocation.

Despite what the world might want you to believe — or what your own doubts might tell you — living this joyful, passionate, grace-filled vision of holy sex is more than pipe dream. It is the promise that God, through his Church, holds out to every couple that says "I do" at her altar. To discover how you can begin to celebrate this kind of soul-satisfying love in your marriage, follow these "five paths to sacred sex."

The Five Paths

1. Guard Each Other's Dignity

Spiritual sexuality cannot exist in the face of cruel humor, blunt criticism, name-calling, neglect (benign or malignant), abuse, or other affronts to one's personal dignity. It also cannot exist as long as either of you has any sense that you are being used by your mate as a mere object for the other's gratification.

Remember that, according to research, the only way to avoid or overcome these obstacles is for you and your mate to be *20 times* more affectionate, generous, complimentary, thoughtful, and kind, than critical, nagging, arguing, nit-picking, or contemptuous. In our personal and professional experience, that is the beginning point of holy sex. Only in this atmosphere, when husbands and wives are fierce protectors of each other's dignity, can couples safely experience the degree of vulnerability necessary for soulful sex.

If you want to achieve a spiritual sexuality, then the only answer is to love. Love more, love better, love every day. Love by doing the little things. Love in a way that is meaningful to your mate, not necessarily because your spouse deserves it, but because your Christian dignity demands it.

2. Be a Servant

There are two sets of behaviors spouses exhibit in their attempt to build a more satisfying sex life with their mates. The first is whining: "When are you going to make time for me? Do you know how long it's been since we had sex?" Or "You never take me out anywhere! How come you're not more like so-and-so?"

Any romance or sex resulting from such pathetic "interventions" will be born of guilt, will not be remarkably satisfying for anyone involved, and will be deeply resented by all concerned — probably for a very long time.

The only way to truly develop the love life you want is to become an expert at the second way: being a servant. Sex will never evolve into the mutual self-gift it is supposed to be until both you and your mate are equally skilled at serving each other charitably, generously, and joyfully outside of the bedroom. To better understand what we mean, answer the following questions:

___ Do you base your spousal roles more on compensation than on complementarity? (See the discourse on the unitive end of marriage in the section "Winning the Battle of the Sexes," in Chapter 2.)

___ Do you criticize your mate?

___ Do you discourage the pursuit of his/her dreams, goals, values, interests, or ideas?

___ Do you pout or act disgusted and/or uninterested when accompanying your mate to some place or function that is meaningful to her but not to you (e.g., shopping, in-laws, corporate functions, church, hobbies, etc.)?

___ Do you use your marriage as an institution of convenience, saying, "Now that I'm married I never have to do *X* again; that's what my spouse is for"?

___ Do you refuse or resist loving your mate in a way that is meaningful to her?

___ Do you consistently give more time and energy to work, social roles, hobbies, or other interests than you do your marriage and family?

___ Do you refuse or resist doing things your mate asks you to do, not because those things violate your morals, but because you "just don't feel like it"?

___ Do you tend to do loving things for your mate and then become resentful if you are not rewarded in kind?

___ Do you or your mate leave arguments feeling beaten up?

___ Do your arguments end with no mutually satisfactory solution in sight?

___ Do you tend to do loving things only when you want something from your mate?

___ Do you tend to be *more* loving than usual when you want something from your mate?

If you answered "yes" to any of these, you now know the reason for your less-than-awe-inspiring sex life. The solution to this problem is not by whining for your mate to change. It is by becoming a better servant yourself. How? By supporting your mate and being actively interested and involved in the things that are important to her. By loving your mate in a way that is meaningful to her. By being a loving, respectful problem solver. By being able to identify all the million or so tasks involved in making your home, family, and social lives run smoothly, knowing how to do each one of those tasks relatively well, frequently doing any or all of them without being asked, and by doing them cheerfully and without expecting any repayment for having done them.

This is a tall order, but it can be done. The *Exceptional Seven Percent* do it most days. You can too. Cheerful, generous, mutual service is the *only* way to achieve a truly satisfying marital sex life. Why? Because a vital sexuality is the *logical, loving response* to joyfully given marital service. Nothing else works. The less joyful service there is in a marriage, the less satisfying that couple's sex life will be (or the more dependent upon eroticism the spouses will become). The more joyful service, the more satisfying the sex life. This is true every time. If you want better sex, don't whine. Serve.

3. Approach Lovemaking Joyfully

Catholics are encouraged to celebrate the sacraments frequently and joyfully. Marriage is one sacrament we hope you will celebrate in such a way. Sex is not about "marital duty." It is not a chore, an extra, or even a "nice thing" to do when you have the energy. If you are married, and you think of your sexual relationship in *any* of these ways, then your sexual mind-set is decidedly out of order. If you are married, then lovemaking is the foundation of your vocation. It is the joyful renewal of your wedding vows. It is your loving response to God's first commandment to all of humanity. (According to the Book of Genesis, when God said, "Go forth and multiply," he wasn't giving math homework.)

A second major obstacle to a joyful sexuality (besides a lack of service) is that too many Christian husbands and wives confuse modesty with shame and awkwardness about their sexuality. While "modesty protects the intimate center of the person" (CCC 2521) and prevents us from being reduced to sexual objects, modesty also "authorizes sexual display where genital fulfillment is allowed, that is, in marriage" (*Our Sunday Visitor's Encyclopedia of Catholic Doctrine*).

Shame, on the other hand, causes us to hold back just where we are called to be generous. It prevents sex from being the "self-gift" that St.

John Paul II says it ought to be. For the Christian, one of the greatest sexual temptations is to dress shame in spiritual garb and use it as a way to avoid confronting our fears of intimacy, while allowing ourselves to feel self-righteous at the same time. (This is the essence of the "Aunt McGillicuddy's Antique Urn School.") Be this as it may, we must never forget that our sexual and bodily shame is a "direct descendent" of the shame Adam and Eve encountered after the Fall, standing before God in their nakedness. If we are ashamed of being exposed and vulnerable before our spouses, how will we ever tolerate an eternity standing exposed and vulnerable before our Divine Lover? Challenge your fears of vulnerability, of "losing control," and you will find amazing joy in the arms of both your earthly beloved and your Heavenly One.

4. Maintain a Responsible Openness to Life

"True, not every upright genital act will originate a new life; neither need one intend that it will," according to Rev. Ronald Lawler, O.F.M. Cap., Joseph Boyle, Jr., and William E. May, authors of Our Sunday Visitor's *Catholic Sexual Ethics: A Summary, Explanation, & Defense (Second Edition)*. "There are other worthy goals of sexual activity also. But the life-giving aspect of sexual activity must always be guarded and respected, or sex is trivialized and made inhuman."

As we explained in Chapter 3, Christian spiritual sexuality represents the attempt to balance two equally important sets of virtues, virtues that are contained within the phrase "responsible parenthood." On the one hand, being open to life enables us to increase our trust in God's providence, helps us identify with the Fatherhood of God, and inspires us to greater generosity, sacrifice, and love, among other things. On the other hand, practicing this openness *responsibly* causes us to exercise such virtues as self-mastery, discernment, chastity, prudence, and temperance, to name a few. For a married couple's sexuality to be truly sacred, the partners can't opt out of practicing one set of virtues or the other; they have to learn to balance both. The best — and only — way to do this is to practice Natural Family Planning (NFP). NFP is the key to having a true, grown-up, joyful, and spiritual sex life. If you don't currently use it, we encourage you to at least learn more about it. Experience for yourself the richness it will afford your spiritual and sexual life.

5. Approach Each Other in Prayer

Some people turn up their noses at the notion of joining prayer and lovemaking, as if prayer serves the same function as reciting baseball statistics. But prayer is absolutely essential to a spiritual sexuality. Greg's prayer goes something like this:

> Lord, let me kiss her with your lips, love her with your gentle hands, consume her with your undying passion, so that I may show her how precious and beautiful she is to you.

Lisa has a similar prayer as well. Every day ask God to make you a better lover to your mate, both in and out of bed. Read the Song of Songs in the Old Testament. It is a beautiful allegory of God's love for his people, and also a model of ideal human love. Meditate on it. Ask God to help you become the lover (literally and figuratively) he would be to your spouse. Develop your own "lover's prayer" and see if the Lord doesn't help you become a more respectful, passionate, generous, loving, and attentive partner.

Another Reason For Makin' Whoopee!

Through her wise teaching, the Church shows us that God *deeply desires* Christian husbands and wives to have a loving, rewarding, fulfilling, and passionate sexual relationship. *It is extremely important to God that you have a satisfying sex life with your spouse.* To those who confuse eroticism with real sex, this statement will be absurdly silly at best or revoltingly scandalous at worst. What can we say? The truth is the truth. It cannot be changed just because it makes some people uncomfortable. St. John Chrysostom had this to say to members of his congregation who were scandalized by his homilies on the goodness of marital intimacy:

> I know that many are ashamed at what is said, and the cause of this is what I spoke of, your own lasciviousness, and unchasteness. Why are you ashamed of the honorable, why do you blush at the undefiled? This is for heretics, this is for such as introduce harlots there. For this cause I am desirous of having it thoroughly purified, so as to bring it back again to its proper nobleness.... (*Homilies on Galatians, Ephesians, Philippians, Colossians, Thessalonians, Timothy, Titus, and*

Philemon: Nicene and Post-Nicene Fathers of the Christian Church, Vol. XIII, translated by Philip Schaff)

God cares about your sexuality because it manifests beautifully a spiritual reality. Sacred lovemaking challenges shame and expands healthy vulnerability. It draws a couple closer together, renews the spouses' vows, celebrates and invigorates their partnership, brings new life into the world, and *helps the spouses experience, in a physical way, how passionately they are loved by God.*

Physical spirituality is *very* important to the Catholic. It is why we have sacraments (which are physical manifestations of a spiritual reality). Take confession (the Sacrament of Penance and Reconciliation), for example. *Of course*, we could confess our sins directly to God. In fact, we do! But the Church understands that people are not just souls — they are bodies too. Just as our spirits need forgiveness, so our *bodies* need to go through the *experience of being forgiven* in order for the process to be complete. After all, it wasn't just Adam's and Eve's souls that experienced the Fall; their bodies' integrity was compromised as well. That's why we die.

We confess our sins to God all the time, but we never *know* his forgiveness as we know it when, *through the senses God gave our bodies*, we *hear* the priest say, "I absolve you from your sins in the name of the Father, and of the Son, and of the Holy Spirit" (CCC 1449).

Through the sacraments of the Catholic Church, God reveals his love to our souls *and* bodies. This strikes many people, especially Protestants, as odd. "Why would God want to minister to our bodies?" they ask. These people would do well to remember that Christians believe in spiritual *and* bodily resurrection (1 Cor 15:12-20 and the Apostles' Creed). If our bodies are to be raised like Christ, God has to get our souls *and* bodies ready to spend eternity with him. He couldn't very well put new wine into old wineskins (glorified souls into unglorified bodies), could he? Being able to *physically* experience the spiritual realities of God's love is extremely important to our sanctification and, ultimately, to our salvation. Seen in this light, certainly you can understand why your sex life is important to God. It is the celebration of the sacrament through which he most powerfully and *physically* (as well as spiritually) reveals his love to us. In marriage, good sex is both a fruit and mechanism of sanctifying grace.

And Another Thing ...

Christians have let pagans take sex from us, poison it for us, and turn it into eroticism. This is tragic, because God gave sex to the godly, to our first parents, who dwelt in original innocence, and enjoyed their nakedness, vulnerability, and sexuality under the loving eyes of the Lord who made them. Remember, every married couple is called to be a new Adam and a new Eve. The completeness of your sanctification hinges upon your willingness to let God prepare both your soul *and* your body to spend eternity in heaven with him. It is time for Christian married couples to reclaim what is theirs; to redeem sex and celebrate it in joy and responsibility.

Well, what are you waiting for?

CHAPTER 12

What If My Spouse Doesn't Share My Spiritual Life?

"Do you think that I have come to bring peace to the earth? No, I tell you, but rather division! From now on, five in one household will be divided, three against two and two against three...."

LUKE 12:51-52

Throughout this book, we have referred to sacramental marriage as a partnership in Christian destiny intended to help you and your mate become everything God created you to be in this life and help each other get to heaven in the next. Some of you may be despairing at this thought, especially if your spouse does not share your love for Christ or the Church.

Don't despair. God is providing you with an admittedly painful, yet wonderfully powerful, opportunity for spiritual and personal growth by being witness to your mate. This chapter will address some of the concerns you may have as you struggle to remain faithful to both God's call in your life and the partner he has given you.

A Painful Problem

Margeaux was referred to the Pastoral Solutions Institute by her pastor. It seems that in the last year she had experienced a "reversion" to Catholicism. The problem was that her husband did not share her enthusiasm for "all that superstition," as he called it, and it was tearing her apart.

Tearfully, she said, "I always wanted the kind of marriage where you could share everything. Now, I finally find something that really matters to me and I can't share it. It's killing me, and I don't know what to do...."

In our work with couples, one of the more painful problems that arises is when one spouse has a conversion experience and the other spouse does not. It is especially difficult to watch something that should be the source of a couple's unity and strength become a club the husband and wife use on each other. While it could easily be the husband who discovers his spirituality first, most often the wife beats him to it. It has been this way since the earliest days of the Church. For example, in the year A.D. 370, the Roman Emperor Valentinian, responding to complaints from his pagan male constituents, wrote a letter to Pope Damasus I demanding that Christians stop converting pagan women. As you can see, this problem isn't something new.

Still, "post-conversion" life is rarely easy on a marriage. How do you grow in your faith in a less-than-supportive environment? And how do you share your faith with those closest to you without being obnoxious (an easy trap to fall into)? The following tips will help you find your feet.

1. It's Not Your Job to Convert Your Spouse

You may be your mate's best hope for arriving properly attired at the heavenly banquet, but anything you can do is secondary to the saving work of Jesus Christ and your mate's own free will. You cannot convert your mate. Nobody ever had a *true* conversion to the faith because of someone else's begging, pleading, scolding, or cajoling. The only thing that makes conversions is a personal encounter with Jesus Christ. The temptation to be your mate's savior is a strong one, but there are three potent reasons for avoiding this trap.

The first reason is that the more your spouse suspects you are out to convert him (it is usually a "him"; but even if this is not true of your situation, the information still applies), the more he will dig in his heels. Nobody likes to be told what to do, especially when it is something as apparently "useless" and "Neanderthal" as going to church. The more you push, the more your mate will push back, and the more everyone loses.

Second, the more your mate resists you, the more you will come to resent him for his resistance. This is especially true if your marriage was not always the most joyful union on the block even before your conversion. As one person we know put it — only half-jokingly, of course — "I always thought my husband was an idiot, but now he's literally a *damned* idiot to boot!" Obviously, this is a poor example of the loving servanthood Jesus is commanding us to share with our mates.

Finally, and perhaps most importantly, the more you argue with your mate about the faith, the less credibility you will have. An example from Margeaux's experience may help clarify this point. Her husband once said to her, "Ever since you've been going to church, all you've been doing is bitching at me. I don't want to go because I don't want to become the kind of person you are now." Margeaux thought her husband was just being cruel; but, sad to say, there was probably a bit of truth in the comment. Often, people who are new to the faith (or have returned to it) don't just become Christians — they become Crusaders as well. And if you know anything about history, the Crusades did not go remarkably well for the Church. For the sake of your marriage, and your sanity, take a lesson from Church history. Get out of the Crusader business.

2. Make Your Spouse an Offer He Can't Refuse

But if you are not to be a Crusader, what are you to be? Simply put, you must be Christ. You must be a cheerful servant, an attentive friend, and a generous lover. Your Christianity must turn you into the spouse your mate always needed you to be but you couldn't become because you previously lacked the grace to do the job.

Remember, only an encounter with Christ will convert your mate. You must be the chief facilitator of that encounter. If your mate won't come to Christ, then by God (and we mean that literally) you're going to have to bring Christ to him — by being Christ for him. Every day make up your mind to serve your mate as Christ would serve him, love your mate as well as Christ would love him, and upbuild your mate as Christ would upbuild him. Stop criticizing him about every little thing. Look for ways to upbuild him, emphasize his competencies, compliment his simple thoughtfulness, and in general, catch him "being good." Also, make a list of all the things your mate ever asked you to do for him, and add to that list all the things you have ever wanted your mate to do for you. Every day do as many of these things for your mate as you can, not because he deserves it, not because you necessarily feel like it, but because your Christian dignity demands it.

Being a true Christian spouse means taking all that Crusader energy and channeling it into becoming a better servant and lover to your mate. Every time you would normally criticize your mate about something, or ask him to go to church with you, or pray with you, stop yourself and instead give him a kiss, or say, "I love you," or buy him a small token of your affection, or write him a love note, or make love to him, or cheerfully do that chore he hates to do — even if it takes you twice as long and means learning an entirely new skill. If you do this with the right spirit, your mate is eventually going to ask you why you're being so nice to him. When he does, simply say, "Because every time I pray, I find out how much more God loves you, and I have to love you that much more too. I'm just sorry it took me so long to figure out how special you really are." Then give him a kiss and walk away.

This is true evangelism. Every day your spouse will see the face of Christ shining through you, and he will be knocked off his "horse" by love, just as St. Paul was.

3. Pray

Being Christ to your mate is hard work, and you will be unable to do it without some powerful help from the Holy Spirit. God will give you his grace, but you must ask for it every second of every day. When you pray, first ask that the Lord would change you. Ask that you would learn to be a powerful witness to your mate, inviting him to Christ without even having to say a word. Second, pray that the Lord would use others and the circumstances of your mate's life to reveal himself in an unmistakable way. Finally, and only after you have first prayed for these other graces, pray for your mate. Pray that the Lord would help him be open to all the love that is being poured out.

It is absolutely essential that you pray in this order to avoid the fate of one woman we knew who — sad to say — was one of the coldest, most shrewish, and most spiteful people we have ever met. After telling us — in front of her husband — what an incompetent, unsupportive, thickheaded man she was married to, she finished her litany with, "I have prayed so many novenas and said so many Rosaries for my husband's conversion! I just don't know what else to do. I guess God is just going to have to zap him one day."

Get help when you pray. Ask St. Monica to intercede for you. She's an expert at converting pagan family members. Though it took fifteen years, her son St. Augustine eventually left a life of debauchery to become a great saint and Doctor of the Church.

Likewise, meditate on the following Scriptures: 1 Corinthians 7:13-14, 1 Peter 3:1-2, and Luke 6:27-49 (especially verse 41). One final caution: If you seek others for prayer support, limit yourself to partners of the same gender. I have seen too many affairs start "accidentally" by having too many clandestine meetings with a sympathetic prayer partner of the opposite sex. Trust me, these relationships are never God's will for your life and marriage.

The key to converting your mate is as simple and as hard as loving him as Christ would love him. Ask God for the courage to be the spouse you are called to be. Preach the Gospel with your life. Be the loving, joyful, passionate spouse you only dreamed of being before you encountered God's grace.

CHAPTER 13

The Little Way of Marriage

An Invitation

It is, no doubt, impossible to prevent his praying for … [her], but we have means of rendering the prayers innocuous. Make sure that they are always very "spiritual," that he is always concerned with the state of her soul and never with her rheumatism….

C. S. Lewis, the demon Screwtape to his nephew, Wormwood, in *The Screwtape Letters*

Despite all the spiritual opportunities afforded us as Catholics, many of us experience prayer as something we do. Prayer, Mass, the sacraments, Eucharistic Adoration, and the many other ways of praying and worshiping as a Catholic Christian tend to be things we are actively involved in and draw comfort from so that we can go out into "the world" refreshed and prepared to take our lumps.

But marriage, as both a sacrament and your sacred vocation, enables prayer to become less something you *do* and more something you *are*. The entire point of marriage is to teach you how to use your *life* as a prayer; how to find God, and spiritual growth, in the "little things," the daily activities, sacrifices, and challenges that are part and parcel of your vocation of husband and father, wife and mother.

Perhaps your work schedule and family commitments prevent you from praying as much as you might like. Maybe you can't get to daily

Mass as often as you want to, or don't have time for adoration or other devotions that were important to you before you were married.

Many people we talk to feel guilty about this, but perhaps it would be help to realize that, in the sacrament of marriage, God has given us a million ways to pray that are hidden in plain sight. As husband and wife, we may reap even greater spiritual benefits by getting off the couch and playing with our children when we are tired, finding more ways to be a better servant to our spouse, and working to trust God's providence in our family's finances. Working each day to become a better husband and father, or wife and mother, can be the most important spiritual exercise we can undertake.

As an example of what we mean, when we were preparing our oldest son for his First Communion, we were reviewing the Corporal Works of Mercy: *give drink to the thirsty, give food to the hungry, clothe the naked, shelter the homeless*, and so on. After hearing the list, he looked up at his mom and said, "You do those things all the time. They should call them the Corporal Works of Mommy!"

We tend to undervalue the tremendous work God can do on our hearts if we dedicate the daily mundane tasks of married life to him and perform them with a desire to glorify him. Through it all, we can learn to identify more closely with the steadfast, providential love of God the Father, the sacrificial love of Jesus Christ, and the transformative love of the Holy Spirit. While it is incredibly important to visit God in church, gathered together with our brothers and sisters in worship of our heavenly Father, perhaps we can learn to appreciate the presence of God in our "domestic church": our family as well. The things that used to be the main dishes in our spiritual banquet when we were single (the Rosary, Perpetual Eucharistic Adoration, longer periods of meditation, retreats, and the like) may, at least for a time, have to become wonderful side dishes we take advantage of as we can. The meat of our spiritual life as husbands and wives is learning to use the nourishment we receive through the Eucharist to live out more fully the sacrament of our marriage. Every day we are called to work to give more of ourselves to our spouse and children in an attempt to grow in our understanding of God's selfless giving to each of us.

When possible, of course, it is absolutely desirable to carve out time for formal prayer, worship, and adoration. But if this comes at the expense of time we spend serving our spouse and children, whom God has called us to spend our days loving and serving, then perhaps we would do better, as St. Frances of Rome once said, "to quit our devotions to God at the altar and find him again in our household affairs."

If we do not make ourselves abundantly present to our children, how will they ever learn to appreciate the eternal presence of their heavenly Father? How will our spouse learn how special he or she is to God unless we make the daily effort to cherish our mate in the small but still incredibly important ways we can? Husbands and wives are, after all, the gifts God gave to each other. Perhaps we should make it our prayer that the Lord would never look at our marriages and say, "Some gifts *they* turned out to be."

Again, taking time away from my family for "formal prayer and meditation" is important and helpful if it can be done thoughtfully, with the needs of those we love in mind; but if we aren't careful, it can be easy to become like the Levite in the parable of the Good Samaritan, who was in such a hurry (probably to get to the synagogue) that he couldn't serve the man God placed in his path. For many married couples — especially those with growing, noisy, busy families — it can, at times be too easy to use church commitments, parish service, and more formal devotions as an escape, an opportunity to avoid the sacrificial love and service God requires us to give to our family.

Of course, we should always do what we can to return to more meditative prayer times and other devotions — and as our children mature, we can share these jewels with them. But until that time, it is important to learn to appreciate God's presence in the service we give to our family and to recognize the rich spiritual treasures that are hidden in plain sight, right there on the altar of our domestic church, where we, through the common priesthood of our baptism, consecrate our little corner of the world to Christ. Every day we can continue to offer up our frustrations and setbacks. We can give praise for the joyful moments of laughter and grace. We can listen for God's voice speaking to us through that child's cry, that unwashed dish, the messy family room, and the warmth of our spouse's embrace when we collapse into bed at the end of the day and — in happy defiance of the exhaustion — join together to celebrate the life we are building together with God's help.

God gave us our unique and unrepeatable spouse and children because loving and serving them is our best hope for becoming the people God wants us to be. They are our best hope for arriving, properly attired, at the heavenly banquet. We must hope to be theirs as well. And yet, we still have so much further to go before we can be the spouse our mate needs us to be, the spouse Christ would be. So let this be our prayer. Today, and every day for the foreseeable future, may God help us give more of ourselves — and his love — to the family he has entrusted to our care. May God help us give more of ourselves to our spouse and children so that we might better understand all the ways God makes himself a gift to us.

More Than Techniques: A Spirituality of Marriage

If all you got from this book was a handful of techniques you can use to make your life and marriage a little more easygoing, then we have failed you. More than presenting interesting information, practical techniques, or anything else, our real purpose all along has been to suggest how you might turn your everyday married life into a prayer, because whether you realize it or not, everything you do in the context of your sacramental marriage — from your work and other roles, to the little pecks on the cheek you give each other, to your getting off the couch when you're tired in order to play with or serve your family, to the arguments you have, to your lovemaking — *is prayer.* Marriage is perhaps the most beautiful prayer in the world. It is a prayer that was written by God at the beginning of time — "the primordial sacrament," in the words of St. John Paul the Great. It is the prayer our first parents spoke with their mouths, souls, minds, and bodies in order to most completely glorify God and actively participate in his creating and sustaining love. Marriage is a powerful reality. It is like the "pearl of great price" (see Mt 13:45-46, NABRE) buried in your own backyard. It is one of the most profound ways God is reaching out to you, calling you to him, deepening your appreciation of his love for you, and preparing you to spend eternity in his holy presence. Please, don't ever take it for granted.

Parable of the Generous Man

There was once a kind and generous man. He attended church faithfully. He ran a successful business. He gave generously both to charitable causes and to the poor and homeless he met on the street.

His pastor praised him because he always took the hours no one else wanted at Perpetual Eucharistic Adoration. His community praised him for being such a wonderful civic leader. He was a great witness because everywhere he went he brought his rosary. When he would have a few minutes, people would see him quietly praying in the back corner of the room. He felt full of the Spirit. He defended the faith. His wife and children admired him. Everyone said he was a good man.

One day, this generous man died. He was surrounded by a beautiful light and warmth, but also filled with a strange sadness. Standing before him was Christ — a vision more awesome, tender, and fierce than the man could have ever imagined. But when the Lord looked into the man's eyes, a tear rolled down Christ's cheek.

"Why are you crying, Lord?" asked the man.

The Lord said nothing, but pointed to something the man hadn't noticed before. There was a small group of people huddled in the darkness behind him. The man walked over to the people, and then stopped. He couldn't go any further. The sight sickened him. There, at his feet, were the emaciated forms of his wife and children. They were alive, but barely. Terrified, the man cried out, "Lord, what happened to them?"

"You are looking at the souls of your wife and children. They are starving for me. You did not show them how to find me while you were with them. Now, they don't know where to look."

"But, Lord," stammered the man, "how can you say that I didn't show them how to find you? I led scores of people to you. I donated money. I served my community. I gave my time and effort to the Church and a hundred other worthy causes."

The Lord just shook his head, saying, "Oh, child. Do you still not understand? Your family admired you, but they never knew you well enough to love you, much less see me in you. You gave to others so that you could avoid giving to the ones I gave to you."

Whatever your prayer life is like, whatever spiritual exercises you are currently practicing, we invite you to pray your marriage as well. Every time you give more love than you think your spouse deserves, you are being Christ to your mate, and you have a better chance of understanding what it is like for Christ to love you. Every time you make yourself vulnerable by giving more to your family than to your own comfort, work schedule, and other "priorities," you join your suffering to the Lord's. Every time you serve the members of your family, you show them the generous face of God. Every time you do something to make your spouse fall even more in love with you, you demonstrate God's own passion for your beloved; and every time you bring a smile to your partner's face, you are giving your beloved one more reason to praise the God who gave you to each other.

Saints are transparent. Their love and service always lead their admirers to God, who shines through them. Be a saint to your spouse and children. Let the Lord shine through the loving, generous service you give — joyfully — every day. Pray your marriage, and let God's grace transform you and your loved ones through that living prayer.

May the Lord bless us and keep us.
May the Lord make his face to shine upon us.
May the Lord grant us pardon and peace,
All the days of our lives.
Amen.

Traditional blessing based on Numbers 6:24-26

APPENDIX 1

Marriage: An Owner's Manual

Cars, boats, homes, gardens — all have them. In fact, just about every valuable thing has them. Why don't marriages have maintenance schedules? Most people know how often they have to change their oil, till their garden, rotate their tires, replace their furnace filters, etc. But do you know how often to oil your marriage? This "owner's manual," dear reader, is offered as a guide for the regular care and feeding of your marriage. Simply follow the schedule below for a well-maintained relationship.

Regular Marriage Maintenance

Do the following as indicated.

Every Day...

- Pray. Ask God to help you become the lover he would be to your spouse.
- Ask yourself, "What can I do to make my spouse's life a little easier today?" Then do it.
- Find small ways to demonstrate affection. Catch your mate being good. Be generous with kisses, hugs, compliments, and calls from the office.
- Find small ways to practice rituals of connection. Take at least a few minutes each day to make time to work, play, talk, and pray together.

Every Week . . .

- Attend Mass together at least once a week. Make sure your kids come with you.
- In addition to your daily rituals of connection, make time for somewhat more lengthy (an hour or more) opportunities to connect around work, play, talk, and prayer once a week. Do a household project. Go to Mass, or an additional devotion, together. Go on a regular date of some sort, even if that means making time to do something fun at home after the kids go to bed.
- Review your "Twenty-Five Ways to Make Love Stay — Every Day" list. Are you keeping up? What new loving actions should you add?

Every Month . . .

- Assuming your children are developmentally ready or physically healthy enough, leave them at home so that the two of you can go out as a couple at least once per month. If you can't go out, make time for "couple time" at home. Set the kids up with a video, or even have the sitter come to your house while you and your mate enjoy a piece of pie and grown-up conversation over candlelight in the dining room.

Every Three Months . . .

- Review problem solving in Chapter 10. How are you doing? What skills do you still need to develop and/or practice? How, specifically, will you develop those skills?

Every Six Months . . .

- Ask your mate how you could be an even better spouse to her. Receive any criticism graciously, give criticism kindly, and act on the discussion.
- Read a book together on some aspect of marriage and/or family life.

Once a Year . . .

- Go on a retreat together. Do a Marriage Encounter weekend or some other marriage-enrichment program. Or spend a whole day in a favorite park or other place with your spouse and children, playing, praying, and discerning what God has in store for you and your family in the coming year.

Following these recommendations will help you assure the continued growth and health of your marriage.

Emergency Maintenance

Sometimes certain problems occur that require your taking your marriage into the "repair shop." Yes, it can be expensive; and yes, it is always a pain. But keeping a marriage in good working order sometimes requires some professional assistance. How can you tell when it's time for a checkup?

Counseling is automatically indicated if...

- Your arguments are becoming physical.
- Many of your arguments occur while one or the other of you is drunk or high. Or many of your arguments are over drinking and/or drug use.
- You are fantasizing about having an affair.
- You are spending more and more time with a friend of the opposite sex who you feel understands you better than your mate (even if your intentions are pure).
- You or your mate seems to be avoiding the other.
- When you look at your mate, you get a sinking feeling in your gut, or become angry and/or irritable for no good reason.

Not every issue is cause for counseling, but some other issues may warrant immediate attention or special interventions. Take the following quiz to see if you are due for a marital tune-up. Mark each statement *T* or *F*:

__My mate and I keep having the same arguments over and over.
__I often feel picked on by my mate.
__I often feel disappointed in or let down by my mate.
__I wonder if my spouse really loves me.

__I feel that my mate is a controlling person.
__I think our arguments get out of control.
__I wonder if I married the right person.
__I intentionally avoid spending time with my mate.
__I feel that my mate doesn't understand me.
__I often think negatively about my mate.

Scoring

0–1 No special maintenance required. Follow regular maintenance schedule as described above.

2–3 We recommend taking a marriage-enrichment course (see Appendix 2). Check out *When Divorce Is Not an Option: How to Heal Your Marriage and Nurture Lasting Love.* Also, review some of the exercises in this work, especially "Twenty-Five Ways to Make Love Stay — Every Day" (Chapter 7).

4+ We would recommend considering some counseling. Most couples wait four to six years from the onset of problems to seek help. Don't wait until the cancer is inoperable. Contact the Pastoral Solutions Institute at 740-266-6461 or visit us online at www.ExceptionalMarriages.com.

APPENDIX 2

Where to Turn: Resources for Couples

A Challenge

When you were in high school or college, did you learn everything you needed to know to be successful in your present work or role? Of course not. We never stop learning about things that are truly important to us. What is more important than your marriage? We read business books and seek additional job training all the time. But when was the last time you took a "training course" to learn how to be a more sensitive, loving, understanding, generous, communicative, *Christlike* spouse? Even if it was yesterday, pick up the phone and call one of the following organizations today. Don't wait until your marriage *needs* serious help. Act now so that it never will.

Pastoral Solutions Institute (www.CatholicCounselors.com): We offer Catholic counseling for couples and individuals by telephone. Learn more at the website or by calling 740-266-6461. Tune in to our daily radio program *More2Life Radio* airing weekdays, Monday through Friday, at noon (Eastern). Check your local Catholic station or listen online (live or podcasts) at www.AveMariaRadio.net.

ForYourMarriage.org: This is a website sponsored by the United States Conference of Catholic Bishops (USCCB) to support marriage and family life. It features articles, resources, and referrals.

Marriage Encounter (www.WWME.org): Marriage Encounter's history and reputation speak for themselves. I have known couples who have attended over a hundred Marriage Encounter weekends, and each time said they learned something new about themselves and each other. What are you doing this weekend? Call your Family Life office for dates, and contact people in your area.

Retrouvaille (www.HelpOurMarriage.com): This French word (pronounced REH-troo-vie) means "rediscover." Essentially, this is Marriage Encounter for couples that need a little more help. Utilizing more intensive seminars and training, plus optional, one-day, once-a-month follow-ups for at least six months, Retrouvaille provides both wonderful training and an exceptional support system for couples that are struggling to remain faithful to their vows. Call your Family Life office for dates and people to contact in your area.

The Third Option (www.TheThirdOption.com): The Third Option is an ongoing skills-based group program to build better marriages. Each 14-session cycle covers a comprehensive set of tools useful for developing better understanding, sensitivity, and trust, while learning more-effective speaking and listening skills. It is designed for all married couples and can be used both as marriage enrichment or crisis intervention. For hurting couples that see only two options, painful endurance or divorce, The Third Option means reconciliation.

PAIRS (or Practical Application of Intimate Relationship Skills; www.PAIRS.com): More skills-based than Marriage Encounter or Retrouvaille, this is also a wonderful resource for couples who are serious about growing in intimacy, understanding, and love. PAIRS is not specifically Christian in its outlook, but some counseling professionals consider it to be more effective than Marriage Encounter in teaching couples important relationship skills. I recommend doing both — often. Call 888-PAIRS-4U.

Your Diocesan Family Life Office: Call the Family Life office of your diocesan chancery to learn about marriage and family-enrichment programs, NFP (natural family planning) classes, recommended counselors, and a host of other resources *in your area*. These folks are working hard to help you get the most out of your Christian marriage and family life. Contact them, whatever your needs are, to discover what rich blessings they have to offer you.

Couple to Couple League: This organization has training and newsletters supporting NFP. Interested in learning more about NFP (or perhaps becoming a teaching couple)? Call 513-471-2000.

Équipes de Notre Dame (Teams of Our Lady; www.TeamsofOurLady.org): Founded in post-World War II France, this international organization helps married couples learn to "pray their marriages." Through regular small-group meetings and simple prayer exercises, married couples support one another in fulfilling the spiritual mission of their marriage. Contact your diocesan Family Life office for information on a local chapter.

References

Andersen, L.; Fiis, S.; Hallas, J. (2014). "Hormonal contraceptive use and risk of glioma among younger women a nationwide case-control study." *British Journal of Clinical Pharmacology* (April).

Cameron-Bandler, L. (1985). *Solutions: Enhancing Love, Sex, and Relationships*. Futurepace.

Catechism of the Catholic Church (1994, 1997): English translation for use in the United States of America copyright © 1994, United States Catholic Conference, Inc. — Libreria Editrice Vaticana. English translation of the *Catechism of the Catholic Church: Modifications from the Editio Typica* copyright © 1997, United States Catholic Conference, Inc. — Libreria Editrice Vaticana.

Centers for Disease Control (2013). Condom Fact Sheet: Condom Effectiveness. Retrieved online January 15, 2015, at http://www.cdc.gov/condomeffectiveness/brief.html.

Chrysostom, John. *Saint Chrysostom: Homilies on Galatians, Ephesians, Philippians, Colossians, Thessalonians, Timothy, Titus, and Philemon: Nicene and Post-Nicene Fathers of the Christian Church*, Vol. XIII. Trans. by Philip Schaff.

Doughty, S. (2010). "Cohabiting couples twice as likely to part as married couples." *The Daily Mail* (March 26). Retrieved online January 30, 2015, at http://www.dailymail.co.uk/news/article-1260774/Cohabiting-couples-twice-likely-married-partners.html.

Eammons, R. (2007). *Thanks! How the New Science of Gratitude Can Make You Happier.* Houghton, Mifflin, Harcourt.

Fincham, F.; Lambert, N.; Beach, S. (2010). "Faith and unfaithfulness: Can praying for your partner reduce infidelity?" *Journal of Personality and Social Psychology* (October), 99 (4), 649-59.

Gallagher, M. (2015). "Why more women are ditching the pill and turning to 'natural' birth control." *Well+Good* (January 19). Retrieved online January 31, 2015, at http://wellandgood.com/2015/01/19/more-women-are-ditching-the-pill-and-turning-to-natural-birth-control/.

Gottman, J. (1995). *Why Marriages Succeed or Fail and How You Can Make Yours Last.* Simon & Schuster.

Gottman, J.; Gottman, J. (2011). "Bridging the Couple Chasm: Gottman Couples Therapy. A New Research-Based Approach." The Gottman Institute.

Greeley, A. (1992). *Faithful Attraction.* A Tor Book.

Grigg-Spall, H. (2013). *Sweetening the Pill: How We Got Hooked on Hormonal Birth Control.* Zero Books.

Groeschel, B. (1984). *Spiritual Passages.* Crossroads.

Hermann, P.; Heil, J.; Gnoth, C. (2007). "The effectiveness of fertility awareness based method to avoid pregnancy in relation to a couple's behavior during the fertile time: a prospective longitudinal study." *Human Reproduction*, 22 (5).

Hochschild, A. (2012). *The Second Shift*, rev. ed. Penguin.

Hogan, R.; LeVoir, J. (1992). *Covenant of Love: Pope John Paul II on Sexuality, Marriage, and Family in the Modern World.* Ignatius Press.

Hughes, M. E.; Waite, L. (2009). "Marital biography and health at midlife." *Journal of Health and Social Behavior* (September), 50 (3).

Janus, S; Janus, C. (1994). *The Janus Report on Sexual Behavior.* Wiley.

Jay, M. (2013). *The Defining Decade: Why Your Twenties Matter and How To Make the Most of Them Now.* Twelve (Hachette Book Group).

Kelly, M. (2005). *The Seven Levels of Intimacy: The Art of Love.* Beacon Publishing.

Kenrick, D.; Griskevicius, V.; Neuberg, S. (2010). "Renovating the pyramid of needs. Contemporary extensions built on ancient foundations." *Perspectives in the Psychological Sciences* (May), 5 (3).

Kunang, N. (2015). "For birth control, what's new is old again." CNN.com (January 8). Retrieved online January 31, 2015, at http://www.cnn.com/2015/01/08/health/fertility-awareness-methods/index.html.

Lawler, R.; Boyle, J.; May, W. (1998). *Catholic Sexual Ethics: A Summary, Explanation, & Defense (Second Edition).* Our Sunday Visitor, Inc.

Lederer, W.; Jackson, D. (1990). *The Mirages of Marriage*. W. W. Norton and Co.
Lewis, C. S. (1943). *Mere Christianity*. Simon and Schuster.
———. *The Great Divorce*. Macmillan (1946).
———. *The Magician's Nephew*. Harper Trophy (1955).
———. *The Four Loves*. Harcourt Brace (1960).
———. *The Screwtape Letters*. Macmillan (1964).
Madanes, C. "Brief Therapy for Managed Care" (seminar, November 1997). The Family Therapy Center of Maryland, Pittsburgh.
Maslow, A. (1943). *A Theory of Human Motivation*. Martino Fine Books (2013 reprint of original edition).
May, W. (1995). *Marriage: The Rock on Which the Family Is Built*. Ignatius Press.
Mayer, R.; Davis, J.; Schoorman, F.D. (1995). "An integrative model of trust." *The Academy of Management Review* (Vol. 20, No.3).
National Cancer Institute (NCI) (2012). *Oral contraception and cancer risk*. Retrieved online January 31, 2014, at http://www.cancer.gov/cancer topics/factsheet/Risk/oral-contraceptives.
National Institutes of Health (2015). Medline Plus: Birth Control Pills Overview. Retrieved online January 15, 2014, from http://www.nlm .nih.gov/medlineplus/ency/article/007460.htm.
Parry, W. (2012). "Water pollution caused by birth control poses dilemma." *LiveScience*. Retrieved online January 15, 2015, at http: //www.livescience.com/20532-birth-control-water-pollution.html.
Popcak, G. (2002). *The Exceptional Seven Percent: Nine Secrets of the World's Happiest Couples*. Kensington Press.
Pope Francis (2014). Address to the National Association of Large Families on the Feast of the Holy Family (December 28).
Pope John Paul II (2006). *Man and Woman He Created Them: A Theology of the Body*. Trans. by Michael Waldstein. Pauline Books & Media.
———. *Original Unity of Man and Woman: Catechesis on the Book of Genesis*. Daughters of St. Paul (1981).
———. *Laborem Exercens* — "On Human Work" (1981).
———. *Familiaris Consortio* — on the role of the Christian family in the modern world (1981).
———. *Letter to Families* (1994).
Pope Paul VI (1968). *Humanae Vitae* — "Of Human Life."

Rhodes, G.; Stanley, S. (2014). *Before "I Do": What Do Premarital Experiences Have to Do with Marital Quality Among Today's Young Adults?* The National Marriage Project. University of Virginia.

Rushnell, S.; DuArt, L. (2011). *Couples Who Pray*. Thomas Nelson.

Schwartz, P. (1994). *Peer Marriage*. The Free Press.

Shaw, R. (1997) *Our Sunday Visitor's Encyclopedia of Catholic Doctrine*. Our Sunday Visitor, Inc.

Sullivan, H. (1966). *Conceptions of Modern Psychiatry*. W. W. Norton and Co.

VandeVusse L.; Hanson, L.; Fehring R. (2004). "Couples' Views of the Effects of Natural Family Planning on Marital Dynamics." *Journal of Nursing Scholarship* (April), (Vol. 35, No. 21), 171-176.

VanderDrift, L.; Lewandowsky, G.; Agnew, C. (2010). "Reduced self-expansion in current romance and interest in relationship alternatives." *Journal of Social and Personal Relationships* (May), 28 (3).

Vatican Council II (1964). *Lumen Gentium* — Dogmatic Constitution on the Church. Retrieved online January 15, 2015, at http://www.vatican.va/archive/hist_councils/ii_vatican_council/documents/vat-ii_const_19641121_lumen-gentium_en.html.

———. (1965). *Gaudium et Spes*. Retrieved online December 8, 2014, at http://www.vatican.va/archive/hist_councils/ii_vatican_council/documents/vat-ii_cons_19651207_gaudium-et-spes_en.html.

Wallerstein, J.; Blakeslee, S. (1996). *The Good Marriage: How and Why Love Lasts*. Warner Books, Inc.

Way of the Cross, The (1965). Barton Cotton, Inc., 1965.

Weiner-Davis, M. (1992). *Divorce Busting: A Revolutionary and Rapid Program for "Staying Together."* Summit Books.

Wilcox, B.; Marquardt, E. (2011). *The State of Our Unions: When Baby Makes Three*. The National Marriage Project. University of Virginia and the Institute for American Values. Retrieved online January 25, 2015, at http://www.stateofourunions.org/2011/SOOU2011.pdf.

Wuerl, D.; Lawler, R.; Lawler, T.; Stubna, K. (1991). *The Teaching of Christ: A Catholic Catechism for Adults*, 5th ed. Our Sunday Visitor, Inc.